For the University

For the University
Democracy and the Future of the Institution

Thomas Docherty

BLOOMSBURY ACADEMIC

First published in 2011 by

Bloomsbury Academic
an imprint of Bloomsbury Publishing Plc
36 Soho Square, London W1D 3QY, UK
and
175 Fifth Avenue, New York, NY 10010, USA

Copyright © Thomas Docherty 2011

CIP records for this book are available from the British Library and the
Library of Congress

ISBN 978-1-84966-615-2 (paperback)
ISBN 978-1-84966-631-2 (ebook)

This book is produced using paper that is made from wood grown in managed,
sustainable forests. It is natural, renewable and recyclable. The logging and
manufacturing processes conform to the environmental regulations of
the country of origin.

Printed and bound in Great Britain by CPI Antony Rowe, Chippenham, Wiltshire

Cover design: Burge Agency

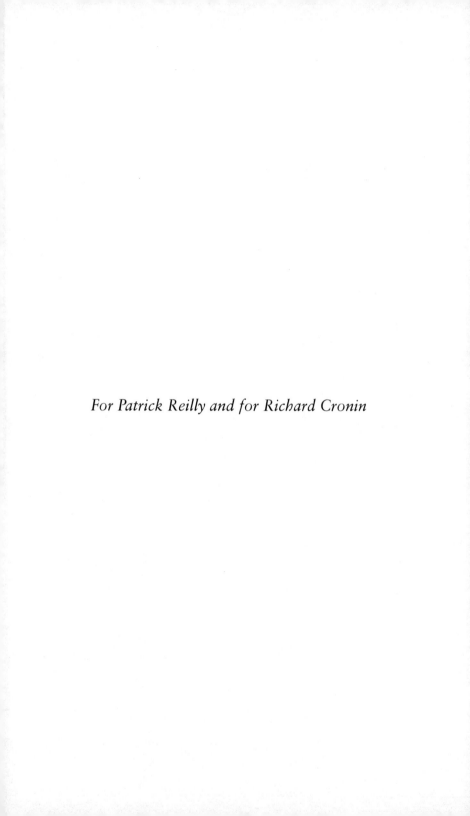

For Patrick Reilly and for Richard Cronin

Contents

Preface and Acknowledgements

In some ways, this book has been many decades in the making; but it has taken its actual form during a critical moment in the latter half of 2010. The thought and research that has informed it has taken at least the entirety of my own career in the University sector to mature and to emerge; but that 'emergency' is shaped by an 'urgency' that derives from a very significant change that is now proposed for the future of the University as an institution. The change in question, driven by the UK's first peacetime coalition government, is really an attack on the fundamental principle that the University exists as a key constituent in a public sphere. That is what gives a pressing urgency to the arguments of the book.

The making of the arguments that emerge through these pages, nonetheless, is a work of much longer duration. My academic career began as a student in Glasgow in the 1970s. There, I was taught by, among others, the two colleagues to whom the book is dedicated: Patrick Reilly and Richard Cronin. It was in the seminars and tutorials offered by Patrick and Richard that I realized a number of possibilities. Their teaching showed me that my future was much more open than I could ever have imagined when I entered the University. In short, through a profound engagement with the language and history of literature, they allowed me to find a sense that I, too, could have a voice, that I was enfranchised in some basic ways; and that it was important that such a widening of autonomy and of a democratic franchise should be further extended. Thus it was that I, in turn, became a teacher.

My experience as a teacher took me to Paris, where I taught both secondary level and adult Continuing Professional Development (CPD) classes. From there, I moved into University teaching, first in Oxford while pursuing a doctorate and doing my first postdoctoral research. At this time, the first major attack on the University system in the UK took place, with the drastic cuts in education funding made by the Thatcher government. Accordingly, I moved abroad to find a position at University College Dublin, followed by five years as Chair at Trinity College Dublin. When I returned to the UK in 1995, I taught in Kent for some nine years before taking up my present position as Professor of English and Comparative Literature at the University of Warwick. Along the way, I taught in many other institutions within the UK and abroad, in a guest or visiting capacity.

This broad experience, then, forms some of the bedrock of the argument in the book. It allows me to illustrate what has been happening to the transformed environment both in the UK and much further afield over the last forty years, as those changes are experienced 'on the ground'. That experience, though, is combined here with a deeper historical research into the condition of the institution, especially through the twentieth century and to the present crisis. In that research, we can trace the vigorous debates that have helped shape a vibrant University. The book is written in the hope of continuing that debate, and thus reviving the very possibility of our establishing a viable future for the University.

I am indebted not only to my teachers and colleagues in all the institutions where I have worked, but also to a number of individuals and audiences elsewhere. Some brief passages of the book have appeared in very different form in the pages of the Times Higher Education magazine; and I am grateful to Ann Mroz and to Phil Baty, who published several 'Opinion' pieces there. Those pieces provoked some lively response; and I hope the book will do more.

Introduction

For the University

The University today is in need of friends. For some time now, in the advanced economies, the institution of the University has found itself increasingly besieged and beleaguered. It is difficult to find any simple or straightforward reason for this, given that most governments repeatedly stress how important the University is in an era where the success and increasing prosperity of the nation is increasingly determined and driven by a 'knowledge-economy' and by 'intellectual capital'. Further, the last few decades have also witnessed a massive increase in the number of people attending a University, especially in the UK; and we have also seen a great rise in the number of institutions that have acquired University status.

It would be reasonable, given this, to ask how I can claim that the University stands in critical need of support and friendship. Notwithstanding the good words of politicians, however, there has been a sure and steadily generated encouragement of a culture of mistrust around the institution and its activities for some time. This goes well beyond the vagaries of a routine anti-intellectualism from parts of the popular media that sees scientists as eccentric boffins divorced from reality and that characterizes arts or humanities intellectuals as dangerous subversives plotting against ordinary lives. It has deeper roots than this.

There are at least two aspects of this negative mood directed at the University. First, there is a long historical legacy in which the University is construed as a site of privilege, and especially of class privilege. Such a view is perpetuated in television adaptations of novels such as *Brideshead Revisited*, the effect of which is to portray Oxbridge (as a synecdoche for the University as a whole) as an institution from another world. The people here have nothing to say of everyday life, for they do not live it; in the portrait, they are presented as cocooned and cosseted. This, while a powerful negative image, is also quite clearly dated. Of more pressing contemporary significance is the preservation of an entirely different kind of privilege, but a privilege that is cast in terms of 'rights'. Specifically, what has been at stake here is what politicians have construed as the right of a government to manage things in a society without fearing contradiction from another source of potentially critical authority.

It is the latter that has shaped attitudes to the University, as also to a more general education, for the past forty years or so at least. That is to say, the culture of mistrust that dogs and threatens the sustained viability of the University is something that is at least tacitly endorsed, if not actually inaugurated, by political discourse. The debate here, over the question of social and cultural authority, might have its roots in real politics. We should recall that, in the 1970s, miners in the UK successfully challenged the centre of political authority. Edward Heath, faced with a powerful strike, went to the country explicitly inviting people to decide 'who rules Britain?' The people duly did decide and, in the election, they ejected Heath from office. That political mistake was not to be repeated. When miners again went on strike a decade later, in 1984, the question of who rules Britain was not posed. Instead, the government established a new kind of language for a new debate. Set against 'the right to strike' that had been long fought for across decades of history by the trade union movements, the government started a rival claim for what it called 'the right of managers to manage'. At issue here was not the crudely posed question of who rules Britain, then; rather, a more subtle discourse came into play. However, the effect was the same: the government wanted to ensure that there could be no real rival to itself as a centre for determining *how* things would be run in the nation.

Thus began, in the wake of a political victory over the miners and their communities, a process whereby the government would set about calling into question many other such possible rival centres of authority. There was a sustained attack on the standing of the professions, a calling into question of 'experts' and the beginning of the doubts about education. This began at school level. On one hand, government complained that school-children showed little respect to teachers anymore; on the other hand, and simultaneously, it was the government itself that showed least respect. Not only did government consistently depress teachers' rates of pay, but in addition government started to call into question teaching methods and the standing of teachers themselves. Given that many of these teachers had themselves been products of University, and had indeed gained their teaching qualification from Universities, it was not a great leap then to start calling the University itself into doubt.

When pressures mounted, for various reasons, to increase the number of young people attending University, some more radical changes occurred. First, in 1992, John Patten (then Conservative Secretary of State for Education) abolished the 'binary divide' between the University and the Polytechnic sectors. At a stroke, the number of institutions in the UK with University status doubled. Although the Polytechnic sector was full of academic colleagues who had effectively been doing work that was very similar to that carried out in the Universities, there was also pressure now to start to try to assure people that this sudden eruption of University institutions would not damage quality.

At this point, we have a great paradox. Government establishes an agency that is designed to assure the people of the quality of what is going on the University sector. The very existence of this agency invites the question – an essentially mistrustful question – that goes, 'if they need to set the agency up, there must be something to worry about'. Unsurprisingly, the culture of mistrust then flourishes in the wake of this.

And now, everyone mistrusts everyone. Teachers mistrust the Quality Assurance Agency; students question teachers; government questions everybody else; funding mechanisms have to be rendered 'transparent' because no one trusts the judgements made by funding bodies; examinations have to be mechanized into exercises governed by transparent criteria rather than judgement; and so on. Within the institution itself, likewise, everyone is now expected not only to do their work but also to justify their existence as workers, through endless monitoring processes and procedures. This is all well known.

In what follows in this book, I am taking sides *for* an institution that increasingly is riddled with difficulties, not always of its own making; and these difficulties are such that they frequently obscure and obstruct the real actions that a University exists to further. The argument requires several stages.

In the first place, I try to revive a certain sense of purpose regarding the University. At the present time – an extremely pressured time and a time when everything is pressured by a sense of urgency – there is not often enough a reflection on the principles that should govern the University. Instead, principles too often have given way to the demands of the moment; and thus, principle cedes place to pragmatism. In some cases, this is necessary; but in other cases crisis management becomes the excuse for failing to address or to respect principles. My opening chapter is a reflection on what might be the first principles governing the University as an institution. However, I argue that those first principles cannot be fixed and stable, if the University is to be allowed to exist as an organic institution, adapting to and evolving for an ever-changing social and cultural environment. It is no longer appropriate for us to have 'the idea of a University'; but it is extremely important to replace that with what we can call the search to make 'the University of the Idea', as it were: the University is where we can figure out the future in terms of imagining possibilities through the making of an idea. Thus, the University becomes that institution in which the first principle is actually the search for first principles.

The key word here, beyond the self-reflexive paradox, is *search*. I contend that the University is above all governed by actions of discovery; and that such discovery and inventiveness – the adventure that is a University – is shaped by a demand for an ongoing openness to possibility. The word that we usually give to that openness to possibility, of course, is just *freedom*. The chapter argues that the University exists for the extension of freedom; and that it addresses this demand by attending to questions of *judgement*. Judgement, in turn, allows us to search for whatever constitutes *justice*; and, if this is to be a justice in a public sphere that is shaped by and shared among a community, then it will depend upon a certain demand for *democracy*.

I articulate these concerns, however, by attending fundamentally to the faculties that a University will typically embrace: faculties of science, social science and arts. It is through the *search* for that which we call true (in science), for that which we call good (in social science) and for that which we call beautiful (in aesthetics, arts and humanities) that we practise this fundamental activity of extending freedom in just democracy. Above all, though, the search dominates here: there is no single and certainly no stable quality of truth, goodness or beauty. These are matters for the public sphere and for just judgements within that sphere – but the University exists to underpin that sphere.

Chapter 2 looks at the question from the point of view of the student and their relation to knowing. That is to say, it addresses teaching and learning. The claim here is that our sense of what constitutes learning and teaching has been skewed in recent times. To examine this, I look at what I call 'the myth of the student experience'. In these days, the category of 'the student experience' has become central to our ways of understanding learning, teaching and the life of the student while they attend our institutions. My claim here is that this category is there, paradoxically, precisely to *preclude* the possibility of the student actually having the experiences involved in genuine learning and teaching. I thus analyse 'the student experience' attending in particular to two things. First, I offer a brief philosophical inquiry into what constitutes experience as such; and in this, I prioritize the notion of material transformation. Experience is both something undergone (a passive sense), but also something that founds the possibility of new agency (an active sense). I place learning and teaching in that transformational intersection. Secondly, however, I also address explicitly the realpolitik of the agreed Policy Statement of the 1994 Group of Universities regarding the student experience. The close analysis of the content of that agreement indicates clearly a trajectory in which any sense of transformational learning and teaching has become increasingly irrelevant within the language and thought of those who promulgate the myth of the student experience. Transformation, indeed, is entirely replaced by a logic of consumerist conformity in the documents. I use this to help prove my case that 'the student experience', as this near-mythic category, systematically downgrades the classroom experience of learning and teaching.

The third chapter is an exploration of space. This may seem an unpromising way to go about exploring the place of research in the University. But it nonetheless yields instructive results. The chapter begins from a consideration of the relation of science research to government policy in the 1960s, and especially in relation to the technologies involved in the exploration of outer space at that time. I then trace what I see as the gradual but insistent modification of an attitude to space in the intervening decades. We begin from an exploratory looking beyond the inhabited space of humanity, and we gradually recast space in other terms, arriving at the point where space has become 'managed space', a restrictive environment – a nano-space, as it were – in which we look insistently within, in an activity that comes close to blending research with surveillance. My examination of managed space within the organization of research reveals a mode of thought that is concerned to restrict research. In this, I attempt to get at the underlying philosophy that has driven us towards the narrowness of 'applied research', focused introspectively on a specific problem, and away from the open reach of discovery that is often called blue-skies research.

The argument driving this case is one where I can then trace the ways in which the managing of space has replaced the occupying of space in our mentalities. Space, in this analysis, becomes instrumentalized. It shrinks because it is 'costed'; and, in shrinking it also compresses or, better, contracts the imagination in a rather anorexic fashion. The governmental policy of 'concentrating' research in located clusters is one direct manifestation of our spatial attitude; and my case is that there is an implicit politics here, and one that is concerned at the potentially emancipatory powers of a research imagination that threatens a polity in which I 'know my place'.

This, I argue further, has a consequence for teaching, especially in those institutions that claim to be 'research-led'. The consequence is one that thinks of disciplines in spatial terms; and it sustains an atomization of our knowledge in terms of 'modules'. The chapter then explores further the relation of research to teaching, and the negative effects of modularization on education and on learning. To counter this, it proposes a different attitude to research, but one that prioritizes what we might call the temporal imagination.

Having explored teaching, learning and research, I turn attention in chapter 4 to the question of leadership. In this chapter, my analysis focuses on leadership within the institution as well as on the role of the University in terms of leadership within the public sphere. The initial draft of this chapter was the briefest I have ever written. It comprised three words: 'There is none.' However, in the revised drafts, I was not interested in lamentation and jeremiad, however well-deserved and well-founded these might be. Rather, I wanted to analyse what I see as a profound lack of self-confidence within the institution regarding leadership. Leadership happens at many levels in the University.

Vice-chancellors lead, certainly, as do registrars. However, leadership also happens at many other levels: deans, heads of department, peers among the faculty; teachers with respect to students; students among themselves. That view looks very hierarchical; and, in my exploration, I discovered that any form of leadership that remains within this hierarchical structure is intrinsically problematic. Through an exploration of the formation of leaders in the University environment, combined with an analysis of theories of leadership gleaned from within the discourses of business and management, I arrive at a version of leadership that is intrinsically more dialogical and democratic. In one way, I still believe that I could close this chapter with a four-word sentence: 'There still is none.' However, I at least try to offer a sense of what a leadership that serves my underlying first governing principles of the University might look like.

One of the most important things that shape everyday life within a University is assessment. Chapter 5 considers the role of assessment in the modern institution. It would be true to say that in recent decades assessment has become a major and abiding concern for the University. Not only have we witnessed the endless proliferation of new modes and manners of assessment, we have also borne witness to increased anxieties regarding how we can legitimize the assessments that we make. This chapter looks back at some of the reasons why we moved in the University from a system of examination (and especially of finals examination) to a looser version of continuously assessing the work and progress of students – but also of peers in, for example, research assessment exercises or peer-review of funding applications.

The argument is that assessment is a big improvement on the faults and shortcomings of the examinations procedure. However, along with the progresses here, there comes also a train of unwanted consequences. In some ways, this may prove to be a most contentious chapter, for in it I argue that assessment has been tacitly politicized, and that the purpose of assessment is to ensure that we produce students trained in the practices of mental or intellectual conformity. That is to say, assessment starts out as an attempt to bring a wider range of positive modes of achievement into our institutions; but it does so in order to 'contain' them, and to ensure that what the University produces in its graduates is a mood of unquestioning conformity with social norms. Those norms are given not by government as such, but rather by a wider set of ideological practices and beliefs. The chapter, having analysed various modes of assessment, and having studied the science of assessment, proposes that we need to make a further change. The change in question here is not necessarily an abandonment of the bathwater of assessment, but certainly a saving of the baby whose imagination and invention – a spirit of critique of norms and of conformity as such – is enhanced.

Finally, in chapter 6, I come to the question of how we pay for all this. My overall argument is that our present mode of funding makes perfect sense, but only in relation to an ideology (or idea) of the University that is flawed, self-contradictory, and essentially extremely limited. That is to say: if we have a view of the University simply as an institution dedicated to the growth of Gross Domestic Product, and in which the institution becomes a two-faced service provider (on one side, business that needs graduates; but, turning the other cheek, 'student-customers' purchasing some commodity), then our funding mechanism is suitable. However, this is a drastically limited and parochially narrow view of what a University is, and it is a view that is helpful neither to the institution, nor to the wider public sphere (including business and commerce), nor to the student.

In this chapter, then, my argument involves a kind of reversal of our usual priorities. I replace the idea of searching for 'value-for-money' from the University with a new question: the question becomes how we will find money-for-values. That is to say, I turn back here to the values described in the opening chapter, and I ask how we establish the political will required to fund those. In the body of this argument, I also make a number of hypotheses about the possible future shape of the higher education sector as a whole. The chapter accepts that it is going to be difficult, at least in the present climate, to establish a political will that would adequately fund around 150 University institutions from general progressive taxation. Nonetheless, it argues that there is still a major case that can be made for a substantial input from taxation. It also suggests different kinds of institution, however, and different possible models for funding them.

The rest, as some might say, is up to politicians. However, my argument is that it is not. The rest is up to the public sphere and the community as a whole. We need to decide whether we do indeed want to have institutions like a University that can help us search constantly for justice, freedom and democracy. My wager in writing this book is that we do indeed not only want those things, but that we also need them, and we need them with increasing urgency.

That is why I am *for the University*.

1

First Principles

The University of the Idea

One of the significant 'events' of 1968 happened in a University. In Nanterre, on the outskirts of Paris, Daniel Cohn-Bendit confronted François Missoffe, who at that time served in the government of Georges Pompidou as France's first ever Minister for Youth and Sport. Missoffe, who in his own youth had played jazz alongside the French polymath, Boris Vian, had an already distinguished career as a servant of the State. His political star was in the ascendant and he was certainly a very well-intentioned politician who took the issues around youth, including their physical health, very seriously. Indeed, the French had endured a very disappointing Olympic Games in Tokyo in 1964; and Missoffe was effectively being charged with improving things in order to avoid similar embarrassment in the future. To that end, he had written a 600-page White Paper, detailing how best to improve things – literally, quite physically and even bodily – for the future of French youth. When he came to open a new swimming-pool facility in the University of Nanterre, however, he found that he had made a misjudgement about the mood and character of the times.

The young, and equally serious-minded, Cohn-Bendit shouted across the pool that he had read Missoffe's White Paper on youth, describing it as 600 pages of ineptitude; and, specifically, Cohn-Bendit said that he had noticed that nowhere in the White Paper was there any proposal for how the French government planned to address the many sexual issues relating to student life. Missoffe suggested – prudishly but imprudently – that Cohn-Bendit should take advantage of the new pool to cool off a bit. Replying that this was the kind of response you would expect from fascist regimes or from the leaders of the Hitler Youth, Cohn-Bendit and some 142 of his fellow-students proceeded instead to occupy the administration building in Nanterre, this action being the formation of the '*Mouvement du 22-mars*'. This escalation of an action became a significant determinant of what was to happen in the next few months, as first Paris and then the rest of France found itself in the near-revolution of *les événements*.[1]

There are several things worthy of note here, at the start of a book that is written *for* the University. The clash at the swimming pool reveals that there is a sense of massive frustration, even tension, between government and students; and the frustration, on both sides, relates to something physical: the youthful body, its value and the relation of youth to politics. From the point of view of government, the young people of France were not as strong and healthy, physically, as they might have been; and thus they projected a national image that was embarrassing. Meanwhile, from the point of view of the students, and especially of the male heterosexual students, the frustration derived from the fact that dormitories were segregated according to gender, in institutions inhabited by adults. What they wanted was access to the girls' bedrooms, to find themselves bodily in other ways than those envisaged by the State.

The key interest here is that the University becomes the site not for the struggle between ideas, but between different attitudes to the body, to its control, and to what constitutes healthy socio-cultural relatedness. That relatedness was to take a significant further turn, in the linking of arms, not between courting youngsters, but between students and workers. One of the most notable developments of 1968 was the establishment of connections of solidarity between students and the factory workers at the Renault buildings in Boulogne-Billancourt, south-west of Paris. When these groups came together, Universities were allied to workers in a class struggle. That, of course, is an early version of what might now be thought of as the 'impact' of a University upon a wider social sphere, even if it is not the kind of impact favoured by most governments. It is a form of impact that brings education, the body and politics together in a rather explosive fashion. This book will explore further those relations, and will ask about how they impinge upon what might be seen as the first principles that should govern our University institution.

These historical events all came at a period of expansion of the University sector in Europe and the United States. The myth of 'May 1968' provoked much discussion in the developed world of the time, and also elsewhere, about the proper function of the University as an institution. In the 1970s, Daniel Bell attempted to address this question schematically. Bell had been a key sociologist in the so-called 'end of ideology' debates in the 1950s. Those debates spread from within sociology into political philosophy. While at one level the very idea of an 'end of ideology' is indebted to Karl Marx, it can equally well be argued that the debates instigated by Bell lead, albeit very indirectly, via a seeming acceptance of the rule of technocracies, towards the more recent political movements and tendencies often associated with the

US neo-conservatives. The coming to prominence in this new century of a neo-con agenda has had important side-effects, not least for our understanding of the public sphere and of the place of education within it. One interim figure here might well be Francis Fukuyama, whose 'end of history' and 'last man' theses gained much ground in the wake of the fall of the Berlin Wall and the next cycle of revolutionary activities in 1989.

A key part of Fukuyama's thesis was that there would now be no further ideological developments beyond a free-market capitalism that was supposed to be intimately linked to expanding and potentially worldwide democracy. These ideas start to help shape, or at least simply to articulate, what comes to pass in our time for an often unspoken sense that the public sphere is itself but a marketplace of various kinds; and, in what follows, I want not just to explore and criticize this but to advance an alternative view of how things might be. That alternative view is a view *for* and in favour of the University as an institution that can help restore a sense of the possibilities of historical change and of personal autonomy: in short, that the University is central to ideas of freedom and justice.

Bell argued that there were essentially only two real models of the University, which he called the 'classical' and the 'pragmatic' models. In the classical model, he says, the University is 'that institution in the society endowed with the special function (and the extraordinary immunity) of searching for truth and evaluating the culture of the times. In this sense, it is free to question everything – *in theory*'.[2] This classical University has no practical function, therefore; but rather exists as a kind of conscience of society. It is a free conscience, roaming over anything and everything, but it is purely speculative: its ideas exist in what the prevailing ideology would think of as a 'market of ideas'. If the ideas are to be realized in any form of material action or history, then they will be so *beyond* the institution, and the actions will be taken by those who are not part of the institution.

There is an important corollary here. In this mode of thinking, the society is now first of all split into separate spheres of activity: one called 'scholarship' or theory, the other called 'citizenship' or action. This represents an atomization of life – of the body itself – that is not yet theoretically justified. According to this, further, if I, as a 'scholar', do indeed take my thoughts out into the streets and enact them in some form of activity, I have at that moment ceased to be a scholar, but have instead become a 'citizen'. Atomization, as it were, goes all the way down, and even fractures our sense of individual selfhood and identity: my identity here is but an agglomeration of discrete self-descriptions, as it were.

Bell's pragmatic model, by contrast, gives us a position where 'the function of the university is primarily one of service to the society: service in training large numbers of persons, service in the application of knowledge, service of the members of the university in government and elsewhere'. The pragmatic University works within the realm and domain of the material and historical world, and avoids being reduced to the condition of a mere 'conscience'. It plays its part in determining matters through service to the financial market, and is designed to contribute to growth in Gross Domestic Product, in personal prosperity and in power.

In this model, the problem of atomization is addressed; but the cost of that is to leave scholarship in an awkward position where it loses any real autonomy. While scholarly research is supposed to be finding out new things in terms of how the research will fulfil its pedagogical conditions, it is also now supposed to be finding out things that are designed to serve others and their interests. In short, in this model, thinking cannot be freely unconstrained but is rather predetermined by the choices of whoever is master. We deal with atomization by entering ideology, as it were; and, instead of being a conscience, the University becomes an 'agency', an agency beholden to the thinking and preferences of others.

These two models – the only models available, argues Bell – give us a crude and schematic if extremely helpful choice. Bell explains the choice neatly and succinctly: 'If one chooses the first [the classical model], then one is barred, in the role of scholar and researcher (though not as citizen) from political advocacy and partisanship.' This is clear: the classical model is a kind of model for free thinking, but a thinking that has no direct historical effect. It may have such an effect, of course; but, to do so, the thought has to be transferred, as it were, into a separate domain – the domain of action.

Bell then goes on to say that 'If [one chooses] the second [the pragmatic model], the question becomes "Who shall decide?" "Should the Universities serve the military? Or the urban poor? Or the radicals? Should the criterion be national interest, social need, the command of money, the influence of power groups, or what?"' This modern version of the ancient *Quis custodiet* question – who will decide? – raises the fundamental issue of where it is that *authority* lies in terms of the relation between University and society. Yet more fundamentally, it raises the question of where authority lies in terms of the relation between consciousness (thought) and history (action).

This scheme opens up some of the key issues facing us in our own times, after what some might see as another failed revolution, the incompletion of 1989 as it were, and the further massification of University education. There can be little doubt, I think, that, in line with a neo-Fukuyama thesis that a capitalist free-market liberalism gives us the best political settlement historically available, the contemporary world has broadly favoured the second of these models, the pragmatic model. The result of this is that whenever we argue about the function of the University, we end up having a debate about 'who decides'; and that means that we have an argument not about the University, but about which government to choose. Governments of all persuasions seem to *require* that the University sector now serves whatever happens to be government policy.

In Britain, specifically, a particular change in the model of funding for the University sector is important here. It should be recalled that, until the nineteenth century, England had only two Universities, while Scotland boasted four. Although Scotland was much better served, especially in proportion to population, this is still not a large number. It is only really in the 1870s that civic Universities started to develop in England, and it is not until 1889, when the numbers of institutions start to rise significantly, that the State took a direct interest in the sector, voting financial subsidies towards the establishment and sound financial maintenance of a substantial University sector. The effect of that State intervention at this stage was that by about 1914, just at the breakout of war, we can see the emergence of the first real stirrings of something like a national University system.[3]

The University Grants Committee (UGC) was founded in 1919, with a view to establishing a secure financial foundation for what was now coming to be seen explicitly (in the wake of war especially) as a system of higher education whose national standing was high enough that it deserved State interest and State money. However, such a system was rather undercut by the fact that it had more than one 'centre'. Precisely because it was a national system, with University institutions dotted geographically around the country, it seemed to lack a stable and single centre. While many in government would have recognized Oxbridge (and more recently the so-called 'golden triangle' of Oxford, Cambridge and London) precisely as such a centre, it was nonetheless the case that the Scottish institutions in particular continued to assume an extremely important role in tying the identity of their students to their own locale.

A further pressure was exerted on the idea of a national University culture during the post-Robbins expansion of the sector in the 1960s. It was not just the case that there were now regional institutions (in Keele, York, East Anglia, Sussex, Kent, Leicester, Warwick and so on – some of which pre-date Robbins, in fact); rather, it was the case that with the introduction, in 1962, of 'mandatory' grants for students, those students began to leave their own home regions almost as a condition of becoming students. The consequence of this is a fracturing of the tie between student and home-locale, between student and parental generations. This affects how we view tradition itself: instead of simply carrying on certain modes of behaviour that are handed down as if by legacy, tradition now comes to mean the assumption, by the new generation, of forms of authority that essentially require a break with the legacy of the past and of parents. Most significantly of all, there now results a fracturing of the idea of the 'national character' that had supposedly been there when Oxbridge was the core or centre of national values. Just as 'received pronunciation' or 'the Queen's English' starts to sound stilted and to be replaced by a cultural validation of regional identity and accent, so also instead of there being a 'received' or standard version of a national character, diversity and eccentricity become the new value.

For government, this quite radical decentring of things, along with the radical distribution of University affiliations, represents a potential lack of control over the nation and its affairs. 1968 was, for many, precisely such an anarchic loss of control; but, of course, the events in France and elsewhere were, in the end, quashed, and the potential reorganization of society was halted in its tracks. In the years after this, there is a whole series of manoeuvres designed to give a kind of 'licence' to what the Establishment sees as 'misbehaviour' of various kinds, most of all in the sphere of popular culture and popular music, where 'underground' and semi-clandestine types of activity were validated. In all areas of aesthetic life especially, we see a wild explosion of 'experiment' with various styles and forms of life. In many ways, though, these are but moments of permitted release whose effect remains entirely local: there is no real motor of social change, but instead the satisfaction of local desires. In short, experimentation and play in the realm of the aesthetic becomes a kind of substitute for political action; and aesthetic revolution quells any demand for socio-political change.

This all forms the backdrop against which the policy for the funding of the University sector comes under scrutiny over a ten-year period; and it helps explain how and why that funding mechanism was changed. There is then a fear of large-scale alterations to the social order; and that fear, for precise historical reasons, is partly associated with the Universities as centres of dissent. It is partly to deal with this that we find the establishment of a new way of thinking about the functions of the University. Thus (though for other reasons as well), in 1992 the

UGC (by then, UFC) became the Higher Education Funding Councils for England (HEFCE), Scotland (SHEFC) and Wales (HEFCW). Prior to this moment, governments, in dealing with the UGC, were constrained to keep a distance between themselves and the institutions. The UGC was a buffer-zone that helped maintain the independence and autonomy of the (not very large, not very well-distributed) University sector. However, the brief for HEFCE and its partner councils in Scotland and Wales is different. It states explicitly that the funding council is answerable directly to the minister in government and that the duties of the Chair are to ensure that HEFCE acts in accordance with the wider strategic policies of the Secretary of State. The consequence of this is that the funding councils no longer have an *authority* but instead they become, essentially, government *agencies*. There is to be a revival of the national interest; but that interest is identified exactly with the interest of government.

This is part of what can be seen historically as a growing and explicit politicization of the entire education sector, a movement that began under a Conservative administration that saw the Universities as being hotbeds of radical dissent, but that was continued and extended under a New Labour administration that wanted to maintain good headlines for itself and its achievements – achievements that would be effected by the education sector, though credit would be claimed by government ministers seeking renewed terms of office. If it is indeed the case that we are now constrained not to ask what is the function of the University but rather which government we wish to have, then not only is there an explicit politicization of education here, but also a link (that I'll explore in what follows) between the question of the function of the University and the fraught and contentious issue of contemporary *democracy*.

Indeed, if we need further proof of the politicization of the tertiary sector, we can look at how inaugurations such as the Research Assessment Exercise (now the REF or Research Excellence Framework) are also explicitly designed to speak directly to government requirements. Consider the trend for interdisciplinarity, for example. On one hand, this looks like a good thing (many scholars have been advocating it for ages, suggesting that the existing disciplines are constraining and narrow). The result is that we now have interdisciplinarity almost as a precondition of getting any research funding at all; but this is managed by having not a freestanding and open kind of interdisciplinarity, but rather the exploitation of 'themes' for interdisciplinary research that are identified by government. The research councils (all eight of them, costing millions of pounds to run) are, like HEFCE, given their brief by government. It is not the case that government explicitly tells us what to do; rather, government tells the funding councils that they (the councils) *will of course want to address* certain priorities.

It should be understood here that I am not about to argue for a version of the University that is based on the ideals – sometimes extremely sound, sometimes simply anarchic and also sometimes frankly conservative in terms of a rampant individualism – of 1968. One very important thing to note about the episode with which I began this study is that, when the French government wanted to expel Cohn-Bendit, it was none other than François Missoffe who stood up for him and who fought on his behalf. If I want to retain anything from the period, it would be this attitude, in which vigorous and contentious debate, where the stakes are very high, finds its proper and comfortable place in the University. There is an obvious generosity in Missoffe's position here; and this is the single most admirable thing about the whole episode. If the myth of 1968 offers us anything by way of example, it would be precisely this sense of an intellectual generosity of spirit.

If we, as academics, want to take a different and critical view of all of this, then the contemporary state of affairs seems to push us inexorably into advocating the classical model; but that would reduce our 'impact', for it places us (as scholars and researchers) into a neo-Arnoldian, allegedly ideology-free zone, one that used to be called 'disinterestedness' in the pursuit of truth. This model has certain attractions, of course; but it does rather have the effect of reducing the scholar to the condition of Cassandra, bewailing and warning from the margins, going unheard and unattended to. It thus explicitly denies us our position as teachers or as colleagues who see the role of teaching as something transformative, in whatever sense.

In what follows, I want to examine the *limitations* of our being placed in the position of having to make what looks like an invidious choice; and to advocate a different view of the debate. To do so, I will urge us to consider what we might call an argument from first principles, which will turn out to be an argument *for* first principles.

1

We should begin, then, as in all matters of policy, from some first principles.

There are a number of reasons why it is a difficult task to begin from such first principles. I will explore some of those reasons below; but here, let me state the case clearly, if seemingly paradoxically. The function of the University is precisely to be engaged in the search for first principles: that is to say, the first principle is the search for the first principle.

It follows that whatever I put forward here as first principles is necessarily done so by way of hypothesis, as something to be tested and debated. If I can succeed in establishing such a debate, I believe that this, in itself, will be an indication not only of success locally, but also of the continuing vibrancy of the function of the University as an institution. When we think of the University, we tend to think in terms of plant and buildings: specific institutions in specific places. In what follows, I want to propose a slightly different way of thinking about the institution. In the very early days, of course, scholars were rather more peregrine and not at all tied to a specific location. In much more recent times, the University has operated as a kind of 'third space' between a parental and childhood home and the wider social sphere; and, in this it operates as the site of a *Bildung*, or a *formation* of sorts.

The position I want to advance here is one where we retain the idea of the University as something linked intrinsically to a special kind of mobility or, more precisely, to the possibility that fundamental transformations may occur. The important word here, though, is 'occurrence': instead of thinking of the University as site-specific plant or as a place, we might think of it as an 'event', as something that happens; and it happens (for one example) where we get the kind of high-stakes vigorous debate about the proper conditions of living and of our living together. The University is an idea, so to speak, first and foremost; but it is not just an abstract idea, divorced from material history: it is indeed something that happens or that *takes* place, and assumes its place in a social formation. If we are lucky, these happenings become systematic and not episodic; and, if we are luckier still, they are systematic in a specific place, the location of the group of intellectuals that constitutes the action that is a University.

With this in mind, let me now advance the fundamental position of this book *for the University*. In some ways, the University that I describe will be seen to match up with a broadly recognizable picture of the kind of institution that we already know. Typically, for example, our Universities are organized into faculties and disciplines in various ways; and, most typically, these would cover the hard sciences, the social sciences and the arts. In the hypotheses that I will lay out, I will follow that structure but will suggest a new way of thinking of this.

Thus:

1 *The hypothesis*: is that the University is where we pursue the true, the good and the beautiful; it is a place for the establishment of

specific 'faculties', which we might now identify as science, social ethics and aesthetics.

2   *The claim*: is that the University should be about the extension of freedom, the progressive pursuit of human possibilities, edification.

3   *The corollary*: is that the University is the motor of a particular kind of contemporary democracy.

Here, then, we have some first principles – hypotheses, perhaps more precisely – for the form, function and idea of a University. The University exists as a focal point that unites three fundamental and essential forms of human inquiry. It is that institution that exists in order to allow us to search for what is true, what is good and what is beautiful: in the true, the good and the beautiful, that is to say, we can have our contemporary equivalent of the medieval trivium (grammar, rhetoric and logic) and quadrivium (arithmetic, geometry, astronomy and music).

Under the heading of the search for what is true would go the pursuits that are typically followed in faculties of the hard sciences; under the pursuit of the good go those activities pertinent to the social sciences; and under the beautiful we will find the proper place for thought in the domain of the arts and humanities. Clearly, these three areas or faculties are not entirely discrete with respect to each other: there is of necessity a good deal of cross-fertilization. Consider, for a simple and fairly typical or paradigmatic example from within the domain of literary studies, the work of Gillian Beer. How might she be able to write a book such as *Darwin's Plots* (where the nineteenth-century novel is seen in the light of Darwinian science) or how might she examine the novels of the 1930s, as she does in an essay such as 'Modernist Futures' (where she relates literature in the modernist period to various developments in medicine), without having made some inroads into the domain of the hard sciences, medicine, history and politics? In regard to this kind of cross-disciplinarity, her work is not at all unusual. In fact, interdisciplinary study is at the core of all that we do in the University; and, as I shall argue later, what we call the separate disciplines are themselves products of what is essentially a normative interdisciplinary thinking.

What I mean to indicate by my version of the three 'faculties', then, is simply the organization, within our institutions, of the presiding faculties that govern the mobilization of knowledge and research (including the funding of research, and the knowledge-priorities established through that funding) within the University. While the arts might focus on the beautiful, they are not constrained to do so in a simply belletristic fashion, for example. Indeed, they are better when they do not so limit themselves. The beautiful here is itself something that actually *constitutes* a version of the good and the true within the field of the literary or that of music or painting, we might say, for examples. Likewise, while physics might focus on the true, nonetheless it is also concerned with the ethical, philosophical and political questions regarding the pure good of science, and with aesthetic issues regarding the form of the universe and how we perceive it. The world cannot be cut into two or three cultures; and any attempt to do this is simply either an attempt at the fragmentation of intellectual life (an intellectual atomization, as it were) or an attempt to substitute the principles of managerial organization for the more fundamental requirements of critical thinking.

These are also practical matters, full of actual historical 'impact'. The three faculties I describe here are not 'ivory tower' faculties; but rather, they have a profound and material effect in our historical being. Medicine, for example, is the pursuit of the true fulfilment of the human body and its possibilities: it is, as it were, the site for the fullest expression of what it might mean to be embodied at all. Embodiment is not something that is limited to the carefully demarcated space of a biological entity: bodies exist in a social domain, for example, as gendered or as aged or as purely physical entities. Missoffe and Cohn-Bendit would have agreed at least on that. Likewise, law goes under the pursuit of the good in that it is concerned with the material realities of justice and judgement, themselves categories that benefit philosophically from an engagement with the arts and aesthetics, as any critical legal studies scholar can show. One very important aspect of our legal system depends upon hermeneutics in the widest sense of the interpretation of sensory data; and this field is one where specialists in aesthetic matters have a primary interest. In short, the thinking that goes on in these domains is intimately tied to action or historical materiality.

We might rethink or rename our three areas, in the light of this clarification. The true would become more precisely described as the pursuit of experiential knowledge; the good can be redesignated as the pursuit of justice; and the beautiful might be usefully rethought in terms of the pursuit of pleasure or happiness, love and freedom.

What unites the three areas, however we name them, is edification. The University is about – we might go so far as to say that the University *exists for* – the edification, extension and exploration of our possibilities and potential. Key to this is what we might call complexity, with 'confluences' among disciplines. The University is a site for the complexification of thought, not for its simplifications. In some ways, this would be in line with the thinking of a philosopher such as Edgar

Morin. Morin's grand project is one where he is concerned to reverse Descartes, in some fundamental ways. Where Descartes contended that the way to knowledge is through separation and reduction of all complexity to 'clear and distinct' ideas (tied, in my own terminology, here, to the 'atomization' of wholes), Morin argues, on the contrary, that any knowledge that we might gain will depend upon our realizing the complex interweaving of all aspects of the world together. To believe that we can have a proper attitude to the world in which we are fully enmeshed through its fracturing into discrete atoms is a fundamental error. Instead, our relations are such that any pursuit of the real state of affairs depends upon our realization that relatedness is endless, and thus endlessly complex. I may have a relation with you; but you are not some simple, discrete entity, much less one whose entire existence is determined by your relation to me. In turn, you form part of a network of relationships with other people past, present and future; and you and I both are also partly constituted through our networks of relations with the things and events of our multiple worlds.

Consequently, we might now see that the University exists in a kind of paradoxical contradistinction to knowledge, especially in the form of knowledge-as-information. It is probably by now a commonplace that there exists in our contemporary situation an often quite profound confusion of information with knowledge. It is for this reason that assessment has become difficult, for example (and I explore this in detail in chapter 5 below). As we codify examination classifications and gradings, it follows logically that we must be able to characterize those gradings not in terms of knowing things but rather in terms of managing information. It may be the case that we will receive an essay where all the information is (by and large) 'correct'; but it may equally be the case that this essay shows no knowledge of its subject matter. We reward the vacuity of information, not the more difficult – and often aesthetically judged – matter of knowledge.

Against this, we might try to recapture the University as the site in which we contest and struggle with information, in an attempt to make knowledge. If we follow this logic, then, the University is where we go in order to find not what we know but rather the extent of what we do not know; and to find ways of dealing with the fact of that ignorance. Indeed, it is the institution that has the ostensibly paradoxical responsibility to *extend the field of what we do not know*, in order to extend the possibilities of human consciousness, human thinking and action as we strive to engage with and deal with the resulting ignorance. It is the place that we should turn to whenever we literature teachers have that horrible feeling that goes by the phrase, 'I think I understand this poem'.

Within such an institution, the task of teaching becomes one where we endlessly defer the gaining of those forms of apparently stable and secure 'knowledges' or 'informations' that would assert some intrinsic and absolutely incontestable truth-value. It would follow from this, of course, that we would have no easy relation with the much-vaunted commercial priorities of an allegedly simple 'knowledge-transfer', then; and, likewise, it would also follow that our relation with a business-oriented 'skills agenda' should be seen as but one minuscule aspect of the function of the institution. The University is, if you will, a place of humility, even of love (more on that later). It is a place where we cultivate our humanity.

2

Here, we come in the phrase 'cultivating our humanity' to what is by now a standard kind of variant on the Bell position. The University is a site, it is argued by some, for the development of culture; and that culture, insofar as it is a cultivating of our humanity, depends upon the University being an institution that has, as its priority, the establishment of a deliberative model of the social. In short, the University is an agora – an open and public space – for democratic debate and discussion. We remain within the classical model here, but we do so in a way that limits the University's claims to make the truth absolute, seeing it instead as a place for the establishment of pragmatic orders of truth, of what it is good for our society to believe.

Bill Readings offers the analysis of this institution in *The University in Ruins*, where he discusses the formation and opening of the University of Berlin in 1810 under Wilhelm von Humboldt. Humboldt also wanted to start from first principles when he was charged with opening this new institution, and he took soundings, in particular from Johann Gottlieb Fichte and from Friedrich Schleiermacher. Out of this grows Berlin as a specific type of University, one that Readings characterizes as a 'university of culture' to be set against what he shows to be the vacuities of our own contemporary 'university of [so-called] excellence'. For Readings, Humboldt's institution 'draws its legitimacy from culture, which names the synthesis of teaching and research, process and product, history and reason, philology and criticism, historical scholarship and aesthetic experience, the institution and the individual.'

It is this last synthesis, of institution and individual, that is central to the development and character of Berlin. Readings goes on to describe what happens in this set-up: 'Thus the revelation of the idea of culture and the development of the individual are one. Object and process unite organically, and the place they unite is the University, which thus gives the people an idea of the nation-state to live up to and the nation-state a people capable of living up to that idea.'[4]

Here, then, in Berlin as a 'university of culture', the institution exists in a dialectical relation with the people and the nation-state. The function of such an institution is to address and even to constitute an emerging 'national character'. It will make the nation and its ideals available to the people; and it will also and simultaneously provide the people who can carry and embody those ideals, people who will be the practical and living embodiment of whatever it is that the University decides constitutes 'Germany'. That 'decision' does not lie in the sole hands of the institution's members; rather, the institution listens to the people (of which it is also a constituent part). The dialectic is also a dialogue. While this is infinitely better than the 'university of excellence' so well and thoroughly excoriated by Readings, and while it may also be the type of institution so nostalgically desired by a liberal left, it is not at all the kind of institution that we should be trying to revive, as I shall show.

Intrinsic to the 'university of culture' is the idea of dialogue and what we will now call a model of citizenship. Martha C. Nussbaum is one of the most vocal defendants of what she sees as the Socratic ideals of a democratic citizenship forged by and through the University. It is probably in her *Cultivating Humanity* that Nussbaum addresses most directly the stakes of the argument regarding the future of our academic institutions. In that book, she finds a legitimizing ground for her preferred kind of University within Stoicism, and specifically within a Stoicism shaped by Socratic modes of argument.

Nussbaum takes her source in a reading of Aristophanes' comedy, *The Clouds*. This is appropriate since, among many other things, *The Clouds* stages a debate on education. On one hand, we have a 'traditional' form of education, as embodied in the Argument that Aristophanes called 'Right'. Right is a militaristic figure in Nussbaum's description, but he might be more accurately construed simply a kind of explicit reactionary traditionalist harking back to the old days, and arguing that the student's task is to imbibe and internalize existing knowledge and to be able to so embody it that its rehearsal becomes second-nature. Against this, we have Aristophanes' conservative and satirical depiction of the Socratic view of the philosopher-teacher, 'Wrong', who proclaims himself an avowed 'modernist', and who argues that it is the task of the student to think more independently, to doubt the existing knowledge and to ask some fundamental questions of it, so that he can better discover himself and his own values. In the play, Wrong is presented essentially as a form of tongue-twisting Rhetoric, a rhetorician with the ability to ensure that the Wrong argument always wins, even in the face of reason and justice as embodied in Right.[5]

It is the case, argues Nussbaum, that we persist in this same argumentative contestation in the contemporary moment. 'Socratic questioning is still on trial,' she writes, and it is the case that 'Our debates over the curriculum reveal the same nostalgia for a more obedient, more regimented time, the same suspiciousness of new and independent thinking' that are critiqued in Aristophanes.[6] While it is the case that the populist media caricature of the contemporary University – as a place of rebellion by blacks, gays and lesbians, the working class and so on – is obviously false, nonetheless it remains true that the liberal or critically aware education that this populist caricature attacks is indeed under threat. Universities are no longer – if they ever were – hotbeds of Trotskyite radicalism; but in caricaturing them as institutions that threaten the existing order, a populist media shifts the stakes of the argument. It is not that the University is under attack for its radical credentials; rather, the University is threatened more now by a drive to homogenize the whole public sphere. The biggest threat to our institution is what we might call the potential triumph of 'the banality of blandness'.

It is factually the case, then, that liberal institutions are indeed under various forms of threat, as Nussbaum recognizes; and the picture is not specific to the United States (which is Nussbaum's primary area of interest in this). To put it briefly, in a culture where the University has become 'pragmatically' the serving agent of the government of the day, independent thought – of whatever stripe or colour – cannot be encouraged; rather, we are to be viewed as 'human resources' carrying out functions as given to us by governments that claim a mandate from the fact that they have been elected into office. Yet, if the University is anything, it is a place of thinking – and thinking is a faculty that is beyond the capacity of mere 'resources'.

It is this contradiction that gives Nussbaum and those who will defend liberal education their focus. The result is a vigorous and spirited defence of the legacy of Socrates, as it were. Nussbaum points out that the Stoical view of education (following Socrates in this) requires that the teacher confront the passivity of students. The point of that is to do as Socrates does in Plato's dialogues: to challenge and even shock people into making arguments for themselves, or to achieve a kind of intellectual independence. Tellingly, Nussbaum writes that:

> All too often, people's choices and statements are not their own. Words come out of their mouths, and actions are performed by their bodies, but what those words and actions express may be the voice of tradition or convention, the voice of the parent, of friends, of fashion. This is so because these people have never stopped to ask themselves what they really stand for, what they are willing to defend as themselves and their own.

In this condition, students are not really extending themselves at all; and education would be precisely characterized as the stimulation of the passive mind into active and independent thinking. This way, people can begin to find their own capacity for thought; and, through that, they can make informed moral and other choices.[7]

In Nussbaum's eloquent formulation of the position, we have the emergence of a number of themes: teaching as a mode of encouraging independent thought; the emergence of embodied belief; and the claiming of a full humanity in the examined life. The position here is uncannily reminiscent also of the biblical 'parable of the talents' (Matthew, 25), for it is one in which the student is encouraged to fulfil her or his inmost possibilities in order to render a return, with usury or interest, to the master (i.e. to pay off the costs of the education – a question addressed also, incidentally, in *The Clouds*). Perhaps yet more importantly, it is also a principled defence of autonomy. The problem being dealt with is that, too often, the things which we identify and consider as our own thoughts are but ideological and rehearsed truisms masquerading as thought. Yet more pointedly, of course, what we may call our own thoughts are but 'what is taken for granted' by government. This is the corrosive power of the banality of blandness, of course: anything identified as thought at all – any independent activity of thinking – suddenly becomes construed as 'oppositional'. Worse, it is construed as being in opposition to an alleged 'natural' state of affairs or 'what is taken for granted'.

For Nussbaum and other defenders of a liberal education, this is an obvious major difficulty. And, in fact, the response is to suggest that the institution should become the site for the sustaining of deliberative democracy. The student or University teacher ought to be enabled to say 'No', to question, to debate with the political powers that shape the being of the institution. In short, a liberal education would be a critical education, an education in scepticism.[8] Of course, the danger of this is that we will emerge simply with a questioning not of government but of truth itself. The University becomes the place not for Socrates, but for a jesting Pilate saying that there are many truths, but in that situation, who will win? We are back to the *Quis custodiet* question: who will decide?

When we reach this level of the problem, Nussbaum's response is clear: the point is not to create a marketplace of competing ideas, or to localize truth according to individual interest-groups; but rather to use dialogue and debate to pursue something that she calls 'the common good'. In this way, she argues, we will find and encourage that form of democracy that is genuinely reflective, thoughtful and able to adopt a deliberative approach to shared citizenship. The good citizen is she who is able not only to take an informed view, but also to be able to reason about what it is that she herself believes and advances as true.[9]

In this state of affairs, then, the University becomes aligned with a version of *participative citizenship*. This represents a stage beyond the 'university of culture'; for it says that the citizen produced is herself a site of debate, not simply a receptacle or vehicle of the University's imbibed and pre-existing truths. It is no longer simply a question here of the debate between citizen and institution; it is now more pointedly a debate among citizens themselves, a debate that is enabled by the institution which now operates as a kind of catalyst for whatever reactions and combinations of new ideas will emerge when citizens engage each other in dialogue or debate.

In the United States, this kind of position is ultimately indebted to John Dewey; but it may be the case that it has parallel Scottish roots, in the much-discussed 'democratic intellect' that is engendered by a generalist education favoured by the traditional Scottish University system (and I will return to this in my final chapter below). We should note first of all, though, that there is nothing *intrinsically* democratic about a University of liberal culture. Dewey was among the first to give the kind of analysis of the German system that we find reiterated in Readings; and, as he pointed out in 1916, that German system 'made the national state an intermediary between the realization of private personality on one side and of humanity on the other'. The result of this is that 'it is equally possible to state its animating principle with equal truth either in the classic terms of "harmonious development of all the powers of personality" or in the more recent terminology of "social efficiency".' It follows from this that, to have an idea of education as a social process requires that we have a prior idea of the kind of society that we want.[10] In fact, we might add, it is precisely *because* of this confusion – the confounding of harmonious development with social efficiency – that we are allowed to have a liberal education at all. What the University offers as harmonious development of full human becoming is received by government as social efficiency.

We can see this yet more clearly if we recall one of Dewey's fundamental observations. A democratic society is, by his definition, an ever-extending society: it requires that each individual within the society reaches out to embrace others. It is an exponentially expansive system. This, Dewey writes, 'is equivalent to the breaking down of those barriers of class, race, and national territory which kept men from perceiving the full import of their activity'. If we thereby establish a greater complexity of social relatedness, we also produce a greater diversity of stimuli to which we, as individuals, are called to respond. In this way, we edify and extend our own human being. Further, in this condition, we generate also a variety in our action: we do not 'conform' to a single stable model of the self. As a result, we are provoked into a greater range of activities and powers. In short, we grow as individuals and as participants in relation with others or civil society. Anything else, in fact, leads to exclusiveness and a society based upon exclusions of groups from a central power; and this is anathema to democracy.[11]

When Nussbaum validates her model of deliberative democracy, it is something like this – a release of previously unheard voices – that she has in mind. However, lurking within Dewey here is a clear critique of any resulting form of identity-politics, any form of politics that thinks of democracy as being the liberation only of a number of identified 'group' voices or 'communities' as we will call them. That is to say, for democracy to be democracy, it has to be ever-moving, ever-expanding. It cannot rest in any value judgements that derive from 'communities of interest', be they based on class interest, racial interest, gendered interest and the like.

A government that is avowedly democratic needs assent from its people; and education is actually one of the ways that it will gather such assent. It does so either by securing agreement or by ghettoizing dissent (or often, in fact, by the adoption of both these manoeuvres), identifying dissent as merely the relativism of different 'community interests'. Thus, what begins as the liberation of human possibility becomes precisely the effecting of social efficiency. In short, any form of critique that is based upon identity politics is profoundly conservative and, let me go further, anti-democratic. It thus has no place in the University, if we see the University as the site for democratic actions. In short, identity is constricting, where the University should be edifying and expansive.

Given that the 'university of culture' is grounded precisely in the formulation of such an identity (whether it is a national identity or an individual one), it has now a clear limitation in respect of its democratic credentials. Further, given that deliberative democracy also depends upon the identification of different points of view and, within that, a claim upon truth that is grounded precisely in such an identity (on both sides of the deliberation or argument), this too offers a limited version of democracy. Let me repeat two things: the University, properly construed, is intrinsically related to the extension of democracy; and democracy is itself intrinsically ever expanding.

3

While the pragmatic model that dominates our institutions and governance in the advanced economies is obviously inadequate to the demands of the modern University as such, nonetheless the corollary of pragmatism – material action – remains fundamental here. Once one considers the University less as a place and more as an event, as something that happens from time to time, then one becomes aware of the essential importance of action. For those who follow Cartesian rationalism, the University can be *merely* an idea (in studies that examine 'the idea of the university', such as we see it in Newman or Jaspers, say). However, in advocating the sense of the University *of* the Idea here, I want us to bear in mind that the idea is nothing unless and until it is action. Rather, more precisely, ideas are what we abstract from actions in the first place. The University of the Idea is not a place for disembodied thinking, for the *preconditions* of deliberative democracy: it is – or should be – democracy itself, as it were.

John Macmurray, the undeservedly neglected Scottish philosopher, is often credited with the fundamental arguments concerning the primacy of action. Especially in his Gifford lectures, but also in *Conditions of Freedom*, he was at pains to show that the human is defined precisely by action. Although his own motivating ground for this lay in a kind of religious impulse, I want to advance the sense of the University-as-action here by some different, and avowedly secular, means. Hannah Arendt, taking a line that is not so distant from Macmurray, argues that the human being is free precisely by dint of the fact of our having the capacity for action. As she puts it, 'while we are well-equipped for the world, sensually as well as mentally, we are not fitted or embedded into it as one of its inalienable parts. We are *free* to change the world and to start something new in it'. Such action depends, she argues (following Martin Heidegger on this) upon our capacity for a kind of *Destruktion*: 'In order to make room for one's own action, something that was there before must be removed or destroyed, and things as they were before are changed.'[12] This action further owes its existence to *imagination*. Imagination, as we will see, is central to the University of the Idea.

I suggested parenthetically here that Arendt had followed Heidegger; but she is also following Hegel more fundamentally (though without explicit acknowledgement). Specifically, her thought here bears all the traces of one influenced substantially by the Hegel of the *Introductory Lectures on Aesthetics*. In those lectures, he – like Arendt after him – explicitly associated the establishment of freedom precisely with the ability to imagine things as other than they are; and for both Arendt and Macmurray, following in this tradition of thinking, it is not the case that we imagine and then act; rather, we reveal our imagining precisely by the facts of our actions.

Actions come first here, as the fundamental condition of our becoming human; and such an activity of becoming human is also now, clearly, identified as a becoming free. Now, the 'university of culture' would see this freedom as being the freedom not of the consumer, but of the citizen. It is interesting to think again about Aristophanes and *The Clouds* in relation to this. When the play was first performed, it did not win the prize in the theatre festival of 423 BCE. Disappointed, Aristophanes rewrote the play, this time inserting an attack on the audience, given by the Leader of the Chorus. We might recognize this from recent times as the kind of thing we can find in the theatre of Bertolt Brecht or, more recently still, of Peter Handke; and the desired effect is the same. The address to the audience quite radically implicates the audience in action. At the first performance of *The Clouds*, Aristophanes suggests, the audience was mistaken in preferring the plays of others, 'But if you now accept my work with ready ears and eyes, / Posterity will reckon you a generation wise.'[13]

This is of significance because the popular and immediate success of these plays was given by a form of radical democratic public assent. Value depended on votes, as it were; and the votes for the prizes legitimized the works and their authors, literally giving them cultural authority. Aristophanes clearly felt that his work had been wrongly judged in its first competitive performance; and 'Right', encouraged by 'Wrong', follows the Leader of the Chorus in launching a fierce attack on the audience, doubting the value of their collective judgement, on the grounds, this time, that they are all allegedly gay. For Aristophanes, citizenship was marked by particular qualities (including, obviously, intelligence, but also heterosexuality, especially manliness or what would later be known as *virtù*); and the logic is that, unless you embody those qualities, you do not actually count as a citizen.

In some perhaps surprising ways, the modern British version of this lies in F.R. Leavis. Leavis is, at some points, not so very far removed from the idea of the Scottish 'democratic intellect' as he would probably have wanted to be. Like Aristophanes, he was not an enthusiastic democrat, preferring the idea that the University (and he meant specifically Oxbridge) was the proper province of an elite, a small group of individuals, who could form a kind of Platonic 'Republican' guard of all that is good in humane culture.

For Leavis, the key thing that was under threat was what he saw as a common core of culture, a kind of agreed set of norms, and specifically the norms of a shared *English* culture or culture of 'Englishness'. He thought of this 'centre' as something that could be identified with fundamental values, and as a kind of vanguard elite that could guide others to share such values. In some respects, he is a re-embodiment of Humboldt, while also being (and there is a massive paradox in this) rather like a voice for a (more obviously Scottish) generalist and anti-specialist kind of tertiary education. He explicitly asks for a kind of rapprochement between a defined and precise specialism on one hand, and a more general but well-informed social sphere. As he put it, in this defence of a common culture (or what I am calling the public sphere), 'An urgently necessary work is to explore the means of bringing the various essential kinds of specialist knowledge and training into effective relation with informed general intelligence, humane culture, social conscience and political will.' He then assigns this task to the University, almost as its definitive and determining trait, going on to say that 'In this work, we have the function that is pre-eminently the university's; if the work is not done there it will not be done anywhere.'[14]

Leavis's concern was that a narrowing of thought by disciplinary specialization and its rapid advance was killing off this idea of a generally available culture, and isolating the University from a more general social state: 'the idea of liberal culture has been defeated and dissipated by advancing specialization; and the production of specialists ... tends to be regarded as the supreme end of the university, its *raison d'être*'.[15] Against this tendency, he argues that a small, if still significant, number of individuals benefit from University (and here he means Oxbridge), but that this is not down to the curriculum or to the measurable quantities that we now use to account for teaching and its outcomes. He is indeed helpfully clear on this, and his characterization of what is essential also offers a sense of what might be his version of the University.

He argues that 'Curricula, at best, give opportunities, and if these are profited by it is mainly owing to the stimulus derived from the general ambience, to the education got in that school of unspecialized intelligence which is created in informal intercourse – intercourse that brings together intellectual appetites from specialisms of all kinds, and from various academic levels.' In this, he is validating the notion of a

University as a space where well-informed people, from diverse fields of interest and inquiry, get together *beyond the classroom* and share, in their dialogues, the more general culture that he seems to value. From this, he then proffers a sense of the University as something that exists beyond the study, as it were: 'It is, it might be said, because they are so much more than educational institutions that the older universities have this measure of educational virtue.'[16]

There are limitations with this, of course. Leavis's version of being 'beyond the study' is one where the academic and student go into a common room; it does not yet, in this version at least, reach beyond the space inhabited by his vanguard elite. However, this is at least a solid acknowledgement that the classroom or study has permeable walls, as it were. We might see here the seed of a better position, where the University likewise has no walls; but that, at this stage, is farther than Leavis himself will go, for he wants to preserve the idea of the core central values being guarded by a small elite.

Yet there are also real strengths in Leavis's position, however limited in social terms it may be. Efficiency, for example, is not to be measured by outcomes, as it were; it is a *mode of living* that we are discussing here. In fact, Leavis is arguing that it is precisely the real and experiential actions that derive from his ideal of University study that are of value: it is *action*, not any kind of pure or abstract formal thinking, that matters here.

Now, for Leavis, the fear was that what he regarded as the common core of this humane knowledge – a common core that was given specifically by the disciplines of 'Eng. Lit.', wherein sense and sensibility were trained together – was under threat. He was right in his fears; and the results are clear for any and all to see in our present version of the University sector. In an age of massification of tertiary education, we have replaced the idea of the *university* with the idea of *diversity*, as it were; and this democratizing move, going hand-in-hand with massification, would have been anathema to Leavis.

Yet, if we are indeed linking the University to an idea of democracy and, within that, to an idea and a fact of extended freedom, it follows logically that we must embrace such diversity. For a thinker such as Leavis, or a writer from antiquity such as Aristophanes, the problem was that not all citizens would conform to the idea of the elite, so to speak. We were not models of the required 'social efficiency', but were rather too much interested in pursuing our individuated human possibilities. Let is now look at how we might see the University of the Idea in relation to such freedom, such democracy.

Being a citizen is a necessary but not yet a sufficient condition for the foundational principles of this kind of University institution. By definition, if the University is trying to go beyond that stance in which it sees its task as the production of a 'national character', then we need to be alert to the simple fact that the University is about the *production* of difference or diversity or change: action such as this being the founding condition of our humanity and our freedom. One attends University in the mode of a reader of Rainer Maria Rilke, faced with the demand to 'change your life'.

The inappropriateness of a 'university of culture' for our time might be thought to be obvious: there is no single culture, as Leavis was right to note. However, while he lamented that fact, he lamented it as an anti-democrat. What happens if we welcome it, if we celebrate diversity and difference? For many, the result is a flight from the idea of a normative and coercive 'national character', certainly; but a flight that heads directly towards the comfort of identity politics. In this, the critic finds themselves at odds with what is proposed as a 'dominant culture', and, in their assumed marginality (or, worse, victimhood) in the face of that culture, they will find the solace of identity with a sub-community, a *sous ensemble* as Alain Badiou refers to it. The critic's position in this sub-group also gives to the critic a position of authority from which to critique or attempt to undermine the allegedly central core culture and its values. The position thus looks 'critical' and 'oppositional' – the very basis of a deliberatively democratic constitution.

There are difficulties with this stance. First, it alleges that the idea of a central core culture is false (there is none), and then takes its stance against it. Next, it sees its task as being *theoretical* in that it attacks the foundational principles of cultural criticism; but it also assumes that this formal critique is substantive. In its formality, however, or in its theoreticism, it contains no action. Richard Rorty is clear on this. In *Achieving our Country*, he makes the convincing case that radical critical theory has made significant changes in American culture, for the better. As he points out, it is no longer acceptable within the academy for colleagues to be casually homophobic, racist, sexist and so on; but he also points out that while this is a necessary amelioration of things, it is so *within the academy*. Meanwhile, 'out there' in the streets of the United States, the poor continue to be exploited; and racism, sexism, homophobia and other regressive attitudes continue to expand their reach, even if occasionally in more subterranean fashion than before.

More than all this, however, is the fact that a mode of criticism grounded in identity-politics is actually complicit with the very object of its supposed critique. The problem is the flight from one identity to another, when democracy would entail, by contrast, a flight from identity into difference, from a University to a diversity, as it were. Alain

Badiou makes the salient point here, when he considers this emergence of myriad sub-cultural relativistic truths. When we identify sub-cultures and ascribe to them a local, relativized series of truths, what we do, effectively, is to set up a marketplace of truth; and, for each identity or for each alleged victim, there is a new market:

> What an inexhaustible future for mercantile investment in this surging up, in the figure of redeemed communities and supposed cultural singularity: women, homosexuals, the disabled, Arabs! And then the infinite combination of adjectives here: what a dawn! Black homosexuals, disabled Serbs, Catholic paedophiles, moderate Islamists, married priests, young green managers, oppressed unemployed, the already-old-young. Every time, a new social image authorises new products, specialist magazines, adequate commercial centres, 'free' radio stations ...and so on.[17]

This, a condition that Badiou calls 'barbaric', is a condition that begins in the search for democracy, but eventually coerces all participation into cohabitation with a so-called 'free-market' and purely economistic 'liberalism'.

Against this blind alley, we might place Jacques Rancière's observations that, within identity politics, what happens is that 'a voice is given to people solely within the framework of an identity that they would have to realise or even to express'.[18] In other words, what is being authorized here is the voice of an already prescribed identity, and not that of an experiential subject, caught in their action. Thus, for example, individual women, especially those rightly persuaded of the values of feminism, might find themselves compelled to speak as if they were an embodiment of something like *Woman* as such: the individual becomes purely and simply a representative of a more abstract generality, with its prescribed characteristics and qualities, regardless of the specifics of the particular woman speaking. The same would apply to all those sub-groups and sub-sub-groups identified by Badiou. As a prescribed identity, this is pure form, devoid of the content of lived experience that would be necessary for a proper democracy of freedom. It is, in fact, no step beyond Nussbaum's observation that we tend to speak in the voices of others, perhaps most tellingly precisely when we believe we are being most authentic, most 'ourselves'.

The question here is how we find, through the University, a form of engagement that is genuinely civil, as it were. Any genuine citizenship cannot be defined in terms of individuals inhabiting prescribed positions. Indeed, we might go further, and agree with Rancière when he argues that 'citizenship is not the defence of one's own culture nor of one's group'. There is a logic here that leads with inexorable force to a conclusion that democracy itself cannot be served by identity-politics, and that it requires the University to become a force for the emergence of diversity, in fact. That diversity and its increase is precisely the extending of democracy and freedom that Dewey sees as intrinsic to any democratic will. The logic is stated clearly by Rancière when he writes that 'culture is always a form of disidentification: the possibility of speaking something other than the tongue of one's ancestors or of one's group or interest-group'.[19] If there is to be a public sphere at all, then it follows from this that it is constituted by the ever-ongoing search for difference and diversity, for new forms of speaking, and for forms of speaking that will turn one's self-identical voice into a voice of alterity.

4

We can begin to sum up the position in terms of our exploration of my hypothesis. I began by suggesting that the University is that institution that seeks edification through the pursuit of the true, the good and the beautiful. However, I have also argued that these pursuits are related intimately to democracy and to freedom, and that they have historically had something to do with a culture centred on an idea of a normative national character. Where have we got to?

First, it is the case that, in the age of a massification of education, there is no single and unified version of what constitutes the true, the good or the beautiful. It would be an error to try to return to such a view and to impose a single version of such a view on a diverse totality. This is the way of centralized or totalizing government, centralizing power and value systems. It has been tried in various totalitarian states and has been shown to be coercive, and inimical to freedom and to edification. It has also equally been tried by different governments, especially avowedly 'democratic' governments that might seem to desire the autonomy of the University institution. These latter governments tend to assert that the University is indeed free to do as it will, while using other means (sometimes financial, sometimes cultural and ideological) to ensure that 'what it wills' coincides entirely with government policy. This is not a delegation of power to centres beyond the government leading to a diversification of interests and freedoms. Rather, it is purely and simply a delegating of blame in which the government can distance itself from accountabilities.

By contrast, then, we might celebrate the end of the idea of the University, and look at the consequences of a culture of diversity. In a plural society, what constitutes the true, the good and the beautiful is multiple, historical, ever-changing. There are many goods, many beauties and many truths; and none of these can be guaranteed as eternally stable or immutable. However, we now reach a second proposition by way of conclusion: it does not follow from this that we should accept a *marketplace* of truths. As most economists well know, the power, purpose and even the intrinsic logic of the market is to establish, eventually, a monopoly: the market is, as it were, the 'scandal' that covers and occludes the fact that we live in and through an oligarchy. As Rancière has said, the minority always wins – and, if we are interested in a genuinely emancipatory democracy, we need to oppose this. Another way of putting this is to point out that it is in the interests of 'the winners' in any market to make of themselves a minority and to draw the bridge up behind them as they retreat into their elite positions. This is anathema to our preference here for a genuinely democratic impulse as a driving force for our institutions.

In his recent exploration of the idea of justice, Amartya Sen has revived a definition of democracy that is indebted to John Stuart Mill, whereby democracy is defined in terms of 'government by discussion'. This is a different formulation of the kind of 'deliberative democracy' for which Nussbaum says that we must fight. It is certainly necessary, as a condition of democracy; but it is far from sufficient, even in its own terms. In many 'discussions', we know already what our correspondent is going to say: discussions are often ritualized dialogues between known points of view. In this, we have the illusion of debate and of thinking; in fact, all we have is the rehearsal of already circumscribed routines. This is so in terms of parliamentary democracy, where discussions between parties follow unashamed ideological lines; and it is so in some personal discussions, as between lovers, say, or friends. Genuine discussion, however, is what happens when we cannot predict what is going to be said. We might say that genuine discussion requires us to open our ears to a different – even a foreign – language; and it requires us to have the generosity of spirit to try to understand and hear what that language says. This way, both parties to a rehearsed debate can be forced into hearing the possibility of change that we call the future. Just as in politics more generally, our 'foreign policy' actually determines the shape of our domestic policy. It is for this reason, among many, that the study of foreign languages, ancient or modern, is and should be a central condition for any University education that sees the extension of democracy as being important.

Third, then, we might try to re-characterize democracy in this context. Alain Touraine has argued that, at the opening to modernity, democracy undergoes a major shift. Prior to modernity, it was the case that the subject, 'I', used to affirm itself by identifying with Reason (the Enlightenment) or with Labour (Marxism, but also Capital). Now, however, in societies that have been invaded by the techniques of mass production, mass consumption and (above all) mass communication, liberty detaches itself from instrumental reason. In fact, at times (and we know this following Adorno and Horkheimer) instrumental reason can become part of the problem, can become carceral itself. I would add to this that it is no longer simply instrumental reason that is the issue, but what we could call the provinciality and insularities of *bureaucratic reason* that have left us in the position of being governed by bureaucracy that is coercive and carceral.

In the face of this, suggests Touraine, the subject wants to defend or to recreate a space of invention as well as of memory: that is to say, the subject finds herself or himself at the crossroads between a past that has informed her or him, and a future that is to be invented, or – in my preferred terms above – *imagined*. The subject needs to do this 'to bring about a subjectivity that is at once both being and becoming ... and the great task for democracy becomes the defending and production of diversity within a mass culture'.[20] In this, democracy is not a system of institutional guarantees; nor can it be defined by any demand for a growing consensus; rather, it has to be defined in terms of respect for freedom and diversity. I add to this that such diversity depends also upon an alertness to foreign discourse, so to speak. Behind that, of course, it has to be oriented towards at least the possibility of change or of diversity in the form of historical movements. In such historical mutability, in the possibility of change, we find a fulfilment of our ideas of the University as that 'event' or occurrence that is determined by its search for justice and for the extension of freedoms. The search focuses on the areas of the true, the good and the beautiful; and, when we find this, we have imagination as action, so to speak; and the site for such imagination is the University of the Idea.

2

The Student Experience

Living Learning, Living Teaching

1

The ancient Greeks posed a problem for learning, asking the very simple question, 'How can we learn?' Simple though it seems, this is actually a conundrum. In its most recent formulation, the conundrum was famously reiterated by Donald Rumsfeld, when he tried to make distinctions and discriminations among 'known knowns', 'known unknowns' and 'unknown unknowns'. While this may have been linguistically amusing, it nonetheless was addressing matters of grave importance in relation to international conflicts and, yet more pertinently for our purposes, matters of grave importance in relation to military and related intelligence. The question of learning – of intelligence, broadly understood – is a question of profound and substantial importance.

Let us examine the conundrum and its consequences, especially in relation to the actual experiences of learning and of teaching in the University. Either we know what it is that we are after as we try to learn something, so that we will recognize it when we find it; or we genuinely do not know, and therefore we do indeed have something to learn. If we know already, then we are not learning, but rather simply repeating or reiterating the already known. If the latter is the case, and we genuinely do not know, then we may well certainly find something but we cannot know whether it is what we are after, since we did not already know what it is that we are after. To sum up: in the first instance, we do not learn for we already know; and in the second, we may find something by way of answer, but we cannot confirm this as a learning process, for we do not know if we have found what we want or need.

This second case certainly looks more like what we think of as learning: finding out something that we did not already know. However, if we decide that this is indeed learning, then there are now two new and corollary problems. The first consequence is that we have a problem with the validation of learning. Instead of asking simply, as the ancient world did, 'How can we learn?', we pose the different question, 'How can we know or be sure that we have learned?' This becomes the problem of the legitimization of knowledge; and it will lead us into a kind of eternal regress. Even if we find a satisfactory answer, it will simply generate the next level of questioning: 'How do we know that we know that we have learned something?' The word we give to this potential proliferation of checking and validating (or introspective navel-gazing), in our present predicaments, is 'quality assurance'.

The concept of this quality assurance opens the door to the second problem directly. This second consequence – of our adopting the view that learning is finding out something that we did not already know – is a problem concerning teaching. Someone else (a teacher) must have already known that what we have found is what was already known. It was already known by the teacher, who can now confirm that what has been found is a satisfactory answer for whatever was being sought. But how did the teacher learn this in the first place? Teaching, like learning, now also enters the endless narcissism of self-questioning, submitting to quality assurance in exactly the same way as the process of learning does.

Putting this philosophically and seriously, what happens is that we enter the domain of the Chinese box or Russian doll: a potentially endless regression in an attempt to find the origins of knowledge. How did we first get any knowledge at all? That, of course, is an almost entirely intractable problem. In some ways, it is not a question that is susceptible to any answer; and it is close to what physicists might call the 'non-question' of where the Big Bang came from. However, and perhaps more importantly, the effect of this within an institution is to turn attention away from any *actual* learning and teaching – activities full of real content, full of the content of thinking and of intellectual work – towards an endless monitoring of the *processes* through which we monitor how it is that we *can be assured* that we are learning, and how it is that we *know for sure* that we are teaching. At least we can pretend that we do have answers to this, for we can provide documentation to show that we are always considering it.

Obviously, there is an element of paradoxical thinking here; and it revolves around the implied stability and certitude of knowledge and its objects. If it were the case that 'knowledge' was something that could be parcelled into bits of stable information – let us perhaps call them 'modules' – then it may well follow that such knowledge could be passed on, like a baton in a relay race. We would eventually learn to disregard the problem regarding eternal regression; and we would simply accept and take for granted that what has always passed for knowledge and truth is still indeed what constitutes knowledge and truth at the present time, just as it did in the past. We would accustom ourselves to 'just how things are', so to speak. One word for this, of course, is tradition; but another way of putting it, as far as knowledge is concerned, is the refusal to think. It is a recipe for docility, for passive acceptance of whatever we are told. We become like the fourth runner in the relay-race, aware only of the present goal, unconcerned about the previous runners except as things that may have disadvantaged us, and certainly entirely oblivious of the big bang at the start of the race.

Further, in this version of knowledge, we are forced to compart-mentalize and to establish certain 'levels' of knowledge. If it is the case that we eventually abandon the endless regression of 'How did my teacher's teacher's teacher know this?' then we can only do so by positing some unquestionable self-asserting 'first cause'. In many cases, of course, such a first cause is called God, a kind of infinite 'I am' who, in pronouncing the words 'I am' thereby constructs a world that is outside of God, outside of this first cause, but always dependent upon it. In short, the modular version of knowledge – the view that knowledge has some stable content that can be parcelled into modules and passed on or 'transferred' – is fundamentally theological, even mono-theological; and, to the extent that it is thus theological, it is also incipiently totalitarian. It presupposes a consciousness that transcends all historical reality; and this is an omniscient and omnipresent consciousness that is also effectively divorced from – superior to – any material or historical body.

In a version of knowledge that is grounded in these beliefs, we do not have authority, but rather authoritarianism; and, in many secular versions of this where the State interferes with the independence of institutions of learning and tries unilaterally to shape the content of that learning, the end-result is precisely a totalitarian version of the social. Such a view claims, at least implicitly, that there exists a stable, and indeed monumental, body of knowledge that constitutes the eternally unchanging truth. If you want the truth, look steadily at the existing monuments. The task of the student is to conform to that knowledge, to that truth, and then to repeat it endlessly, in an act whose function is simply to retain the monumental body of truth in an unchanging fashion and to confirm the voice of an earlier authority.

Clearly, this is rather in conflict with the adventurous instinct, not to mention the instinct for critical consciousness, of the human intellect. While some may indeed be content to worship at the monuments of unchanging intellect, others are stimulated into thinking – maybe even into 'begging to differ' – when they examine that supposed stable body of accepted dogma. Therefore, minor variations are of course to be permitted; and we can call this 'discovery' or even 'research'; but even in this, the activity that we call research becomes nothing other than the eradication of earlier error, instead of the production of the new. We get an even clearer view of the monument, as it were, for our researches have essentially been exercises in either purging us of our erroneous ways or of polishing-up and clarifying yet further the essential shape of the monument.

Perhaps it is better now to rename what I have been referring to as 'the monumental' for what it actually is. The monumental body of the past referred to here is really made up of all those works of art that a civilization claims to possess as markers of its identity. The works have to be rendered 'stable' in terms of their meaning if our own identity is itself to be preserved and maintained, or rendered stable and assured in its turn. That is to say: their meaning has to be controlled and regulated, especially if I am to feel secure in my own identity. Thus, we cannot ever learn anything about them, for we have now fallen back into our first predicament: there is nothing new under the sun, nothing new to disturb what has always been known as truth. In this, the task of the student is to conform; that of the teacher to repeat and 'transmit'. The consequence is that we have no need whatsoever to examine the *content* of the activities of learning and teaching; and we can safely and assuredly turn instead to measuring the *processes* of learning and teaching. If we are to be assured of the quality of this, then what we are looking for is simply conformity to the ideology of knowledge as a stable entity, susceptible to modularization and transmission in parcelled packages or units.

As avowed 'moderns', attentive to the needs and demands of the contemporary, aware of our position as the latest runners in the relay, we might feel unhappy with a view that keeps truth in the past. However, the paradox of the activity of making minor modifications that we call 'research' is that we can still claim an essentially modernizing drive in our intellectual work. The net final result – wherever knowledge has become reduced to the eradication of error or the correction of a previously limited view of things – is the peculiar state of affairs in which 'the now' and 'the new' are identified with 'the true'. This, while peculiar, is also reassuring. It is as if all the peculiar and challenging intricacies of research can be caught in a rather Whiggish view of progress, in which we researchers say, 'Wow! Thank goodness I live now, for at last humanity has entered the realms of the true.' This is the fundamental aspect of what we usually blithely and blandly refer to, in self-righteous and self-aggrandizing fashion, as 'modernization'.

Jonathan Swift satirized this thinking in his comic critique of the 'modern' author in *A Tale of a Tub*. There, his avowedly modern author, driven by the madness of endless 'modernization', is able to make the absurd claim that 'I here think fit to lay hold on that great and honourable privilege of being the last writer. I claim an absolute authority in right, as the freshest modern, which gives me a despotic power over all authors before me.'[1] This is not the Optimism of Alexander Pope, writing that we should assume a certain humility before the world, and accept with Leibniz that 'Whatever is, is right'; rather, it is the arrogant hubris that says instead 'whatever I say is right' and that legitimizes this by an assertion of modernization, of being in the here and now. It is the move that, at a stroke, recharges mere opinion as knowledge; and that claims such knowledge as truth. If two people now claim different truths, we cannot any longer argue about the content of their truths: all we can do, if we wish to seek for a foundational ground on which to choose sides, is to argue about the processes whereby they *know* that they have learned.

If the now and new is also axiomatically the true, we are enabled to suggest that those who went before were less developed intellectually. That is also very reassuring, for in the end it allows me to say that such and such a state of affairs is true for no other reason than that I, here and now, believe it to be true. If I 'know' something in this philosophy, my knowing it makes it indisputable. If you disagree, then you are entitled to your opinion; but, being 'you' and not 'I', *you* only have *opinions* while I have truth on my side. Thus, that great philosophical division that was so central to the Renaissance in Europe – the division between *scientia* and *opinio*, between knowledge and mere point of view – is eradicated. By definition now, *I* (as that which is 'here, now') am identified as that which has truth, while, equally by definition, *you* can only have opinion.

Friedrich Nietzsche, of course, is the philosopher who has done more than any other to help us to see that truth may be relative, or dependent upon point of view. Famously, he argued that 'There is no truth. There are only interpretations'; and, at a stroke in this, he dismisses that paradox of our teaching/learning conundrum that would find its solution in an originary God. However, having said that there is no truth, but instead only interpretations, Nietzsche also immediately adds the statement that, 'This, too, is an interpretation'. The statement logically undoes itself or deconstructs itself in a paradox akin to that of the Cretan liar. That paradox is most easily summed up in the sentence, 'I am lying.' If that is true, then it is false; and vice versa, indefinitely and undecidably.

Likewise, in Nietzsche, it cannot be *true* in any fundamental sense that 'There is no truth. There are only interpretations', for that, too, is but a way of looking at things. In any proper reading of Nietzsche, we retain the angst regarding the origin of truth; and, indeed, part of the point of his philosophy is to make us genuinely *experience* that angst in the unsettling of our minds as we try to deal with the inherent paradox of his statement. However, it is interesting to note, in passing, that our contemporary moment, which often salutes Nietzsche in validating the so-called relativism of truth, is a moment wherein what we actually find is that *all* truths are indeed relative – *except for mine*, which remains absolute and guaranteed and stable. That is to say, we have been very poor readers of Nietzsche.

In the existing model of 'monumental' educational thinking that dominates contemporary discussion of these matters, learning and teaching have become evacuated of any sense. They have become mere formal processes without substantive and material content. As Walter Ong put it some decades ago, in a communication model where interlocutors are seen as 'boxes', one full of a message and the other patiently attentive to its reception, the whole mental world has 'gone hollow'. We simply do not 'communicate' by transferring the content of one consciousness into another, and in this respect, there is simply no such thing as 'knowledge-transfer'. Rather, communication is always a much more communally produced activity: there is interference, as it were, between and among all the signals that are being put into play, and there is no such thing as a kind of 'module' that 'contains' the knowledge that we can either teach or learn.

Nonetheless, much of what passes for 'learning' in our times proceeds precisely as if this were how knowledge operates. Our talk of 'outcomes' and of 'knowledge-transfer' presupposes a certainty and a stability in the process of learning or of 'taking' certain modules; and in doing so, it stops learning from being a process, reducing it to the level instead of the commercial activity of the consumption of a product, and of a product that is assumed to be non-organic, non-changing. Is it any surprise that a teaching that goes on in this model is rightly experienced as 'dead', in every sense?

Notwithstanding that dominant ideology, we intuitively are aware that the monumental model is not really a satisfactory model of how knowledge actually works; and it is most certainly not how learning works. I suspect that we have known this since at least 1845, for that is when Dickens satirized it when he described this particular mode of teaching as 'murdering the innocents' in his novel *Hard Times*, published that year. It is there that we meet that particular kind of teacher, Thomas

Gradgrind. Gradgrind is, literally, very matter-of-fact and 'realistic'. He believes that education is about the transmission of facts, which he confounds with knowledge. His reverence for the fact is rivalled only by that of his extremist rationalist predecessors in the Enlightenment, or by his progeny in today's conservative politicians (not simply those of the conservative parties in our democracies, of course).[2] For Gradgrind, the correlative of the fact is the mathematical calculation; but what this amounts to is an obsession with measurement. He is 'a man who proceeds upon the principle that two and two are four, and nothing over, and who is not to be talked into allowing for anything over'. He is to be found always 'with a rule and a pair of scales, and the multiplication table always in his pocket, sir, ready to weigh and measure any parcel of human nature, and tell you exactly what it comes to.'[3] The obsession with measurement comes at a price: the price that his pupils pay is the threat to their potential for grace and sociability, the contribution that we can make to social life, or simply the principle of 'giving' of oneself to a wider public realm that is social existence of any real kind.

Gradgrind is the kind of teacher who 'transmits knowledge'; but he does so in the mistaken belief that his pupils are empty vessels, and thus unworthy of any respect – at least until he has filled them with the image of himself. His purpose is to make his pupils, in turn, into the next generation of transmitters of his own ideas or 'facts'; and this to ensure that they conform to the system of society that he himself upholds. It is also designed to ensure that there can be no change to the social order, and that the historical existence of his 'innocents' will remain devoid of material substance. The innocents are to be denied the autonomy to bring about change, to effect things, or to live a life that could genuinely be called their own. This is why all such teaching is conservative. In this, of course, the experience of the pupils or students amounts to nothing: it simply does not count, should not be measured, cannot be computed.

Facts are, of course, important in teaching; but, if teaching and learning are to be historical, if they are to be allowed to make a difference to people's lives in such a way as to give those pupils the autonomy necessary for the assertion of their own authorities, then facts become subservient to experience. It used to be 'a fact', for example, that the world was flat; but the experience of circumnavigating the globe changes this 'fact', and the experience produces new facts that are themselves, in turn, subject to further modification. If learning is anything, it is a process of *transformation* and most certainly not of *transmission* or transfer. It is a process in which I can become something, and in which I can become something other than I am at present. Learning puts me in possession of new facts; and it does this not simply by a process of abstract rationalization, but primarily through historical experience. Conservative education, such as the Gradgrindian instrumental utilitarianism that we see above, is frightened of the possibility that learning things might bring us the experience of freedom, and especially of a freedom that will allow us to grow intellectually. It thus does all in its power to proscribe the possibility of learning and teaching becoming a genuine student experience.

We need to examine this 'experience' more closely.

2

In 1933, Walter Benjamin published a short essay in *Die Welt im Wort*, called 'Experience and Poverty'. He begins by lamenting the fact that a tradition of passing on experience in narratives or proverbial speech seems to be lost: 'Where do you still hear words from the dying that last, and that pass from one generation to the next like a precious ring?' he asks. He relates the devaluation of experience at that moment to the war of 1914–18, in which a generation had to experience 'some of the most monstrous events in the history of the world'. When the soldiers returned, they returned in a silence, 'poorer in communicable experience', as he puts it. His argument is not just about how terrible sufferings that these men underwent in war have rendered them unable to pass traditions on. Rather, it is more far-reaching: he wants to argue that experience itself is devalued and even 'contradicted', as he puts it, by modern technologies and by certain powers of abstraction that prefer to remain at the level of the theoretical or the drawing-board.[4]

As we might now say: experience of real-life is devalued in preference to the schemes, drawn up in the classroom, that are supposed to capture the reality of that external world. Among the effects of this, Benjamin lists two that are very important, saying that our economic experience is devalued by inflation and that our moral experience is devalued by the ruling powers. In this, what he is getting at is a cultural impoverishing of the facts of experience: these facts of experience are now seen to be less important than the ways we talk about them; and the ways we talk about them are in turn the key to our control and manipulation of them. That is to say, if 'the ruling powers' are defined as those who decide what is legitimate or normative with respect to values in society; and if, further, these powers understand those values in abstract terms, by the force of theorem rather than of material reality; it follows that the material realities of historical experience count for nothing, no matter how substantial or even traumatic they may be. What, then, might we say when we turn to the ostensibly lesser 'trauma' occasioned by learning and teaching: the fundamental transformations of fact, of reality and of the identity of the self that should be effected by learning and teaching?

Prior to Benjamin's 1933 essay (in which, in passing, he refers also to 'the coming war', the Second World War), John Dewey had also written of this kind of experience. In 1916, just as the United States was about to enter the First World War, he published his *Democracy and Education*. In that book, Dewey outlined two different aspects to experience. He pointed out that there are two senses, an active sense and a passive sense, that get mixed together in the word 'experience': experience means trying something (as in an experiment whose outcome we cannot predict); but it also means undergoing something (and thus opening ourselves to the possibility of being transformed). As he put it, 'When we experience something we act upon it, we do something with it; then we suffer or undergo the consequences. We do something to the thing and then it does something to us in return … The connection of these two phases of experience measures the fruitfulness or value of the experience … We learn something'. Learning is precisely the negotiation of an experiment: we may have an idea of what we would like to achieve, but we cannot guarantee the outcome; and we will also potentially be surprised and even changed as we work our way through the experimental process. In this, Dewey is starting to outline a pragmatic view of education: an education that is formed in and through activity and practice – material historical thinking.

He goes on to address explicitly the relation of learning to experience, and he does this in a way that links learning to experience intrinsically. He writes that 'to "learn from experience" is to make a backward and forward connection between what we do to things and what we enjoy or suffer from things in consequence'. This is important in that it puts learning into a historical situation; and it places the subject who learns – the student – right at the centre of an experience. In this, the student finds that they have to negotiate material realities, and that they have to realize that there can be material consequences of thinking in certain ways. Further, he goes on to note that 'under such conditions, doing becomes a trying: an experiment with the world to find out what it is like; the undergoing becomes instruction – discovery of the connection of things'. Learning here is tied firmly to teaching, to an instruction in realizing that our very 'situatedness' in relation to the activity of learning has consequences. There is a materiality to learning and teaching: they literally *matter*. 'Intelligence' is a material entity. It has a historical substance in and of itself. It is not a preparation for action, but is rather itself already constitutive of action. It does things, and changes not only minds but also other things as well.[5]

Dewey here explicitly addresses the ways we learn, and succeeds in his attempt to counter that state of affairs in which a pupil was regarded simply as a passive recipient of knowledge (a knowledge supposedly 'transmitted' or transferred spiritually, as it were). He replaces that moribund and non-organic model of learning with a radically healthier view of the pupil as active – physically and bodily present to the activity of learning and teaching. The account of learning that he rejects is one based upon a profound philosophical dualism, in which mind and body are radically discrete. For Dewey, that was no mere or bland philosophical position: it had a profoundly ethical counterpart, for he saw the dualism of mind and body in these matters as incipiently evil, in fact.

The reasoning is clear: the acceptance of such a dualism led straight to a situation where the body (and with it the entire realm of an exterior or public sphere) is regarded as 'mere' physicality, and meaning becomes instead the province of a realm of spirit divorced from material and historical realities. As he writes, in this condition, 'bodily activity becomes an intruder … it becomes a distraction, an evil to be contended with'. For those who subscribe to the evils of dualism, a major problem lies in the fact that pupils (and even teachers) have bodies. Their bodies are, self-evidently for Dewey, 'wellsprings of energy' and, as such a coiled or potential energy, the body is prone to do things, to act. It is now therefore regarded as the source of a certain potential indiscipline, a threat to the control of the teacher in the classroom; and teaching, in this situation, becomes – in some cases primarily – a policing of the body's physicality.[6]

This is reminiscent of an early modern version of the world, such as we find in Milton's *Comus*, for example. In that text, the explicitly religious aspect of the question comes to the fore. The Lady at the centre of this seventeenth-century masque, threatened with rape, tells Comus, her violator, that the freedom of her mind will remain intact, despite whatever happens to her body: 'Thou canst not touch the freedom of my mind / With all thy charms, although this corporal rind / Thou hast immanacled, while Heaven sees good'. In this, we see an extreme example of a divorcing of mind from body and a profound identification of the self's identity with the mind; but it comes at the cost of the body itself. The religious aspect of this is that it prioritizes spirit with the extreme consequence of the total eradication of the bodily or historically material world.

Such an attitude is also at the root of education conceived fundamentally in theological terms as a necessary policing of the body. In this the 'good' pupil is 'educated not into responsibility for the significant and graceful use of bodily powers, but into an enforced duty not to give them free play'.[7] As we know, certain fundamentalist groups try to effect a ban on the possibility of girls or women learning things: infamously, and disgracefully, the contemporary fundamentalist Taliban have historically targeted girls, and those who teach them, with violence. This actually comes close to the nub of the matter: at the core here is a fear of the body – specifically, in this instance, of the female body – and a madness that says it must be controlled. However, before the more 'advanced' societies congratulate themselves on not being as regressive as the Taliban in these matters, we might profitably consider the more subtle ways in which we have negated the body – including the body as the site of a sexual difference – in our own cultures. This goes all the way from those historical men-only canons of literature and the arts through to ideologies of single-sex schooling. In many of the advanced societies, the governing myth here is not that which shapes the barbarism of the Taliban; but it is to be found in the equally fundamentalist reading of the Adam and Eve myth, where a profound awareness of the body and a shame regarding it is the consequence of eating of the fruits of knowledge.

And yet, the body is at the foundation of all empirical perception, as of all aesthetics: it is through the body that we perceive the world in terms of our material engagements with it, in terms of our experiencing of it. If education, learning and teaching are to be experiences with a real and substantive historical material reality, then the body itself must be engaged. Imagine, for a simple example, the case of a musical education. Music usually involves notation on the page; but the real point of music is the experiencing and the sensation of physical vibration. We hear music thanks to the manipulation of air, the transmission of vibrations that are felt not just within the ear but also deep within the body itself. The response can be various: we dance, we sing, we clap hands, we weep; but all these are material and physical – aesthetically visceral– sensations or experiences.

If we isolate the mind from such bodily experience, Dewey argued, then it follows that we start to prioritize the objects of perception as things also in isolation: we see things and not the relations between things. If we cannot allow for a learning that depends upon the essential relation of our body with material activity, then we cannot hope to see the relations between things in the world. We become removed from the sphere of the social and of community; and the social becomes rapidly atomized. We end up lacking the possibility of sympathy, for we are reduced to living in the mental space of a now vacuous 'I', an 'I' crying out to be filled. Worse, we are an 'I' crying out to be intellectually manipulated into conformity with what already exists. 'Do I dare disturb the universe?' asked J. Alfred Prufrock in T.S. Eliot's poem. In these cases, the answer is clearly negative. But real learning is indeed a shaking of the universe, a disturbing of the ground beneath our feet. More than this, it is a shaking of the ground on which *both* the learner and the teacher stand: it is a communal experience, and an experience of community. We usually simply call that something like 'communication'; and communication is central to education.

But the ground beneath the feet of Gradgrind's children is shaken in an entirely different way. Gradgrind's classes sit in rows, segregated by gender, and their links to their daily life are severed while in the classrooms of his school. Sissy Jupe is even renamed as 'Cecilia'; her father's fondness for her, as reflected in her pet-name, reduced to the pure formality of identification by Gradgrind (who prefers to see her as 'Girl number twenty'). Sissy, though brought up in daily experience of horses, cannot offer a satisfactory verbal definition of what might be a horse. That definition is given by Bitzer instead, and it is given as an abstract and entirely atomized set of discrete qualities: 'Quadruped. Graminivorous. Forty teeth, namely twenty-four grinders, four eye-teeth, and twelve incisive. Sheds coat in spring; in marshy countries, sheds hoofs, too. Hoofs hard, but requiring to be shod with iron. Age known by marks in mouth.'[8] And now, announces Gradgrind, Sissy knows what is a horse.

Sissy is told she must not paper her walls or floors with images of flowers, for that would be to indulge her fancy; and fancy or imagination is what is to be removed. In the eradication of imagination, however, we are left simply with atomized parts of a whole that no one can see or experience anymore. If we continue briefly with the example of music, we do not fully perceive music when we reduce it to the sum of its constituent notes and parts. A major chord involves notes in concert; and, in concert, the tones interfere with each other so that the sound made by the chord cannot simply be expressed as the summation of its three elements of root, third and fifth. As Dewey puts it in relation to a different example, 'A wagon is not perceived when all its parts are summed up; it is the characteristic connection of the parts which makes it a wagon.'[9]

There is a difference, then, between what we can call the mechanization of experience, which is achieved by the reduction of relations to discrete and atomized things; and, on the other hand, experience as learning, which is much less predictable and which involves the body in sensation. Within 'the student experience' it is the former that becomes the quarry, for it is the former that can be ostensibly 'measured' and quantified. It would be like trying to learn how to play the piano simply by reading musical notation, and without ever going through the physical changes required in feeling how to strike the keys, heavily or lightly (forte or piano); or how to stretch and coordinate the fingers; or how to sit or stand. What of those whose bodily sensations are limited or disturbed by some quality or other? What of Beethoven, say? The great percussionist, Evelyn Glennie, who is deaf, can feel and sense her music through the vibrations of the instruments around her: music is experienced neither just as notation nor as a discrete activity of the ear, but is instead an entire physical experience. That experience is itself at the root of Beethoven's own 'imagining' of his own music: the emancipation of the imagination itself has a profound and fundamental relation to experience. And if it is thus for a composer or performer as they learn the music that they will 'teach' us, then it is equally thus for the audience or the learner.

Any craftsperson knows this. Richard Sennett has recently written about the importance of understanding the hand itself in relation to learning. He, too, gives an example from music. As a cellist, he indicates that one learns to play the cello not by an abstract transferring of notation to sound, but actually through feeling how the hand itself makes the notes. Practice is just the name we give to that state of affairs in which our body starts to work as if intuitively in relation to the materiality of the objects (in this case, cello, bow) that it manipulates: the body learns to act in concert with something exterior to it, to make the third thing that we call 'music'. These musical examples are paradigmatic of all learning: ignore the role of the body, and both learning and teaching are radically limited and circumscribed.

Dewey relates his own idea of what constitutes thinking here explicitly to what is going on in the First World War: 'As this is written, the world is filled with the clang of contending armies.' In our response to this dread and factual state of affairs, it is not enough to register individual items (to take an atomized view), nor is it enough to ignore them (or to argue that this has no effect on our other activities, especially those that involve thinking and learning). He writes that, 'To fill our heads, like a scrapbook, with this and that item as a finished and done-for thing, is not to think. It is to turn ourselves into a piece of registering apparatus.'

First here, we should note the necessary attention to the specifics of detail – we do indeed have to try to perceive things; but we should note also that Dewey is saying that, though necessary for thinking, this is not yet a sufficient condition for thinking to take place, for the *transformative event* that is a thought to happen. It is not enough to parade across our world, registering blandly the events that surround us, as if we were some kind of neutral camera. When Isherwood described his writing as being characterized by the formulation 'I am a camera', even he knew that the camera is positioned, that its holder is repelled by certain things and wants to turn from them, while being seduced by the possibilities of other things. To present oneself as a mere 'registering apparatus' is not yet experience, and thus also not thinking, especially if we consider thinking to be something that has a material and historical substance: that is, if we consider thinking to be an action, every bit as real and historical as a bodily action. Instead, Dewey writes, 'To consider the *bearing* of the occurrence on what may be, but is not yet, is to think.'[10]

Thinking is related not simply to registering what happens, but actually to imagining what might be the case, that is, to imagination as such. However, this is not some dreamy-eyed imagining, done in the seductive charm and cool of one's room late at night; rather, it is imagination as action, imagination in the midst of battle. Edward Said always took the view that critical thinking – the only serious kind of thinking that there is – is tied up with the demand for liberation. As he put it, describing his own preferred modes of literary criticism, 'criticism must think of itself as life-enhancing and constitutively opposed to every form of tyranny, domination, and abuse; its social goals are noncoercive knowledge produced in the interests of human freedom'. This, together with his political writings, give a real substance to his view that 'even in the very midst of a battle in which one is unmistakably on one side against another, there should be criticism, because there must be critical consciousness if there are to be issues, values, *even lives* to be fought for'.[11]

Where does this get us to? Both Dewey and, before him, Dickens are in essential agreement with these formulations of Edward Said. The question of learning and teaching is really a matter of a battle, even a physical battle, a battle for the future control of our own bodies and thereby for the future ways in which we will occupy and relate to each other and to our environment or ecology. Ask Sissy Jupe.

3

And what now of our much-vaunted and debated 'student experience' crowed over by University marketing managers, surveyed endlessly by student associations whose surveys – perhaps ominously, and presumably not entirely disinterestedly – are sometimes financed by banks? Has it anything whatsoever to do with this? If it has not, then it is missing the point. And, of course, in the hands of those who describe and manipulate 'the student experience', it really does have nothing whatsoever to do with this. 'The student experience' is there, we might say, in order to ensure that our students *do not have any experience*. It is a myth designed to preclude the experiences of learning and teaching. Teaching and learning take place, certainly; but they do so *despite* the demands and norms of 'the student experience'; for it is really but an exercise in consumerist branding. As such, it is a sinister threat to the fundamental point and function of the University.

Real and genuine experience, we might say by contrast, is precisely contentiousness, the kinds of battle for and with the imagination – and for the possibilities of freedom in actual lives and futures – described by Dewey and Said; but it is a physical battle every bit as much as a mental or spiritual one. Dewey thought of it as an engaged thinking. He pointed out that, in a situation such as war, whether we are directly involved or not, we take sides, at least 'emotionally and imaginatively', for 'We desire this or that outcome'; and if we do not have such desires, then we are not thinking: 'One wholly indifferent to the outcome does not follow or think about what is happening at all.'

Importantly, this shows the consequentiality of thought. As Dewey put it, 'Born in partiality, in order to accomplish its tasks it [thought] must achieve a certain detached impartiality'; and this is so because we share in the consequences of the action, of the experience. It follows from these observations that thinking, thus, happens always in a state of doubt, of uncertainty as to outcomes: 'all thinking is research, and all research is native, original, with him who carries it on, even if everybody else in the world is sure of what he is still looking for'. It thus follows that 'all thinking involves a risk'.[12]

'Risk' is precisely what 'the student experience' cannot accommodate. The very language of its documentation is dominated by 'guarantees' and assertions of what the University *will* 'provide' or 'deliver' by way of this commodity. But genuine experience is, as we can now see clearly, something that is oriented towards the future, towards the ongoing emancipation of human possibilities or potential. Insofar as it is future-oriented in this way, it is by definition *unpredictable*. As Dewey and Said make clear, such unpredictability is not ill-judged recklessness: at each and every moment, one can be 'unmistakably' on one side or other of a division or decision. However, if the experience in question is such that it will lead to the assertion of autonomous and free authority, to the ability to make the world anew in the light of one's learning, then it cannot know exactly where it will end up. Further, any such orientation to the future is also always an orientation directing the self towards others, towards the community with whom we enter into relations as a condition of the possibility of learning and teaching. It is thus not simply in my sole gift to make the future this or that: it depends on my level of association with others, and theirs with me, and ours with the environment that we both find and make, that we receive (undergo, in Dewey's words) and imagine or realize.

It is important that we note here that learning is about the release of potential. However, this is not the kind of potential that is exhausted once it is exercised as a kinetic activity. The Italian philosopher, Giorgio Agamben, can help us understand this. Following Aristotle, Agamben points out that there are at least two kinds of potential. The first is that which can be exhausted through a form of realization. For example, certain liquids have the potential to expand and, when they do so, they usually lose their form as liquid and become a gas. In this, the liquid 'exhausts' its being as liquid, and replaces it with a new identity, that of a gas. However, against this, consider a different type of potential. The architect, let us say, is an architect because she has the potential to design and build a building. When she does this, she does not exhaust the potential that she had: indeed, she may even increase that potential. Furthermore, that potential is there even if she never builds again. This kind of potential does not need to be used up in order to prove its existence. It can be an ever-renewing and, indeed, ever-growing potential.

The modes of learning and of teaching that are based in genuine experience are related firmly to this second type of potential. They shape the possibility of ever-increasing liberation and of an ever-expanding association or relatedness that we can call society or the environment. 'The student experience', by contrast, focuses on the first kind of potential here: in this, one has the potential to fulfil the requirements of a module, and one exhausts that when the module's course has run. The logic is one of 'student progression': in other words, 'That was that; and now onwards to the next one.' Such a logic has everything to do with consumption and nothing whatsoever to do with education.

In sum, 'the student experience', in foreclosing the possibilities of genuine learning and teaching, precludes the possibility of genuine – critical – thought. For Dewey, such thinking involves us in a) an initial perplexity, due to the fact that we are in an organic and evolving situation called history; b) a tentative interpretation of where we stand in relation to this evolving situation, and especially in terms of how we interpret relations and consequences of possible future actions; c) examination of data; d) a trying out of things to see if we can bring our initial perplexity into a calmer condition, thus allowing us our next thought; and e) a commitment to this thought, if it seems to work for us by opening up a possible imagined future.

This is open-ended, risk-driven, physical, critical; and, above all, it is *transformative*.

Transformation – of the self, of the social, cultural and political sphere, of the natural world and our modes of inhabiting it – is at the heart of any serious University education. The University is where we can open ourselves and our students (indeed, ourselves *as* students) to the discovery of things previously undreamt of in our philosophies; and, having discovered them, no longer merely interpret the world differently but actually do something substantive to change things. Changing the world is what we usually call politics; but changing the self is what we call *experience*. Through an education, we go where angels fear to tread, into a contest with the bounds of knowing.

Just over a century ago, E.M. Forster opened his first major novel, *Where Angels Fear to Tread*, with a paean to such experience. Philip tells Lilia, on the eve of her departure for Italy, that if she wants the real thing, she must go off the beaten track. The injunction is common enough for us: we eschew the plasticity of tourism – the faked-up 'Italy experience' – for the authenticity of the hidden, the unknown – Italians living whatever lives they are living, lives that are for themselves and not acted out for the benefit of the short-stay tourist. It is thus that we validate our experience at all: the experience, as such, requires a confrontation with the unknown and a negotiation of it. It means an acknowledgement that, while there are rules and *forms* there that govern what we can do, those rules are there to be questioned, even broken, if they bar our way to the real *content* of a positive engagement. While regulations may *govern* experience, they should never *become* the totality of the experience.

Confronting the unknown is some major part of what it is to be a student, to experience living as a student. However, today, there seems to be a terror of acknowledging this. Who, among us, feels encouraged to be easy in saying to a student's question, 'I don't know'? In the marketized consumerist model of education, the relation of the student to knowledge is cheapened to the point of utter falsification: there exists a body of knowledge; the student pays to get it; and I, as teacher, reach back into the store and provide it. Such a transaction is anathema to the very idea of experience itself: it denies experience while promising to provide it.

Yet, this managerialist fabrication lies behind all models of thinking that want us to dignify the myth that we call 'the student experience'. It is rather like giving the student the brochure, replete with images of terracotta pots and frescoed walls, as a substitute for talking and living Italian. The alleged concern for 'the student experience' is actually a concern to *manage* and *administer* students, as part of the consumerist process. Theodor Adorno knew what was at stake in this. In flight himself from Nazi persecution, he argued in 1944 that what happens is that enlightenment (which should include a struggle for knowing things) is converted into positivism (where certain facts are assumed as self-evident truth). Then, the world can be presented as the unchanging realm of those facts, and knowledge becomes reduced to the managed 'worship of facts'. We end up in a situation where, as he put it, 'Not Italy is offered, but evidence that it exists.'[13] By analogy, today, we do not offer a proper experience of being a student, but instead an image of what might be such an existence and experience. And then we sell it: education as kitsch.

This, at least, is what the architects of the mythic 'student experience' want. However, there is still a place for experience in University education; and it is an entirely legitimate pedagogical task to seek out its possibilities. Building on Dewey above, we can say that there are two senses of experience: first, there is the *undergoing* of a transformative event; and, in this, the experience partly consists in our not being in control of the situation. Pedagogically, it is the negotiation of uncertainty; and the word we used to have for that is 'learning'. Secondly, there is the *amassing* of such negotiations; and, once we have amassed these, we talk of our authority, an authority that derives from actual experiences undergone: and we used to call this 'teaching'. Experience in the University is the interweaving of these two senses.

And surely these are at the core of anything that we call a University experience? That, surely, is the establishing of a situation where the coming generation can find their authority from an engagement with the constant transformation – of self and of world – that we call reality, the place where angels fear to tread, but where we ourselves must.

4

It is well known that young children learn a great deal through play. It is perhaps not so often accepted that things are no different at any later stage in life. Play is central to learning and to teaching; for, in play, we exercise imagination and we explore possibility; we take the 'what is' and ask 'what if' instead. Play allows us not only to imagine the world and ourselves as other than we are, but actually to become other than we are. That, of course, is why it can be subversive; and that is why governments and administrations are suspicious of it. In its threat to control and regulation, it must be downgraded: it becomes 'frivolous' or 'unproductive' or 'a waste of time'. In hard times (and times are always Dickensian-hard, of course, when a powerful class wants to restrain possibilities that others might become free), play becomes construed and mediated as a threat to efficiency.

Yet, as even the mythmakers of 'the student experience' know, play is serious business. The 'student experience' is thus characterized not just in terms of teaching and learning; rather, it reaches out to embrace all with which a student might want to engage, including facilities of all sorts. Many of these facilities are what we might call 'hardcore': they include accommodation (for both living and teaching), libraries, refectories, shops on or near campus and so on. There are also other facilities, including entertainment venues, as given by the Students' Union and by all kinds of society; and, in these latter areas, we find 'the student experience' at play. The point, however, is that this is also 'contained' play: it, too, is regulated in ways that are designed to eliminate risk.

We can return to our quadruped graminivorous creature here. When Lev Vygotsky considered the development of the child, he looked at a young boy who was playing with a stick. The stick, in the hands of this boy, rapidly became something other than it was; and the young boy started to 'ride' it as if it were a horse. As a horse, the stick is now in a different physical relation to the body of the boy; and, through it, he can imagine his environment as other than it is. He can become a horse-rider, even though there is no horse there; but he is showing that he has the potential to do something new, and to transform his body and his world thereby. The stick is what Vygotsky calls a 'pivot'; and, around such a pivot, the boy not only learns, but also develops. This is what we might call *Bildung* or *formation*. It involves a transformation of boy and world; but a transformation that is effected through unregulated play.

Friedrich Schiller, in his *Letters on Aesthetic Education*, was also extremely aware of the power of play, or of *Spielen*. In Schiller, the play in question was both the childhood activity that would be later described by Vygotsky; but it was also theatre, play-acting. *Spielen* brings body and mind together in the form of action once more. Theatre, Schiller argues, is a prime location for the activity of learning and teaching as

I have been describing it in these pages. The important thing about this kind of play, however, is that, by trying out a role, one can achieve not only knowledge but also *authority*.

Authority is, as it were, the other side of experience. In saying this, I do not mean to suggest that we unquestionably grant authority to those more experienced than ourselves. In fact, in our time, this is extremely unlikely to happen: experience counts for little, if anything, in the question of authority. In our time, rather than listen to the voice of experience whose loss Benjamin lamented, we are encouraged and enjoined to prefer the mathematical voice of abstract facts and computation.

An anecdote will suffice to explain this. In a certain faculty of Arts, whose plant was built some time ago and suited for very different conditions from those of mass tertiary education, some lecturers complained that office space was too small to accommodate seminars of eight students. The cramped environment made it difficult to concentrate on the intellectual work in the seminar; the door, left open of necessity, meant that disruptive noise could be heard. The University's authorities were invited to discuss this, with a view to improving conditions. Those authorities could not do anything unless and until they had actually measured the space of each office, computed that against the space that the University 'allocated' for each individual student body, and then saw whether there was any mismatch between these sums. Invited to come along and actually witness the open doors, the stuffed rooms, they expressed no interest, as 'that would prove nothing'. This is, as it were, the eventual triumph of Cartesian rationalism: abstraction is closer to truth than empirical reality; and, certainly, abstraction is what we turn to if we seek authority. Experience itself has no such legitimizing power: it is, after all, 'merely' anecdote, merely subjective and thus lacking in an authority that is now identified with pure abstraction, with the cold and untouchable 'reality' of number. Authority in our time is given and characterized precisely by the eschewing of any substantive experience, and the alleged 'objectivity' of this abstraction is what also turns human subjects into objects at the mercy of those in control of the computations or accounts: our very own Gradgrinds.

At some level, surely, the very point of learning is to gain authority; and to gain that authority through the transformations that constitute learning. More than this, the point is to get the authority to seek the release of further potential, for other learners in their turn. Genuine authority, in this way, is rather like a democracy in that it is ever-extending and ever-expanding. That is to say, what we pass on or transfer or transmit is *not* the module or modularized and compartmentalized nuggets of commercially graded knowledge; rather, it is an *activity of imagining* that we pass on, the activity of critical consciousness in action and in history itself. In short, we pass on the possibility of *play*, of trying things out, trying out roles in an experimental fashion. We pass on – and also generate – *potential*; and play is central to the imagining of that potential, as also to our capacities for realizing it in communally engaged or social actions.

Play, therefore – unregulated play, or, better, play that makes its own rules autonomously as it goes along – should be at the centre of a University. By this, I do not mean to suggest that the University is a site for frivolity, obviously: I have already rejected the description of play as frivolity as a conservative ploy that is designed to hamstring people and to force them into specific forms of 'efficient productivity', where 'child number twenty' can be as productive as the next child. Play as *Spielen*, however, is axiomatic to learning and teaching; and this is especially so if we consider the importance of experiment to teaching and to learning. Not only Schiller and Vygotsky, but also Johan Huizinga would back this up, for the social is shaped to a large extent by the rituals that surround the modes of living produced by what he described as *homo ludens* (playing man). Play is that which disrupts the routines of mindless production, the mechanization of life, in order to produce *time*; and that time is where thinking – and thus also learning – can take place, as our bodies try out new roles, new languages, new stances or positions, new arguments, new battles, new loves.

However, something has happened in the developed and wealthy societies in the last few decades. Whereas, in the mid-century, children might range and roam freely, playing in the relatively traffic-free streets, picking up sticks and becoming cowboys or mountaineers, or doctors and nurses, now it is conventionally the case that such play is regarded as too dangerous, too risky. This, of course, is not specific to thinkers of the conservative right, with their basic demand for the policing of people; it is also shared by those on the left who have become dismissive of certain types of role-play, often confusing the play (playing with toy guns, say) with a political reality (being a violent gangster). In place of this unregulated and unsupervised play, play now has become much more structured and organized. Further than this, it has become essentially privatized, and not something that opens up the public sphere for our children to inhabit and shape.

Children do not play in the street any longer; they go instead to play-group. And, as play has become structured and organized in this way, so it has become something that has to be provided. At this stage, the demand for play in turn generates groups of 'providers'; and play, with great rapidity, becomes something that is easily and very rapidly commercialized into a business. Children now pay to play, as it were. It has its own modes and measures of 'efficiency', and is valued in terms of its 'productivity' and so on. Further, once it has become such a commercial transaction, play is subject to exactly the same kinds of 'quality assurance' mechanisms that have evacuated teaching and learning of content. We do not get play anymore; rather, we get the processes and procedures of play. These, at least, can be quantified and measured.

This is the fundamental ideology that has been carried forward into the marketization of life in the playful aspects of 'the student experience'. In short, the discourse of this student experience is there in order to preclude the possibility that students, like children, will construct in imagination a new configuration of the public sphere through play. It is a restraint on play, so to speak; and it is thus also a restraint on learning and on teaching. As such, it arrests the development from play into learning; it arrests the transformation of experience into authority. The net result of this, ostensibly paradoxically, is a state of permanent infantilization of culture. That is paradoxical because play, as we have seen, is itself determining of *Bildung*: it helps growth and edification.

All of this may help to explain why it is the case that, once they have graduated, students find it difficult to exercise their authority in the workplace. Corporate business – the graduate's employer – has nothing to learn from our graduates; on the contrary, the graduates have everything to learn from the business in question. Is it any surprise that business routinely complains that Universities do not provide the specific qualities that business requires? The one thing that business does not require is the authority of its workforce to change things: conformity and regulation – efficiency – is again the dominant code.

We can consider the emergence of 'the student experience' as a specific new element in the management of higher education. Broadly, it goes hand in hand with the introduction of elements of a supposed 'free' market in higher education. In other words, 'the student experience' can be fairly precisely dated, like sex for Philip Larkin. Where sex began for Larkin in 1963, 'the student experience' started, as it were, in 1998, between the abolition of the binary divide (between Polytechnic institutions and Universities which happened in 1992) and the Blair-inspired political target of having 50 per cent of school-leavers benefiting from a University degree.

Obviously all of this is not to suggest that students had no experiences prior to 1998; but they did not have 'the student experience'. The new 'student experience' is related directly to questions of the market and to the transfer of cash. The issue of fees is addressed later in this book; but suffice here to say that the introduction of fees to the higher education sphere in 1998, and its first tripling in 2003, did not signify that students were now paying for their education whereas they had received it 'free' before. In fact, before 1998, students typically did indeed pay for their education; but they paid for it through a system of progressive direct taxation, on the assumption that, if their education got them a job, it then required taxed payment into a general pot for others to use in the future and for future further extension of freedoms. Payment is thus subject to their potential for payment, and varying upwards according to the benefits they received in their salaries.

But the story of 'the student experience' begins not in the cloisters of Oxbridge, nor on the leafy campus of Sussex or Keele. It begins, in fact, in the period of a certain kind of scarcity of resources in the lead up, during and after the Second World War; and it can be said properly to begin in a relatively small seaside resort town on the east coast of England: Skegness. Skegness is where Billy Butlin opened his first holiday camp, with a novel kind of business model. The idea – which really developed fully in the after-war years, inspiring Pontins as well – was one where you paid an initial global sum as an entry-price to the attractions, and then got access to an entire raft, or a 'suite' as it is now called in business jargon, of facilities. The model was one where, by paying a fee upfront, you were entitled to what would ostensibly look like 'free' access to all the facilities. The basic facilities were all included in the entry-fee, and so too were many playground-style attractions such as funfairs. Soon, of course, there were some notable exceptions to this; and participants or customers had the possibility of paying extras for some facilities that were considered special.

For the child visitor, typically unaware of the high cost of entry, everything was 'free'. The experience was one of untrammelled consumption; and, in what has been characterized as the post-war 'age of austerity', such consumption would have appeared as, and have been felt as, a return to real living, as opposed to mere surviving. The child ran from amusement to amusement, from helter-skelter to swimming-pool by way of the roller-coaster and merry-go-round. All around, there were the staff, dressed in uniform as 'Redcoats' and these staff not only acted as hosts but also as tour guides, showing how to use the facilities, and as entertainment. When one tired of the amusements, one could turn to the staff, who perhaps would be in the midst of putting on an evening show of songs and dance; when one tired of the surfeit of facilities, one could go and watch them acting out their comedy routines, into which they would sometimes invite the audience for a widened form of participation. The audience could then do 'presentations' of themselves.

What has this to do with 'the student experience'? Everything, in fact. The growth and development of Universities, after the first major expansion in the 1960s, led to an emergent *national* University system, rather like Butlin's in that respect. While the emergent Universities were all different – located in towns or in campus – nonetheless there was a drive to some sense that all students were enjoying similar kinds of life; and, as in the proto-'theme-park' experience of Butlin's, there was the implicit demand for consistency across the patch. No matter where in the nation you took your studies, there had to be comparability if we were to be able to claim this as a national system and not merely a series of local institutions with their own regionalized priorities. As with the holiday camps, there would be obvious minor local differences (the Stirling campus is famously beautiful; others are more utilitarian), but there would be some sense of comparability in terms of the 'experience' (you would want your holiday this year in Rhyl to be as good as last year's in Bournemouth, say).

The students in the now expanded national University system would be away from home, for the most part; they were gaining some independence; they were finding themselves as a pressure group and as a community of interest. The teenager generation of the 1950s were now the student generation. They took an interest in music and so on, and the media of the period again ensured that there would be shared priorities in this domain. In short, there was something close to an idea of a unified national system of education at the higher or tertiary level; and, however quickly it was to be threatened during the 1960s, also the emergence of a sense of a national culture and identity. As the Universities developed, especially given the fact that students were away from home, it was important to ensure that they had things to do outside their class-time. Hence the development of student clubs and the like as a vital aspect of *student life*, as it used to be called.

This was an experimental period. It was also a time when students would start to assert a certain kind of group identity, often associated with a cultural avant-garde. This led to the break-up of an easily maintained national consensus regarding values. Thus, for a cultural example, instead of everyone favouring the Beatles in music, new types of interest started to gain their own followings: progressive rock; hard rock; singer-songwriter melancholy; crossover jazz-funk; and so on. It was a time when students would be trying themselves out, forging new identities, experimenting in all senses with the post-Larkin world, so to speak. It was, as is well documented, a period of some radical experimentation. It might even be called a period of playful experience. It led inexorably to 1968.

After 1968, the question of control of this experience soon becomes necessary. Experience has to be managed, lest it might actually change things. Throughout the following decades, a new student identity begins to take shape. Students are seen as potentially revolutionaries, radicals, free-thinkers. The Open University makes this worse and more widespread: now everyone and anyone can be such a student, can adopt such an identity. The national centre cannot hold as easily as before; and terrible beauties start to be born – above all, the beauty that is freedom achieved through the play of an autonomous imagination. In the late 1970s, this system is brought down to size through a series of economic cuts imposed by the new Thatcher administration; and any resistance to those cuts and their effects is neutered by that explicit change in regimen from UGC to HEFCE, ensuring that the government has a fuller control of what the University institution will do.

This is the backdrop to a specific financial and economic 'initiative', brought into being by the Conservative administration, with John Patten as its then Secretary of State for Education. In 1992, the government proposes the abolition of the 'binary divide' between Polytechnics and Universities. This shift doubles, at a stroke, the number of Universities in the UK, for those specialist institutions that had been previously called Polytechnics were now renamed as Universities, and given the same type of research-and-teaching mission. Suddenly, funding is a new and critical issue in this state of play: it is difficult to increase funding uniformly now across the entire system. As a result, both research and teaching now have to be 'costed' and 'priced'; and, to bring this about, teaching itself has to be compartmentalized more fully than ever before. Play has no role whatsoever in the resulting structure of efficiency demands.

The solution to this emerging predicament is the introduction of upfront fees; and, with it, the encouragement to subscribe to the view that higher education (HE) is part of a market economy. While education at HE level has always contributed to the economy, the trick now was to say that this external relation to business should be replicated internally. Everything now becomes part of a purchaser-provider contract; and everything interior to the University should be marketized. Key to this is the sense that, as with Butlin's, when you pay your fee upfront, you want a good 'experience', and an experience that is to be homogenized as much as possible nationally. All must become 'excellent'.

This is not to argue that the University is now a theme-park; but it is to suggest that the thinking that informs 'the student experience' as opposed to student life is informed by the same kind of marketization as that of the holiday camp or theme-park business. The business model is exactly the same. Lecturers have become the moral equivalent – or, more precisely, the commercial equivalent – of Redcoats in this business model. The activities of learning and teaching become simply one among the now wide-ranging 'suite' of facilities that constitute a specific institution's 'offer', as it is called.

Prior to the emergence of 'the student experience' as a major element in our marketing and branding of ourselves, it was always certainly the case that learning and teaching were at the centre of the University's relation – what we would now call 'contract' – with the student; and, it followed from this that some of the other elements of the student life would be taken care of by students themselves. Universities certainly funded things like Students' Unions and the like; but what went on in those unions was largely the responsibility of the students themselves. Accommodation was also a key element in making sure that students had the right environment for learning; and, perhaps above all, the sense of the University a site of play was important – with the equally important modification that this play is now characterized not as a serious activity that is integral to *Bildung* but rather as consumerist-style entertainment and pleasure-production. The University, while not a theme-park, is put in the position of struggling against becoming a mere extension of the 'culture industry'.

5

This becomes clear if we regard seriously some of the University documentation on the student experience. All Universities now have websites showing what a great time students are having; and all have, in their prospectus, paragraphs and chapters on the quality of the student experience in their particular institutions. We can look closely at one very clear example of this, in *Policy Statement: Enhancing the Student Experience* by the 1994 Group, published in 2007.

The 1994 Group of UK Universities has taken this issue of the student experience perhaps most seriously and for good reason: they see themselves explicitly as the market leaders in the field. In all official surveys, their institutions come very close to the top of league tables. It may be worth noting, in passing, that the difference between positions in these tables (and this does not affect simply the student experience) is often extremely marginal. While University X comes above University Y, it may be that the first has scored a satisfaction rate of 93.7 per cent, while the latter has scored 93.6. These differences, especially at the micro-level in relation to individual questions posed in these surveys, are so marginal as to be almost statistically insignificant; but their market effect is enormous, and the economic consequence is potentially devastating for some institutions, as also for the students attending and graduating from those institutions. If the difference between the top position in a table and an institution that lies thirtieth, say, is nothing greater than 2 or 3 per cent, then that potential difference, well within a margin of error or based upon a misreading of data, can cost the 'weaker' institution an enormous sum. In extreme cases, the abstract mathematization of quality that is supposedly revealed in these figures may cost not only institutional reputation but quite serious teachers their jobs.

The 1994 Group statement starts by acknowledging, rightly and exactly in line with my own argument here, that there is no such thing as 'the' student experience. There are so many different types of student, and so many different kinds of life going on, that it is folly to try to categorize and to homogenize. This said, that is exactly what the document will now set out to do.

The self-contradictory position here leads immediately to a certain incoherence or inconsistency. On one hand, the student experience is described in terms that show how well the University adapts to the rapidly changing expectations of the student body: it is thus, we can see, primarily about the satisfaction of prior expectation. However, it is also, and equally and simultaneously, precisely *not* about this. Rather, it is about preparing students for their future, and preparing them for their assigned task of making a significant contribution to society. The net result of this is the resolution of the bland phrase that the University will aim to 'provide the best possible experience'; but this, of course, begs the question immediately in all sorts of ways. How do we 'provide' experience? And how do we provide it if what it actually amounts to is determined by things that are not in our control – such as the expectations that specific students might have had, or, on the other hand, the equally fast-changing demands of future lives, as students carry out their assigned duties of making their contributions?

Interestingly, the *Policy Statement* document abandons the language of *Bildung* or *formation*, and it replaces it with the language of the student 'journey'. Such language is interesting. A journey has a defined end-point: the destination. If we set out on a journey, we do so with a destination in mind that has to be guaranteed; otherwise, we would not be on a journey, but something like a ramble (like Samuel Johnson, maybe) or a meander (like Samuel Taylor Coleridge, perhaps). This journey, then, is entirely different from venturing out on the experimentation that used to be called 'learning', the route-making that we might once have called 'discovery' in which we learn how to 'make our own way' in and through the world. We have the logic of the satnav against the poetry of Wordsworth, so to speak.

The language of the 'journey', of course, is itself indebted to contemporary celebrity culture; and it is designed to replace the ideas of *transformation of the self* that are central to *Bildung* and to formation: to education as I have described it above. Where *Bildung* can be difficult, requiring self-assessment and self-conscious transformation, the 'journey' is a vague term in that celebrity culture. On one hand, it is meant to suggest that there is a very clear direction of travel – in most cases, from tragic disadvantage to sudden success. It is also usually intended as something fast: journeys now take much less time than they used to do. Importantly, however, and above all, the journey involves a change of place, but *not* a change of self.

This is key: as in Butlin's, the consuming self simply consumes, and that which is consumed makes no difference fundamentally to the self that entered the holiday camp or institution. The 'scandal' here is that, whereas the student experience is supposed to show how life chances can be transformed, in fact it is designed precisely to ensure that there is no social mobility at all, no real change of self or of attitude that will encourage or allow the student to change. It is little wonder that, as a result, there might be some levels of dissatisfaction in what goes on. The wonder is that it is not higher than it is.

The 1994 Group gives seven priorities for future work in the field of enriching 'the student experience' after its 2007 *Statement*. The first of these is the provision of transparent data about the student experience itself (which, within the document, is never actually properly defined, in fact, but left rather strategically vague), so that students can make 'informed choices'. The mantra of the market again rules here: it is as if the provision of data will in and of itself exculpate Universities from the responsibility of allowing risk; as if also the transparency of the data guaranteed some supposed truth or reality; and as if also the student-as-consumer is some kind of ideally rational purchaser, unaffected by anything outside the transaction. Further, the mantra of choice in this discourse occludes the fact that the choice is not all one-way: Universities still 'select' candidates, dependent usually on qualifications previously achieved by the candidates. It is not, and never has been, the case that students 'choose' in some kind of untrammelled fashion (there are many constraints, not all of them educational); nor is it ever the case that choice is categorically fulfilled or satisfied. This is so even in the case of a fully marketized and privatized version of the University.

1994's second priority is the provision of a workforce; and in this, we see the University presenting itself in a position of subservience and servility. It and its graduates have no authority; instead, they become mere handmaidens to an undifferentiated realm of commerce or what is always vaguely alluded to as 'business', as if there were indeed something as specific as 'business-as-such'. It is argued that a good student experience – looking to the future of the student's life – will help ensure that students fit into the existing workforce. Again, there is to be no assumption of the possibility of fundamental or structural change carried out by the student who might have learnt something while at University: instead, the student is to be made fit to conform. This, as the punks used to say, constitutes a future that is no future at all; for it is the same as yesterday.

There then follows the third priority for promoting the student voice; and in this there is the valorization of 'consultation'. Ostensibly, then, this offers a glimmer of democratic participation. It explicitly thereby ensures that the University is not seen as coercive with respect to its students; and, of course, this would be a good thing. However, it also instils a sense that the University has no authority either. As with most kinds of managed consultation processes, the end-results are guaranteed by the questions. 'Would you like your morning post delivered by 3 p.m., or by 5 p.m.?' Thus it is that the managers of the postal service can claim that customers *wanted* their erstwhile morning delivery of post changed to 3 p.m.

In the consultations advocated by the 1994 Group, schools and colleges are to be included; so by the time of this fourth priority, the student experience has become pure marketing to potential future customers, in fact. The fifth priority is to do with resources, including the physical infrastructure: that is, accommodation and the like have to be up to a high standard. Sixth is a further element of marketing: the internationalization of the student experience. This does not mean the kind of compulsory foreign-language tuition that, in my first chapter, I placed at the centre of a democratic institution where we listen to voices that are difficult or foreign to what we usually expect, nor does it in fact mean anything so academic; rather, it means simply bringing in more high-level fee-paying international students.

For its seventh and final priority – and by this stage one wonders if it can still be called a 'priority' at all – the 1994 Group *Policy Statement: Enhancing the Student Experience* remembers, almost as an afterthought, something that many might have thought rather fundamental: teaching and learning.

There has been here a complete reversal of the kinds of priority that shaped the University sector prior to a marketization that started out as incipiently creeping but has now become fast-racing; and the reversal has the effect of embedding commercialization at the centre of the institutional mindset and management. It is not long, once these changes have taken place, before vice-chancellors start to style themselves as CEOs and to describe their institutions crudely as 'businesses'. Yet more importantly for the purposes of this present chapter, these changes also have the consequence that the actual life-transforming possibilities of experience – in this case specifically those associated with teaching and learning – can now safely be relegated to the realms of the appended afterthought. The centre of the University's activity has moved elsewhere; and teaching and learning have now explicitly become the least important of the priorities for future development of 'the student experience'.

6

Against all this, let us introduce a brief final moment of philosophical thinking in this present chapter. Hegel, in his *Introduction to Aesthetics*, points out that there is something about beauty that is inherently excessive, unnecessary. He is arguing his case that art is, in some ways, 'higher' than nature: the world of nature is marked by necessity, by an intrinsic *essence* that allows of no superfluity. The sun, as it were, is *just there*; but a picture of the sun, a painting of the sun, is contingent. What it is contingent upon, however, is freedom: the image is characterized by 'intellectual being and by freedom'. As Hegel controversially puts it, 'even a useless notion that enters a man's head is higher than any product of nature, because in such a notion spirituality and freedom are always present'.[14] In this lack of necessity, we see the possibility that art, precisely in its 'excessiveness' or in its 'unnecessariness', can yield the possibilities of freedom. Such *playful waste*, as we might now call it, provocatively, is precisely the counter that is required against the triumph of 'efficiency'. As we have seen, the drive for efficiency is what precludes the possibility of experience – and now, we can also add, of freedom itself.

Playful waste, as I am calling it, is that kind of activity that produces *time*, produces time even in the form of a 'waste of time', an expanse of time; but, for experience to happen at all, it is precisely time that we need. Time allows for the possibility of historical change. We will look later at whether the usual undergraduate degree programme of three years duration is sufficient; but, for the moment, let us remain with the philosophical position that says that a University programme should be concerned with the production of time itself, and not with an alleged 'efficiency' model that says more must be crammed in to less by eliminating the time required for play or, indeed, for thinking. Voltaire once suggested, close to despair at the banalities of philosophical Optimism, that we might abandon the grand scheme of things and 'cultivate our own garden'. The analogy here, for my own purposes, might very productively be made with gardening: playful waste is like compost – it needs time to settle in order to generate fresh life and growth.

My final philosophical remark here comes by way of Hannah Arendt. Arendt broadly follows these Hegelian tendencies when she comes to consider authority and historical agency. Specifically, she argues that our very humanity is bound up in our capacity to 'begin' something, to initiate or to 'authorize' something. That is to say, we define ourselves as human subjects, historical agents, precisely to the extent that we can differ from that which has been handed to us. In terms relevant to these present pages, and to arguments about knowledge in the form of modules that are to be transmitted as commercial units, the argument has a great power. If we accept the terms of the student experience as something essentially commercialized and thereby flaccid, then we arrive at that odd state of affairs in which the graduate has no authority. In short, we arrive at the position where the graduate has learned nothing – nothing, that is, except the demand for conformity to established rules and conformity to the practices of consumerist capital. Against this, we might place Arendt's description of authority as something that 'implies an obedience in which men retain their freedom'.[15]

We should note that this authority does not imply some kind of anarchy whereby each and every individual makes their own rules; rather, it is a carefully modulated notion of authority. Implicit in this is a sense that there is a demand – here called 'obedience' – a demand that seeks to base behaviour upon an authority that eschews coercion – including the silent coercion to conform to models of efficiency and consumerism. In short, the authority here – and this is the kind of authority that can only be gleaned through the experience of learning and teaching – is one that is communal, not atomized into the individuated experiences of single consumers. It is an authority that is gained through play; and, as in play, it is an authority whose entire point is to offer authority to other players, to bring more participants into the game. The result is not simply a wider distribution of authority and of power; it is also the establishment of a public sphere in which each player has an interest, but an interest in extending authority and participation ever wider.

If there is to be a future for the University as an institution that has an important social role, and a role that involves an increase in freedom and autonomy for the entire community that sustains the institution, then it follows that we must abandon the myth of 'the student experience'. That myth leads only to coercion and conformity; to abandon it is to take the risk of learning, and with it to embrace the demand for freedom.

3

A Terrifying Silence

Spaces of Research from
Discovery to Surveillance

The eternal silence of these spaces terrifies me.
Pascal

On a sweltering day in September 1962, President John F. Kennedy addressed the students and faculty of Rice University in Houston, Texas, where he held a position as an Honorary Visiting Professor. His lecture that day was extremely important. Among other things, it centrally set out to affirm the place of the University in scientific research, and specifically in space exploration. In then committing the United States to putting a man on the moon and returning him safely to earth within the decade of the 1960s, Kennedy did many things. He invoked the spirit of the early pioneering explorers, thereby tying this exploration of outer space to a foundational myth of the geopolitical formation of the United States. Going to the moon was aligned with the earlier earthbound onwards push westwards that claimed more and more land, as the early country formulated its boundaries through the 'discovery' of new worlds. The history of this push westwards is controversial, of course, related as it is to the issues around ethnic displacement of peoples who inhabited the land; but it was already controversial even in the 1960s, for this and for other reasons. As we will see, those reasons had to do with a negotiation between the demands for introspection (protecting US internal interests) and for further expansion of US ideas and ideologies. The determining factor is an attitude to space.

Kennedy reminded his audience about the Cold War rivalry with the USSR, and stressed that this scientific research – based upon the search for the true – was one that was tied not only to a politics but also to a way of life – the search for the good; and, in some ways, the very continuity of the United States itself depended on the nation assuming the leading role in the research-race. He replaced the direct violence of crude military confrontation with a demand for technological and scientific supremacy;

and, in this, he both aligned science with war while simultaneously arguing that scientific advance was precisely a way of averting war.

In all of this, Kennedy used the idea of open expansive *space* – evoked in terms of aesthetic beauty – as a way of reaffirming an identity tied firmly to *place*: the United States; within the United States, Houston; within Houston, Rice University. In all of this, then, we see Kennedy affirming the links among the search for the true, the good and the beautiful that I have suggested as the core first principles of the University as an institution; and, most importantly, he explicitly and successfully ties these ideals to the activities of University research.

Space becomes place and identity when it is occupied, inhabited and given a character: the artificial flag on the moon bears the marks of the very national identity or national character invoked by Kennedy's speech. The fact that it is made to look as if the flag is blowing in the wind, a wind that the moon cannot have, is testament to an awareness that aesthetic beauty and the sensation of a living and organic experience is thought to be of great importance: the idea is that the national identity *lives* there, and it does so as well and as fully as it does *here* on earth.

The speech that day at Rice placed the idea and the reality of space at the centre not only of a national identity, but also at the centre of an idea of progress based upon research, and upon research that was to be placed at the centre of the University as an institution. Indeed, the University was identified as the primary institution for the advancing of research as such. It is worth considering, now some half-century later, how space – as idea and as reality – has somewhat shrunk or narrowed in our contemporary University world. In these rather anorexic transformations and conceptual or imaginative shrinkages, we will see that our ways of thinking about space are related now to forms of thought that can actually damage scientific research – and indeed, all other forms of research – in our Universities; and this precisely at the moment when governments in the advanced economies are claiming that they put science and scientific research at the heart of government policy.

In Kennedy's speech, space becomes almost a metaphor for the very fundamental principles of research itself. He stresses that the outcomes of space and lunar exploration are uncertain, and that we will be seeking answers to questions that we cannot even begin to formulate: things undreamt of in our philosophies, as it were – or in that less eloquent modern formulation, 'unknown unknowns'. In short, the space-race is predicated upon a free experimentation, where we do not have the very specific questions that would contain within themselves the seeds of their own answers. This is, as it were, the original 'blue-skies' research.

Just one year after Kennedy advanced these ideas, Harold Wilson committed the UK to a rather similar academic and research-oriented priority, arguing that progress for the entire social realm – the good, in other words – would be achieved by the deployment and exploitation of our research communities passionately burning with the 'white heat' of science and technology at the heart of our own government's policy. Not only that but, by 1965, Wilson and his then minister for the arts, Jennie Lee, had committed the nation to another critical moment of democratic expansiveness with the development of plans for an 'Open' University, the very name of the institution being a paean to what would now be called 'widening access', and a tacit hymn of praise to the generosity of space and its exploration. This is edifying, exciting, visionary oratory that calls up the originary spirit of scientific research; and it had an impact in all the advanced economies and in the funding of scientific research in our Universities. In our present times, though, does space have anything of the same allure or significance?

The obvious immediate answer is 'No, not at all.' That answer has little to do with the facts of lunar or space exploration itself, but it is influenced instead by much more mundane matters. Modern management within the institution of the University prefers to think of space primarily as a commodity; and this particular affliction adversely affects not only the University institutions, of course, but also most corporate and other arenas within the public sphere. Work needs plant, for it needs to be located somewhere; plant costs money; expanding businesses or Universities attract more people, who occupy more plant; people in the workplace therefore cost money, and not just in salary terms but also in terms of the fact that their bodies occupy space. Thus, space and its occupation are no longer matters of visionary import, but rather crude factors in tawdry economy drives, related essentially to the price of property and to the location of University buildings (now treated by the managerialist class in exactly the same way as the plant of corporate business). The reduction of space – an intrinsic and even endemic demand for ongoing reduction that is seen axiomatically to be consistent with matters of efficiency – leads, in much of what passes for good modern management, to cultural norms that highlight the 'advantages' of hot-desking or home-working, which are polite ways of telling staff that they are, quite literally, a waste of space. As in the question of experience in my previous chapter, the physical body becomes an obstruction for efficiency-drives to overcome.

Considered in this way, space becomes a concept that drives any institution towards pusillanimous parochialism, sometimes referred to as 'modernization' and 'increased efficiency drives'. In the jargon,

'VfM' or 'value for money', the 'three Es' become the motivating force here through which, supposedly, by starving an institution of resource ('economizing') – including, centrally here, space – that institution somehow magically works more cheaply ('efficiency') and thus gets better results ('effectiveness') than was the case heretofore. More pointedly here, in having thereby to justify the use of space, we effectively are asked not just to do our work or carry out our occupational duties, but also to justify our *occupation* in – *and of* – a place of work (which is what underpins the modern audit culture that stifles invention and discovery). Our occupation of this instrumentalized and shrinking foreclosed space is to be justified in terms of the economic profit that can be securely predicted to flow from the research – itself to be managed equally in terms of certain 'spatial' analogies and priorities, as we will see in what follows below – that is to be carried out within that shrunk environment. Thus, 'managed space' now keeps us firmly within the bounds of the earth and of the already known. It is anathema to research as such.

When the United States began to realize Kennedy's imaginative vision, the Apollo astronauts famously provided us with the great ecological icon of our earthly place as a fragile sphere, hanging lyrically blue and uncertain in the midst of a great unknown. The aesthetically arresting image gave us our own place back, but gave it back to us as a place changed forever; and our identity changed with it. Yet effecting change such as this is, in many ways, the very point of the University. It is what was going on in Kennedy's professorial lecture in Rice, as he gave his audience a new imagined identity, through a visionary concept of space as the organizing and central principle of expansive research.

All University education brings about a form of deracination such as that felt by the astronaut staring back at 'home' on earth. The point – the project – is to change how we inhabit the planet or home in every sense. The sense may be scientific, sociological or cultural: that is, the sense can be determined and described in terms of the true, the good or the beautiful. It most certainly is not the case that we should be simply finding more cost-efficient ways of *exploiting* our space, place and identities. Those working-class grammar-school intellectuals of the British mid-twentieth century – the people written about by Richard Hoggart in *The Uses of Literacy* – lay this bare: they are individuals who are firmly identified with their traditional roots, yet no longer easily able to remain at home in that space. The tension that this situation produces is what we call research, in fact, and it gives us new ways of living, of expanding the spirit or imagination, of changing not just our personal space but also the space where we all live as communities, cities, nations, civilizations.

However, the wayward drive towards the cost-efficient exploitation of space offers, in many ways, a perfect description of the misdirected pressure that governments in the advanced economies have placed upon University research in the decades following the heady moments of hope and expansiveness of spirit that we saw in those grand rhetorical and political gestures of the 1960s. Space, as a commodity, is itself to be exploited; and its exploitation will lead to further manipulations of space that will encourage further exploitation of the resources of the planet we call home. Behind this is an ideological drive in which citizens will start to 'know their proper place', as it were; and, in this, I mean to hint that there is a tacit political and ideological drive here, and one that is meant to 'contain' (if I can pursue the spatial metaphor) the potential or latent demands of the human subject and spirit for edification and expansion of consciousness into unforeseen modes of thought.

For Kennedy and Wilson, science *was* government policy; in our more parochial and miserly time, instead, science in the advanced economies is being forced to act merely *in the service of* government. There is a world of difference. We might now reaffirm, against this prevailing ideology, that space is more than money: it is possibility, imagination, opportunity. Research, in fact, is and should fundamentally be about a certain spatial expansion or expansiveness: generosity is the moral term that we would use to describe this, the generosity that is marked by a hospitality towards the new, towards the foreign and the strange unknown.

1

Kennedy came to power in the elections of November 1960 and took office in January 1961. The president he replaced was Eisenhower who, in his own farewell address on leaving office, gave an equally important speech. As with Kennedy, Eisenhower was profoundly aware of – even shaped by – Cold War ideology. In the speech, he pointed out that the United States now had, for the first time, not only 'an immense military establishment', but also 'a large arms industry'; and he said that the combination of these was a new phenomenon in what he called 'the American experience'. He stated its supreme importance, arguing that it affected the 'very structure of our society'.

He then uttered the phrase for which the speech is now best known, saying that we need to be watchful of the resulting 'military industrial complex', for 'the potential for the disastrous rise of misplaced power exists and will persist'. This is important for present purposes because Eisenhower directly relates this complex to the research that goes on in the University, and with it he raises a question about the function of the University's research within the contemporary public sphere. His concern was that governments might deploy the 'military industrial complex' for direct violent ends and purposes – purposes that, in his view, threatened the United States. What he had not foreseen was that governments might be much more subtle and indirect than this: the ostensibly bland issue of space-management might be able to do the needful instead, reducing human possibilities while maximizing governmental control of our public spheres.

Eisenhower points out that, with the potential rise of the military-industrial complex (and, in early drafts of the speech, the word 'academic' had also been inserted as part of the complex), the very liberties and democratic processes that constitute the identity of America are at risk; and the citizenry needs to be made aware of the risks, alert to the dangers, through increased knowledge. He then links the development of the military-industrial complex to the technological revolution, which, he claims, had been 'largely responsible for the sweeping changes in our industrial-military posture' in the preceding decades.

'In this revolution,' he goes on, 'research has become central; it also becomes more formalized, complex, and costly.' Then, in what is the most telling passage of the speech for our present purposes, he says:

> Today, the solitary inventor, tinkering in his shop, has been overshadowed by task forces of scientists in laboratories and testing fields. In the same fashion, the free university, historically the fountainhead of free ideas and scientific discovery, has experienced a revolution in the conduct of research. Partly because of the huge costs involved, a government contract becomes virtually a substitute for intellectual curiosity. For every old blackboard there are now hundreds of new electronic computers.[1]

Above all, his concern was to get what he saw as the right balance between, on the one hand, an overweening State that would attempt to control research; and, on the other, a scientific-military elite that would try to wrest control of what had been a democratic constitution. Public policy should not be driven by a research elite; but, equally importantly, research should not be driven solely or even primarily by the demands – financial or ideological – of the State.

That is to say: each should have its own designated space, in the interests of maintaining freedom. In the days of Eisenhower and Kennedy, that freedom was dominated and shaped by the fact that their nation was on a quasi-permanent war-footing. These were Cold War days, after all. The question that arises now is whether, in recent times, when politics are dominated by questions of security and terror, we have ever managed to escape such a war mentality. Further, when the potential enemy with whom we are at war is a vaguely defined 'terror' that threatens an equally unclear 'security', it becomes difficult to identify that enemy as something external to the State: the danger is that terror – and the terrorist – has become the enemy within, the new version of reds under the bed; and, further, the question is whether any citizen might somehow, in the dark space of their own interiority, be harbouring such terrorist ideas themselves.

We are in a new era of suspicion, and one where surveillance of spaces becomes thought of as a fundamental condition of survival; and, in almost religious terms, the very inner spaces of our own consciousness or even unconscious become fundamentally suspect. Now, then, the fundamental question for us in this chapter becomes whether the pursuit of research in the University has managed to realign itself with our priorities of justice and freedom, a justice and freedom based in the generosity that should shape the true, the good and the beautiful, and not in the demands for technological supremacy over an implied enemy. If, by contrast, our research is still dominated by the demands of an economy on a war-footing, where might we hear any voices being raised to warn us of the dangers? Instead, we might, like Pascal, start to hear an 'eternal silence', the 'eternal silence of these infinite spaces' that he found so poignantly frightening in his prescient *Pensées* in the late seventeenth century.

The military-industrial-academic complex described by Eisenhower yields a model of research concerned with and even driven by the demands of imperial power in a potential conflict situation. Such power is essentially a way of controlling and appropriating space, bringing space under control, bringing foreign space into domestic law and governance. This is entirely different from a state of affairs that welcomes the foreign or the strange in the mode of hospitality: rather, it is precisely a way of refusing that generosity, driven instead by misery or the avaricious meanness of pure fiscal or arithmetic measure. Crucially, it is important to note that, effectively silently, the academy is brought in this to a state of affairs in which it serves the politics of the State. Its research is funded by the State, but not so as to enable the search for the true or the good: rather, what is at issue is the establishment of political ends, ideological ends. Tacitly, research is driven increasingly by the ongoing shrinking not just of the public sphere, but also of the private space that we tend to identify with the privacy of our own thought. If funded by government, the argument goes, our research – our advanced thought – becomes already public; and we lose the private space of reflection – and also, of course, of critique. This is not what is good for the University; and, as Eisenhower could well see on the day he gave his farewell speech, back on 17 January 1961, it was also inimical to the extension of freedom and democracy, elements in what I would call the just.

Returning to Pascal, the kind of tension that was being addressed by Eisenhower finds a much earlier philosophical expression in his *Pensées*. Among the non-classified papers in the Port-Royal edition of the *Pensées*, we find a series of thoughts relating to what Pascal called the difference between two modes of thought. He called these two different ways of thinking the '*esprit de géométrie*' and the '*esprit de finesse*'. The geometrical spirit is concerned with measure and calculation: it aims to *demonstrate* the truth of a proposition by working from abstractions, logical principles and their consequences. The latter spirit – *finesse* would translate not just as 'finesse', but also as something like 'delicacy', 'nicety' or 'shrewd subtlety' – is concerned with *judging* and with judgements made from intuitions that are not themselves necessarily grounded in abstract logic.

This, in some ways, neatly describes the kind of division in terms of attitudes to space that I claim as central to our considerations of research in the modern University. Where research is carried out in the service of government – that is, where it is instrumentalized, measured and quantified for ideological purposes, no matter how positive those purposes may be – then its primary research component and activity are threatened. They are threatened because the research is done in a measured or audited way – governed, that is, by the *esprit de géométrie* – and the point is, at least partly if not wholly, to conform to and to serve pre-existing principles and abstract ideological themes. In the extreme case, the expectation will be that research evidence is to be produced by researchers in ways that are fully in conformity with predetermined government policy. The result of this is a research wherein space has to be managed, measured, accounted and paid for (as if one could ever actually 'buy' space). When research is genuine blue-skies, then the *esprit de finesse* is prioritized; and, in this, we have the possibility of scientists and researchers expanding space, exploring and pushing boundaries, even following intuitions or hunches in an experimental fashion (that is, *inhabiting* space, posing questions about *place*, which is much more rational than the idea of purchasing it). This latter is research that is consistent with the first principles of the University that I set out above.

Kennedy's speech, while being rhetorically extremely edifying, lapses into precisely the kind of thinking that also shaped that of Eisenhower. In both cases, there are essentially two divergent attitudes to research at work; and the tension between them is palpable. That tension persists to our present times; and it may even be said that that Cold War ideology – probably carried through into questions of terror and security – is still one of the major determinants of how we conduct research in the University. However, the more fundamental question is: can there be a mode of research that is *not* governed by the question of space and its control? An attitude to space might seem to offer only a rather tangential way of approaching the question of research in the University; but, in what follows now, I will show that it is fundamental to our concerns.

2

In some ways, I am tempted to point out that the poets, philosophers such as Pascal and literary critics got there before Eisenhower and Kennedy. Specifically, in 1957, William Empson published an article in the *Kenyon Review* about the seventeenth-century poet, John Donne. It was called 'Donne the Space-Man'. Counter-intuitively, he was applying the terminology appropriate to the most recent and advanced scientific research in his own day to this early modern poet and Dean of St Paul's Cathedral in London. The point of the article was that Donne's interest in space and in the universe, especially in his newly emergent post-Copernican world of the early seventeenth century, offered us a new way of thinking about ourselves and about our own location in place and time. Specifically, Empson's Donne brings about the era of a certain relativism. The tenor of the article, broadly, is that if it is possible – following the Copernican decentring of the earth – that there are many universes, or at least many worlds, then it is also likely that there is no single overarching guarantor of a single and univocal truth: no God, so to speak.

This, genuinely, is the opening of a new age of modern humanist study and thus also of a mode of scientific research that was to be empirical, evidence-based, and potentially merely relativistic and provisional – but yet dominated by the demand, all the more urgently now, for truth. If truth is now elusive, and thereby no longer so easily assured or guaranteed thanks to our understanding of space and of our perhaps less than significant place in the universe, then it becomes all the more necessary that we research, in more fundamentally imaginative 'blue-skies' ways, to try to find it; or, at least, to find ways of imagining – even building – a world in which we can live with the resulting uncertainties.

Donne's poetry is indeed obsessed by space and by its manipulations. He writes not long after the first telescopes have come into reliable use in

Europe; and he starts to see the world as a space that can be manipulated by toying with perspective and the resulting play of space or of point of view. The telescope was regarded, in its early days, not just as advanced technology but also as a kind of expensive toy: and playing with it became central to discovery. The technology of the telescope lens allows the viewer to control space (or at least its perception) and to change perspective, making that which was small into something big, and vice versa. Thus, in his poetry, fleas can contain entire worlds; the universe can be collapsed into the eye or face of a lover; the world of east and west can be united in the space between the reflecting gaze of two lovers, and so on.

In this, Donne is bringing the realm of play – so central to experience – into a direct relation with space and with research into truth. His effort to reconcile technological savvy with intuition results in a new language, specifically and above all a language of love. For Donne, as a poet, the truth that is now always in question is also often related to love, and he will frequently play with space and with exploration metaphors in order to suggest that the truth of the world lies in the goodness of an aesthetic relation based upon lovers reflecting each other:

> Let sea-discoverers to new worlds have gone,
> Let Maps to other, worlds on worlds have shown,
> Let us possess one world, each hath one, and is one.
> My face in thine eye, thine in mine appears ...
> Where can we find two better hemispheres,
> Without sharp north, without declining west ...
>   John Donne, 'The Good Morrow'

We are not yet here in the Keatsian world where truth is beauty; but we are certainly in the world where truth and beauty become aspects of space and of the play of perspective. Indeed, when Donne was writing, many other thinkers are also exercised by the play of space. It becomes central to the constitution of knowledge; and it thus becomes central to the pursuit of the true, to our disciplines of the hard sciences.

There is a set of historical determinants here that also need to be fed into our consideration of the founding conditions of modern research in the University and for the importance of space to that foundation. In the world of the medieval University, the question of space was, at least ostensibly, very different from these present thoughts, and also different from the perspectival play of Donne's early modern world. The University of the middle ages was then really composed not of formalized and managed space at all; rather, the University comprised groups of peregrine scholars who were able to move around to teach, for they were not tied to specific buildings, plant or locations.

As I indicated in my opening chapter on first principles, such an arrangement might very readily map on to the idea that the University is better thought of not as something that exists as a material set of buildings in a particular place, but rather – and more fundamentally – as an *event*. The University is something that 'happens' or, in terms appropriate to this chapter, it can be thought of as something that 'takes place'; and it does this only episodically. When the episodes are repeated in the same geopolitical space, then they become identified with a location; and we thus get the development of federated places, like colleges in Oxford, Paris, Bologna, Salerno, Glasgow and elsewhere. The settlement of the wandering scholars begins. Historically, the location in space becomes something that grows into larger federations; and eventually this is writ large into something like the coherent national systems that have grown up worldwide over the last two centuries.

As it evolves in this way, however, the University as institution makes itself concrete, and it does this in ways that make the domination of place more important than the historical activities constitutive of the University-as-event that go on episodically. Indeed, as we have already seen, the University becomes, in some basic ways, tied to the formulation of a national identity and national character. Something similar then also happens at the micro-level of its conception of space itself. The management and occupation of space supplants the idea of expansion of space as a condition of research: geometry starts to triumph over finesse, as it were. As I hinted already (and I shall say more on this below), we bear witness here to the triumph of the 'module', with its building-brick geometry, over the more organically living and evolving consciousness, and over that very experience that we call human development or just 'thinking'.

I should, of course, make it clear that, in this present chapter, I am not advocating a return to the medieval condition of the University. There are, as we know, too many politicians – and maybe even vice-chancellors or University presidents – who would be keen to see this as a neat way of saving money, by selling plant off and asking us all to work from home, and thus at our own expense. It is important to note that the peregrine scholar was part of what was essentially a privatized institution, in which individuals would pay for what was essentially an atomized set of learning exercises. Such atomization is paralleled by an atomized condition in society: dog eats dog. Some politicians, primarily those of the political right-wing, do in fact see this dog-eat-dog, every-man-for-himself and excessively individualized attitude as a norm; and they will foist it upon the University by arguing that the institution exists for private gain, that one 'invests' in an education for the purposes of benefiting as an individual economically later (for more on this, see chapter 6 below). My concern in this book, however, leads me to address the University as something that is of central interest to the State, because it is of central importance, as one of our instruments of civilized freedom and democracy, to the idea of a community of interlocking and negotiated interests.

In exploring this, Pascal does indeed offer us a useful starting position. Famously, one of Pascal's most poignant *pensées* – and one that I have cited already above – is in the group that he entitled 'Transition' or 'Change'. There, he wrote, in a rather isolated phrase or fragment, that 'the eternal silence of these spaces terrifies me'. The spaces in question are those of the universe; and Pascal is, in this 'Transition' section, considering at length what he calls the 'disproportion de l'homme', the question of the human's relation to the environment considered in terms of our occupation of place and time and our own tendency to self-aggrandizement. Pascal is amazed by the happenstance that places him in this space, 'here', rather than elsewhere in space, and at this moment, 'now', rather than in any other time; and, above all, he is amazed that, given his insignificance in the face of the immensity of an infinite universe, he seems capable nonetheless of thinking of that immensity, of 'containing' it in his own thought or in the interiority of his consciousness. The terror in question arises from the fact that this universe, in its immensity, effectively has no need for Pascal, no need to address him; yet, despite that obvious insignificance, Pascal knows that, in some ways, he actually *contains* that immensity, for he is able to think and to imagine it.

I suggest that this restless and potently terrifying condition is one that describes what research is about, in fact. Part of the task of research is to make the world answer to the possibilities of human imagining; part of the point is to make the world respond and to talk back – to break that silence so frightening to Pascal – to reply to the call of the human imagination. It is also, of course, vital that the human imagination has the subtle shrewdness – the *finesse* – to be able to respond to a mysterious silence, to respond to the fact that we may be insignificant and to find ways of imagining, in the face of the world's indifference, what a viable future might be. For Pascal, the search was for the fundamental good, which he called God; for the humanist, it is the search for the true, but it is carried on under the same aegis as the work and thought of Pascal. What is at stake is an extension of the self beyond the self, beyond the boundary as it were.

In some ways, we might then think of research as being related to *desire*. By definition, desire is something restless, something that does not know quite *what* it wants; but it does certainly and definitively know *that* it wants. Desire is that momentum that makes the self seek alterity, makes the subject of an activity reach out to whatever it may be that is beyond it. The 'beyond' in question here might be thought of as the transcendental; but, in fact, and in secular terms, it is precisely what is meant by the true, the good and the beautiful in that constellation of technological progress that we call modernity, that culture typified by the restlessness of Donne or of Pascal.

Desire, too, is a question of space. Roland Barthes knew this when he wrote a small but extremely important book (*Sur Racine*), in 1960, researching the seventeenth-century French playwright Racine. In Racine, Barthes found many elements of the kind of bodily play that we have already foregrounded in earlier chapters; but, importantly, he founded his book – a revolutionary book in literary research, opening the entire field of poststructuralist work – on an examination of space in Racine's plays. He begins his study by noting that, in Racine, there are three Mediterraneans: classical ancient, Jewish, byzantine; and he rapidly sees that these three spaces form one complete complex, uniting the forces of fire, earth and water. However, those elements, which will become constitutive of desire in the plays, realize themselves in particular scenes or located spaces. Barthes begins from the bedroom or chamber; and, from this, he notes that there is in the complexity of the Racinian stage, a fundamental conflict of *inside* and *outside*. Inside represents a kind of spatial terrain; but outside is marked by temporalities that allow for death, for flight and for the 'event'; and the event, especially the event of the world outside, is never finished. It is an invitation to further play, to continue the play beyond and outside the scene of the theatre; and this, in fact, is both the nature of desire and of research.

This attitude is not a million miles away from the pragmatism advocated by a more recent philosopher and critic such as Richard Rorty. He was always at pains to stress that the point of philosophy – indeed of all research that involves thinking, that involves an unpredictable event – is not to find answers, but rather to 'keep the conversation going' or to keep us discussing things in such a way as to generate further questions and to bring more voices into the discussion. Any answer that we may find, we know, is provisional: the history of research in any discipline indicates that fact. The construction of this proper kind of research – the research that will take us out of the bedroom or study, out of the library or laboratory, and into the blue skies above the Mediterranean, as it were – is one that opens us to time and to the event.

Behind this is a philosophy of desire as constituted by the exploration of space, the transgression of boundaries – and, above all, the transgression of the boundary of the self and of the conversational language in which we articulate that self. The point, always, is transformation – of space or environment, of the self, and of the self's constitutive language.

Barthes quite possibly gleaned a lot of his thinking from the work of Gaston Bachelard, who wrote eloquently in 1958 of the *Poetics of Space*, as he called it. In that book, he pointed out that 'inside and outside form a dialectic of division', a dialectic that has all the force of the strictly demarcated opposition of Yes and No. Bachelard argues that if we consider space in this way, however, we end up with a pure geometry that has to exclude the facts of our historical being in the pursuit of certainty.

Bachelard thus prefers to think of the human subject as taking neither the inside nor the outside, nor even the opposition between them, as fundamental; and, in avoiding that kind of opposition, that spatial structuring, he proposes a situation in which research is absolutely necessary because the door that separates inside and outside is always 'half-open'. That is, uncertainty – and the desire for resolution, but a desire that can never be satisfied – is the stimulus for research. Research is not an activity that allows us to 'gain access' to a hidden truth; rather, it is an event-oriented activity, not pre-programmed, with no already existing but tacit or occluded solutions. The dialectic of inside and outside – with all its attendant ideologies of 'widening access' and the like – is but an aspect of managed space. It is not about the release of imagination into freedom that is constitutive of proper and genuine research; but, on the contrary, it is simply a way of restricting freedoms while merely *pretending* to enjoy them and to widen them.

In political terms, the question of a democratic education – which would begin to satisfy the criterion for the University as the pursuing of justice – is much more fundamental than could be determined by answers to the problem of who has 'access', important though that might be. It is really a question of the emancipation of the imagination, of the freedom from restricted and managed space that so dominates our contemporary predicaments.

3

I have stressed the importance of the body and of experience in the teaching and learning situation; and now I need to turn to the importance of the body and bodily space for the organization of research. We can look at one of the UK Research Councils, the Biotechnology and Biological Sciences Research Council (BBSRC), as an example here. It provides a clear guide to the organization of its research funding on its website. There are four key committees for this council, one of the largest in the UK; and the research that it funds is spread across four broadly overlapping areas. The diagrammatic representation of the relations between various research activities and the separate committees looks rather like a Venn diagram, though it is an open-ended one, with lots of permeability rather than just intersections. It is clear in directing prospective researchers to specific bodies for research funding; and much of it looks non-controversial. For typical and clear examples, work on agricultural systems goes to a different committee from work on food science; or neuroscience is funded separately from mathematically oriented biological research and so on. Right at the centre of the diagram, and seemingly at the core of the entire activity, is genetics.

This is interesting: the spatial diagram, in placing biogenetics at the centre of its overlapping fields, is drawing attention to a certain contemporary phenomenon. It is not the fact that this is all organized in a spatial diagram that is important here (indeed, it would be difficult in the visual plane to present it otherwise); rather, what is important is that, at the centre of bioscience funding, we find the body. More importantly still, we find a deep interiority of the body, a kind of substratum – the genetics – that shape the very possibilities of any body in the organic domain.

This is interesting because of the contrast with the age of Kennedy. Then, in the 1960s, a Cold War ideology has Kennedy looking at the expansiveness of space, well beyond the confines of the human body. The V2 rocket becomes a massive prosthetic weapon allowing the human body to escape the very bounds of the earth itself. Now, though, in the contemporary times, we are looking deep within in a moment of profoundly introspective research. In what has become the conventional parlance, we are looking at the 'building blocks' of life itself.

That conventional metaphor, of the 'building blocks' of life, is telling and is indeed far from innocent. It reveals a mode of thought that helps prove the argument that I am making in these pages. In what follows, remember that the great scientific advance promised by the telescope coexisted with the use of that technology for *play*: many considered it a plaything, a toy. In the late 1940s and early 1950s, another new kind of toy was developed in Denmark. It consisted of small building bricks that could interlock with each other to make a potentially huge number of different constructions. It was called 'Lego', from the Danish words *leg godt*, meaning 'play well'. Importantly, for present purposes, these blocks operated as small 'modular' units of carefully regulated sizes. However, although the toy allows for a huge number of different constructions, it cannot possibly allow for an infinite variety. It cannot do this precisely because the modularized brick units, though perhaps themselves differing in size or coming in precisely measured units, operate as a mode of regulated and measured space. 'Playing well', according to this, means limiting the possibilities of one's play: there are, it turns out, only a relatively *small* number of permutations that are possible, and those permutations are *determined* not by the 'content' of the module-bricks, but by their spatial and modular form. It is this predetermination of possible outcomes that we now call 'regulation'; and, as in Lego, our regulations have become determined by an attitude to space, and one that *limits* our potential.

Lego gives us our 'building blocks' research mentality in how we describe even something as organic as genetic codes. In terms of space and its relation to a war mentality, it is as if the war is now with ourselves: a war with our own destinies or 'internal' programming – or, in the more sinister fashion at which I hinted above, a war with our own inner evil or incipient 'terror', a terror that might reach to include simple critique or critical private thinking. We need to crack the codes, decipher the future possibilities that are hidden within those codes; and that way, our bodies will stop being sites of terror and become the domain of our security. Above all, though, research is now conditioned by a 'looking within ourselves', and a looking within that aims to find our modular and coded roots. 'Roots', however, is the wrong word, for that is too organic; rather, we are looking for our Lego.

This looking within, of course, follows a period when scientific research has concerned itself with the *reduction* of space. First, the miniaturization of transistors allowed for various technical developments to be put into widespread use; and, following that, nanotechnology has led us to that state of affairs in which we now have much more computing power in the most basic mobile phone than *Apollo XI* had when it landed on the moon.

This shift to an introspective research is not specific simply to the biosciences, however: indeed, it affects virtually all of our research practices. In nearly all of the councils of the UK, and for research funding more widely across the developed economies, there are priorities for *methodological* research: that is to say, for work that will reveal new ways of doing research by looking at the structural foundations – those building blocks – of our different disciplines. In the Engineering and Physical Sciences Research Council (ESPRC), we find a heavy stress on materials, especially at the atomic scale. The Economics and Social Research Council (ESRC) prioritizes behavioural studies and well-being. Even the Natural Environment Research Council (NERC), while obviously taking a global view of matters such as global warming, nonetheless turns inwards to address matters of technological progress as a key to world sustainability.

In all of this, we see a kind of shrinking of space. This is not of itself either a good or a bad thing, of course; but it does require further consideration. What we will find is not just that there is a shrinking of space, but an evacuation of space as well. We call it 'modularization', and we have applied it to research every bit as much as to undergraduate work.

4

There are two other occasions on which Pascal addressed space. In the unclassified papers of the *Pensées*, in fragment 407, we find him meditating on the distance between himself and God, between himself and happiness. The Stoics say that we should look within ourselves to find peace, he writes, while others say we need to divert ourselves through the attractions of the external world. Neither is true, he claims; and asserts that our happiness lies in God who is *both* within and without the self. Finding this 'proper' attitude to space, and to our relations with the possibilities of transcendent knowledge (for Pascal here, God), is axiomatic to our happiness. Again, the search for the true here is being construed as a spatially grounded inquiry.

More telling is fragment 68, among the classified papers in the section that he titled 'Misère'. There, he is concerned with questions pertaining to justice and tyranny; and he again records his fear in the face of immensity. More poignantly still, he acknowledges his relativism. What fills him with dread is pure contingency, the question of why he is 'here' rather than elsewhere, why he has been allotted this 'little space of time', as he puts it, instead of living at any other moment. In this formulation, Pascal blends together the questions of time and space; and time, we will see, is also important. In my previous chapters, I have indicated that the production and extension of time is important for teaching and learning; and here, it is equally important for research.

At a basic level, though, the question that Pascal asks is the axiomatic and fundamental research question for all University disciplines, for it asks the question, 'Why are we here?' More importantly, the inflection of the question prioritizes space: 'Why am I *here*?' This gives a historical particularity and a material experience to the research drive. It is fundamentally *not* concerned with the abstractions of geometry; rather, it is concerned with *justice*, with what I will do here, now, by way of my research, in the face of potential tyranny.

I have pointed out that Kennedy and Eisenhower are shaped by Cold War ideology; and I have indicated the ways in which this might trouble any idea of 'pure' or disinterested research. However, what I now need to stress is that all research, properly understood (that is, research governed by the criterion of the desiring of truth, goodness, beauty), is also political – but in the sense that it should always be by definition first and foremost primarily a 'blue-skies-searching' for the just and for freedom. However, this is not the way in which research is usually driven or carried out in the modern institution. The University in our time is afraid of space, afraid of the imagination that drives research; and, as a consequence, research has to be regulated, managed and controlled. It is also afraid of time, of the time that can bring change in the future; and this also leads to a tacit demand for control. This is a *covert* and unacknowledged politicization of research, even of allegedly disinterested research. It is not simply that we have tended to prioritize so-called 'applied' research; it is rather that the research has forgotten its primary aims of searching imaginatively for justice and for democratic freedom.

One primary tool for the resulting constraints upon research is 'space-management'. This management of space relates not just to the costing of square metres; it extends more fully to the attempt, by governments, to determine *where* research will take place. Especially in recent times, when governments in the advanced economies have been reluctant to fund research from public funds, there has been an effort – and in the UK a very determined effort – to limit the places where research will happen. That was one of the key purposes of the Research Assessment Exercises (initially called Research *Selectivity* Exercises) that were in place from the early 1980s: the idea was that, by competitive assessment of research, government would be legitimized in its attempt to fund only a few institutions where 'excellent' research was happening already. In slightly more subtle fashion, there have also been attempts to 'concentrate' research in so-called niche fields, thereby reducing the scope and ambit of research activity. In yet more subtle moves, the idea of 'competition' is being occasionally forgotten, to be replaced by a rehabilitated 'cooperation', in an effort to persuade researchers themselves to 'concentrate' their research activity together. In all cases, the reduction of scope, the reduction of space, is key.

This is not to say that research – good research, consistent with the fundamental principles of the University – does not happen: on the contrary. However, it happens despite the managements of space and of time that otherwise hamper it.

5

One way of explaining this is to consider, quite literally, the 'place' of the University in contemporary thinking. We tend to think of it sometimes, in literally 'utopian' fashion, as an institution that is international, deracinated, fundamentally not tied to any specific geographical location. That is, of course, an idealized view. In practical terms, our thinking is driven by completely opposite demands, which we say are the demands of 'practicality'. Accordingly, we are asked to consider individual Universities as 'regional' institutions, for example. These are supposed to enhance the economy of specific parts of a nation or country, and they are to do this by attracting and stimulating the business-drivers of an economy to a specific place.

Just as we have seen teaching broken up and organized into 'modules' that can be rearranged and combined to produce a whole, so the 'national' system is now to be made up of these building-bricks that dot the country. As with modules, diversity is the alleged commanding order of things with this. However, what we have here is an extremely constrained and regulated 'diversity', a diversity that cannot bear fundamental difference or change, Pascalian *transition*, in which people may start to change their places rather than simply to 'know their place' and rest easy within it. The institutions are very definitely not to be parallel to each other: they will have their separate and diverse 'missions'; and that supposed multiplicity of mission, it is alleged, gives the student something called 'choice', which we too often accept as our poor substitute for what should be a more fundamental freedom.

It is time to explore the culture of the module as part of the compartmentalization of research into managed and restricted space, and as a consequent restriction of human possibility. Modularity and regionalization, in fact, are of a piece and go together; and, in what follows here, we will see that the more or less explicit management of space that is central to both of these inhibits the fundamental aims of research.

At one level, and from a specific and easily identifiable ideological point of view, the modularization of University degree programmes makes perfect sense and has certain obvious benefits. From the point of view of both teacher and student, there is a high degree of organization: the otherwise immense world of knowledge in specific fields can be broken down into manageable units. Very importantly for present purposes, the teacher can supposedly align their teaching more firmly with their research, for the modules that they choose to design and teach are governed primarily by those intellectual interests, and not by any allegedly intrinsic demands of an overarching or transcendent programme. In any case, the programme as a whole is too big to allow any one individual to have an overview; and the breakdown into modules reflects, and morally respects, the individual intellectual freedoms of each participant.

That freedom is respected for the student as well, in this view of things. The student can see a kind of 'map' of the whole of the field of study, but is enabled to negotiate their own chosen 'pathway' or 'progression route' through and across the field. The student is now rather like the peregrine scholar of the medieval world. The claim is that the student now has a number of advantages. In the first place, they have an essential freedom, enacted in and through the *choice* of specific high-quality-because-research-led modules to take. The choice in question, and the resulting configuration of the degree, gives them the chance to express their specific identity, different from those around them, with learning 'tailored' to measure, as opposed to being like a potentially ill-fitting 'off-the-peg one-size-fits-all' suit. In this, what is now released and celebrated, it is claimed, is the individuality of the student. In passing along the way, something also happens to the student: they become a 'customer' or a consumer, making their own 'journey'.

It may seem perverse to attack this as being actually precisely the opposite of what is empirically the case, but that is what I intend here to argue. First, the module is an exact illustration of the triumph of the *esprit de géométrie*, entirely unregulated or unmodified by any *finesse*. The programme as a whole, and any sense of an intrinsic logic of its wholeness, no longer exists; and in its place, we have fragments of a whole that are assembled in idiosyncratic ways. This, say the advocates of spatial regulation and of the module as our basic organization principle for pedagogy, is precisely the point: the idiosyncrasy here is valuable for two main reasons: a) it is impossible to attain a knowledge of the whole, as the field of each discipline is now so massive; and b) idiosyncrasy is precisely what should be glorified, as an indication of our non-coerced individuality.

I adverted above to the invention of Lego, the toy with interlocking building blocks, as a kind of parallel here. It is indeed the case that Lego – and modularization – ostensibly allows for a huge number of possible different permutations of a programme or built system. However, is it not peculiar that modules can all be measured as comparable in size, or at least computable as multiples of each other? How is it the case that 'Deconstruction' can be 'the same' in functional terms as 'Aspects of Modern Literature, Painting, Music', say? How might these 'equal' a half of 'Renaissance Sculpture in Italy' or 'Computational Mathematics II'? As a teacher, if not as a student, one knows empirically that there is a radical shoe-horning effect here, as modules are wrestled into the 'proper' shape in such a way as to make them all comparable or, more importantly, *exchangeable*. No matter how long it might take, in intellectual and academic terms, for one to engage in a course of study of deconstruction, in administrative terms it *must* take precisely the prescribed computable number of hours, series of classroom sessions, essays with their prescribed and matched word-limits, and so on. If the module unit is X, everything must be X or a multiple thereof: there can be no irregular-shaped bricks. The module determines the learning, and not vice versa.

Let us note something important in passing. Even the more modern developments of Lego have realized this and the basic brick-structure is long abandoned for a more varied kind of modelling; but this will never be able to reach the kind of organic shape that is fundamental to and constitutive of learning, or of research. In short, our University models in which research and teaching are caught up in managed space – the regulated module – are, quite simply, out-of-date: they have failed to adapt to the requirements of our contemporary predicaments and needs for more organic research, learning and teaching.

The module is, as it were, the *currency* of a degree; and, measured like currency, it allows for all sorts or mercantile exchange. We usually call this the module's CAT value (the acronym expands as Credit Accumulation and Transfer). As with money, the key thing is that the tokens for exchange – CATs – have no actual material content: they allow for a transaction to take place, certainly; but they do not in themselves act as *transformative* in the ways that I have described in earlier pages. The transactions that take place are always between already settled entities: there can simply be *no research whatsoever* in this structural organization, where research and thought are shoe-horned into units of exchange. The 'research-led module' is, at some fundamental level, an oxymoron with regard to its establishment of relations between research and learning.

Further, such a modular organization does indeed allow, in principle, for multiply divergent end results: some may build a house that is all red, others a one-storey house. The possibilities are seemingly endless – but only seemingly so, since the shape of the foundational units – the limited and prescribed shape of the modules – predetermines and circumscribes what is possible. Moreover, what do these possibilities amount to? In fact, the end result is always a house, but one with minor modifications only. The end result, then, is but the signing of a name, the construction of an identity ('my' house differs from 'yours' because my door is green and yours is blue); and the difficulty – as in Lego – would be in building something that was both entirely individual while also having legitimacy. That is to say: only certain 'buildings' can be recognized as buildings; and only some of them will have legitimacy or will actually 'stand up'. It is the same with the alleged freedom of the module: the spatial organization is designed to *produce conformity* to what we can now call 'official' identities.

We might illustrate this most readily through research and teaching in humanities subjects. We have long ago given up on the idea, in an English Literature degree for instance, of what used to be called 'comprehensive coverage' of a broad canon of agreed core literary works (an extension of what is often called the 'great books' programmes in many US liberal arts programmes). Rightly, many indicated that the agreed 'canon' was essentially rather restricted, eliminating a number of groups of people from literary and cultural history. There were not many works by women; not many by people of ethnic origins other than the Anglo-Saxon, Anglo-American or Anglo-European; writers who were lesbian or gay were noted, perhaps, as writers, but their sexuality was not of interest; and so on. The breakdown of a belief in a centrally agreed canon, and its replacement with a more diverse curriculum, is indeed welcome and very important.

The problem lies in what happens to this in modularization, which proceeds as if we are now 'mapping' a new terrain or drawing out a new series of histories, cultural and literary, in the interests of the edifications of the freedom that I have placed at the core of my University principles. Again, we have a guide in how we might properly think about this. On 9 December 1922, the French philosopher, Alain (the pseudonym of Émile-Auguste Chartier), published one of his many 'propositions on education'. In this small newspaper article, he considers how difficult it is, through education, to advance the possibilities of human change – what I might here call the transformation that is central to any learning and teaching, and certainly fundamental to any research. He asks us to consider the pupil learning the violin, and argues that the adoption of the same method 'is good for everyone' learning the instrument, no matter how different they may be at the start. Some might think that this has the effect of homogenizing them, making them all sound the same; but Alain argues that it is precisely the adoption of this 'common method' that allows them to express their differences at all. He goes so far as to then make the more generalizing claim – and this is the most telling observation that he makes in virtually all of his writings on this – that 'a common culture makes differences flourish'. Difference, or what we might call the exploration of the human's capacity for imagining herself or himself otherwise, is dependent upon a pre-existing ground of some kind: if we are to differ, we need to 'differ from', so to speak. In fact and by contrast, argues Alain, a condition of *initial* diversification leads only to an eventual homogenization, or a conformity that is essentially limiting with respect to human diversity.

In literary study, the argument might then go that, as a first (and good) step, we abandon the idea of an immobile core canon and replace it with a flexible curriculum, which is to be followed more or less at the choice of an individual student. The result is that the student has a fragmented view of parts of a whole, without any 'finessing' delicacy – that is, no capacity for *judgement*, but only for *measure* or *calculation* – regarding that whole. It is like having Lego bricks without a design or without the idea of a house to be built. Faced with this, as the student moves from one module to another, from one research-idea to another, ranging 'freely' across the field, all that is left in the way of making this cohere at all is, fundamentally, a regular and consistent fundamental *method* of study. It is like making a building in which, systematically, it has been decided that each layer of bricks will be done in alternate colours: one red, one white and so on.

Thus we find the triumph not only of the of the 'Stoical' introspection and reduction of our space that we saw discussed by Pascal, but also the triumph of that 'theoreticism' that reduces all texts, no matter what, to exercises in the identity-formation of the student. In principle, this may be admirable; but, in empirical fact, that identity-formation is not at all free for the kinds of mode of inquiry – the methods – are themselves rather limited: Marxist, feminist, postcolonial and so on. Thus, I as a critic find myself *not* as 'differing' but rather as conforming to predetermined identities: the 'working-class Scottish Marxist', the 'Irish nationalist feminist', the 'bourgeois formalist', for instance. It matters not which one of these one is: they are all commodified versions of the self, each with its own 'market' of books, films, T-shirts, styles, TV shows, 'values'.

Instead of an opened ground in which the student can find an archaeology of the culture that they study, and can find that archaeology as being *to some extent* intrinsically determined by the objects of inquiry, the net result is a conformity to a pre-given 'official' identity. This way, in fact, the module-model leads only to conformity, denying the possibility of experience and, above all, denying the very principles of research – blue-skies inquiry into the expansiveness of the field – upon which the modular system is allegedly built.

We can write this large now, at the institutional level. Regionalization, in which the University's research is 'applied' to the economic requirements and identity of a specific region, is a form of parochialism that we might now identify either as the triumph of the *esprit de géométrie* or as the improper restraint upon research by an improperly overweening ideological government against which Eisenhower warned us. In either case, research – as blue-skies expansiveness and edification – is endangered.

6

The 'inward turn' of research, that turn away from the frightening expanse of space to the world within at its nano-levels, is also consistent with a further ideological drive towards self-scrutiny. Research, in sum, is shaped by surveillance, and especially by a drive to doubt one's own authority as a researcher. The auditing of space, and also of time, means that a good deal of research energy is spent and wasted in the researcher 'describing' not just what they are doing, but also in predicting what they *will do*, and thus in foretelling a future, describing an outcome and so on.

I leave aside the politics of surveillance for the moment, in order to turn attention more fully to the question of time and the foretelling of the future as a component of research. I indicated above that, when Pascal wondered about his own locatedness, he was also concerned with the issue of time, with his allotment or allocation of *time* on the earth at this specific moment. That temporal dimension has been lost in research; and, if we are to revive a genuine research model that is not constrained by the controlling mechanisms of the space and Lego metaphors, then we will need to find a way of reopening time and temporality, and of bringing a properly historical dimension into our research mentality.

If one can predict the future, then it is not the future. Let us begin from that simple observation. To explain it, consider the example of capitalist exchange. I go into a shop and see a coat that I would like to have. I give the shopkeeper £100; but I do this *if and only if* I am absolutely sure that, in the very near future, the shopkeeper will hand me the coat. In doing this, I bring the moment at which they hand me the coat back into a complete intimacy with the earlier moment at which I hand over the money. In fact, it is *as if* that second moment (the future) has already taken place (and is thus as fully guaranteed as the past can be or as my present gesture of handing over the money now is). I compress time, in such a way as to make the future (which has not yet happened) really an aspect of the present (as if it is happening right now). Further, the exchange takes place if and only if the coinciding of the two moments is guaranteed. I do not hand over the money in the mere hope that they will give me a coat.[2]

In this exchange, then, the future is, as it were, guaranteed and controlled. The exchange means that temporal unpredictability is removed, as is any notion of experiment. This is how research is too often regarded: it is seen *as if* it were a mercantile exchange in which, for example, a government gives me a certain sum, but will do so *if and only if* I can guarantee the outcome of my experiments. In recent times, this has been described as 'impact'; and it is increasingly being used in order to allocate funding for research. Obviously, however, this has to be a fabrication: if I could guarantee the outcome, there would be no experiment taking place at all. Governmentally driven 'thesis' would replace research 'hypothesis'. What is being 'bought' here is not research; rather, what is being bought is a decision, or a justification of government ideology or policy. The impact required is not the kind that we saw in 1968, with contemporary Cohn-Bendit confronting government ministers; rather, the impact required is purely financial: will this medical research enable a pharmaceutical company to make money? If so, the success is measured in terms of the difference between the money made and the money invested for the execution of the research; and our term for this is 'value for money'. It is essentially a channelling of public funding into private company hands, and the misappropriation of University research to that end.

Against this, let us consider research as a genuine opening of time. In this, we would start to see research as being something that looks both backwards into the past and also, crucially, forwards into an uncertain future. To put this most bluntly, research is a matter of generational change: it is, as it were, a debt owed to future generations, but a debt whose capital is given through the researches of the past that allow the present researcher to imagine the world otherwise. It is only in this way that research can take its proper place, as an *event*, in the strict sense that I have been giving that word: the event as that which is un-pre-programmed, as that which cannot be predicted from the state of affairs prior to its taking place. Perhaps, more simply, we can define it as 'experiment'.

I hand over my £100, but then the question is 'what happens next?' Research is there to answer that question, but to do so by looking for the true, the good, the beautiful: that is, research answers the question 'what comes next' with an answer that seeks to expand freedom and justice. It is entirely inappropriate to fund research on the ideological basis of capitalist exchange: that is simply not how research works, and any such funding is bound to narrow and deform its possibilities. Genuine research (and the only surprise here is that one now needs to say these things) entails a state of affairs in which we cannot guarantee the future, but must rather seek to generate it – and to generate it as different from the present. And this, in a brief word, is also the more genuine and proper meaning of 'applied research'.

I argued earlier that research is about the transcending of the boundaries of the self; but it is now clear that it is also about the transcending of the boundaries of the present. It is about the future generation.

7

It is in this way, in fact, that research and teaching come together. This is close to what Karl Jaspers had in mind when he linked research and teaching in his version of the *Idea of the University*. Jaspers wrote his own manifesto for the University in the days of Weimar; and he was called upon to revise it immediately after the Second World War, when Germany needed to find a new basis for the reconstruction of a nation. This, we should remember, was the nation whose leaders, at one point, had advocated the burning of books. We are never far away from this kind of barbarism, for too many of those who are in power and authority fear the openness that research gives us and its unpredictability; and they fear what may happen if that openness is to be passed on to generations afterwards.

Unlike Cardinal Newman, whose idea of a University in the nineteenth century was one that prioritized teaching, Jaspers argued that teaching and research were interlinked; but research was primary. He saw the University as being the place where we seek truth and, 'because truth is accessible to systematic search,' he wrote, 'research is the foremost concern of the university'. He went on to suggest that this truth is not governed by disciplinary boundaries, but rather is greater than any specific single science or discrete discipline. It involves the whole of the human being, not just her or his intellectual expertise. Thus, this pursuit of researched truth involves 'the serious commitment of the whole man'. Then, finally, the truth can be transmitted; and this is how he described the activity of teaching. This, then, gives us the model for one of our contemporary myths of 'excellence', the claim that quality in teaching is governed – and that it can only be guaranteed – by research.[3]

All Universities now boast of their 'research-led teaching'. This, however, is simply an atomization of knowledge and its reduction into modular forms, as I have already shown. Yet there is a further aspect to this that requires exposure. 'Research-led teaching' is but another myth. It may be reassuring to those who see the University as primarily to be characterized by its brand of excellence; but, in fact, teaching that is 'research-led' is usually poor teaching. Why would one want to teach a first-year undergraduate, for instance, to the limits of one's own research? It would be a little like trying to teach the basic principles of arithmetic by a thorough exposure to and engagement with the intricacies of multidimensional space and fractal geometries. The undergraduate needs *time* to bring themselves up to a certain kind of speed, time to do the reading and thinking required to be able to cope with the advanced searches that constitute research itself.

The prevailing ideology, however, seems to think of the University as a place where advanced knowledge is 'held' in a kind of non-temporal store or spatial repository. The teacher/lecturer is a kind of gatekeeper to this store, while the 'researcher' is the one who 'finds' the knowledge from somewhere and places it, for safe-keeping and then sale, into the repository. The teacher is then charged with the 'delivery' of the knowledge, in its little modularized compartments, to the student, now re-branded as a customer. Needless to say, neither teaching nor research is happening in this ideology. Again, this is not to say that good teaching and good research can't take place in the University; but it is to say that such good teaching and research as does occur happens *despite* the prevailing myths – such as that, in the present instance, of 'research-led teaching' – governing the institution.

Where is that 'reserve' on which our 'research-led learning' can draw? We all know exactly where it is: it is on the Web. This Web, however, in this ideology, is conceived entirely as a spatial entity: it is seen not really as a 'web' at all, but rather as a container of knowledge, a treasure chest that can be plundered at will and without any compunction – or, indeed, 'payment'. We can plunder at will – most will rightly call this plagiarism or internet piracy – because, even when we take from the treasure trove that is the Web, the material is still there: we don't remove it. Further, it's 'free' or at least ostensibly freely available at all and any times.

However, it is not, and cannot be, 'knowledge' at all. What we find, in this spatialized model, is research commodified as 'information'. This 'information' is 'transparently' available; but it is transparent because it has no substance as knowledge or as research. It is only in this mode of thinking that we could ever believe that such research-knowledge can be 'transferred'. It is not simply a matter now of research-based knowledge being 'delivered' to students in the classroom; rather, knowledge can be 'transferred' much more widely. The distribution of research, in knowledge-transfer schemes, is what we usually mean when we talk about the benefits of 'applied' research or simply of applying the results of research to real-life situations and practices. Yet, in our prevailing modes of thought, knowledge-transfer is nothing more or less than moving bits of information around: it is like shelf-stacking in a supermarket. Knowledge-transfer is a bit like taking a journey on the Underground or metro system: at various points, you can make a connection; but the specific connections we make are unimportant, for all we are doing is simply moving about in a controlled space. Research, properly understood, would get us out of the controlled space underground for a bit of real exploration of the great city above.

Research-knowledge, by definition, is much more opaque, then, than anything suggested by our prevailing modes of spatialized practices; yet, it is only by our realizing that knowledge will take time to find, and time to move between generations, that we will find anything approaching truth, not to mention goodness or beauty, justice or freedom. For this to take place, however, we need something called leadership; and it is to this that I now turn.

4

Leadership

Legitimation and Authority

I began this book with a description of the first principles that should govern a University. Those principles, I said, were the search for the true, the good and the beautiful. Many readers will have realized that I am certainly not the first to suggest such a thing. A rather more famous teacher than I could ever hope to be once used almost exactly the same words. In a critique of the politics of Stanley Baldwin, who in his 1929 general election campaign adopted the motto 'Safety first', this teacher said, one Friday in March 1931, while walking with her pupils through the streets of Edinburgh, that 'Safety does not come first. Goodness, Truth and Beauty come first. Follow me.' The charismatic teacher here is Miss Jean Brodie, the character made famous in Muriel Spark's novel, *The Prime of Miss Jean Brodie*, initially published in the *New Yorker* in 1961. Miss Brodie is, of course, a most dangerous precursor for any responsible educator to have.[1]

Yet the problem does not lie in her concerns for the search for truth, goodness and beauty; rather, it lies in the ideas of 'following' (that we see in that slightly menacing and disturbing instruction, 'Follow me') and more pertinently in the ideas of leading that govern her practice as a teacher. The motto 'Follow me' figures quite highly among the worst things a teacher might ever say to their pupils. Miss Brodie's girl pupils, the 'Brodie set', are to be charmed by the unconventional idiosyncrasies of the enigmatic leader that Miss Brodie sees herself to be; and she, in turn, is but a follower of some other, more dangerous political tendencies than those advocated by Stanley Baldwin, for she is an admiring follower of Mussolini ('one of the greatest men in the world', she calls him)[2] and of the *fascisti* who, at this time, are threatening the whole of Europe with a certain kind of authority-worship masquerading as strong 'leadership'.

On the walk that March day, and in one of the many highly ironic passages for which Muriel Spark's novel is rightly celebrated, Miss Brodie outlines her fundamentals of education. She takes the girls of her set out to walk to Edinburgh's Old Town, 'where history had been lived', she says.[3] She marches them there, and, en route, gives only one definite, but deliciously charged, direction: 'We turn to the right', she says.[4] Having made this turn, she is able then to expound her notion of education, which she sets against the practice of the more traditional head-teacher, Miss Mackay. It is worth quoting at length:

> Meanwhile, I follow my principles of education and give of my best in my prime. The word 'education' comes from the root *e* from *ex*, out, and *duco*, I lead. It means a leading out. To me education is a leading out of what is already there in the pupil's soul. To Miss Mackay it is a putting in of something that is not there, and that is not what I call education, I call it intrusion, from the Latin root prefix *in* meaning in and the stem *trudo*, I thrust.[5]

The difficulty with this – Spark's irony – is that Miss Brodie is wrong in the matter of linguistic fact. The linguistic root that she describes here is the root *educere* (to educe) and not *educare* (to educate). She is not talking about education, but rather about *educing*. Although close in some superficial respects, educing and educating nonetheless remain substantially different; and the key difference has to do with leadership and following. To educe is to elicit or to infer, to bring a conclusion out of raw data; and in that sense, it is to 'draw out' or to lead out a reality from a mere raw or implicit potential. This needs 'leadership', in the sense given to that word by Miss Brodie, in that it needs someone to spot the reality within the potential and to draw it out. Education, however, is not the mere realizing of potential; rather, it is the ongoing making of more and more potential, the never-ending *desire*, identified now with the activity of research, to seek out the good, the true and the beautiful.

The key here lies in two notions of authority. To 'educe' is to assert one's own authority as the final word, with one's personal preference as final arbiter. Miss Brodie subscribes to such a view. She asks her set, 'Who is the greatest Italian painter?' and they reply that it is Leonardo da Vinci. 'That is incorrect,' replies Miss Brodie. 'The answer is Giotto, he is my favourite.'[6] The 'authority' for this is nothing more or less than Miss Brodie's assertion of her authority: as 'the greatest' equates with 'my favourite', there can be no discussion, no proof or legitimation of the authority behind the statement – other, that is, than Miss Brodie's own charisma and force, or the weight given to her statements by her institutional authority. In short, it amounts to a form of leadership by whimsy.

Against this would be a version of authority whose purpose is to give authorization to the views and thinking of others, or to bring them to the point where their voice is legitimate; and it is only this latter that can be called education. Education, in this sense, is almost the very opposite of educing. It is the ongoing quest after justice and freedom – and especially for the justice and freedom for future generations; and these things – justice, freedom, the future – are themselves restless and changing. Given the fact that we are oriented thus towards the future, which is unknown, it is axiomatic that the teacher cannot herself know in advance what might be the actual *content* of justice or freedom: education becomes a communal activity, involving teacher and learner, both now involved in an 'inventing'. Here, I mean to signal in this word two senses: one sense of 'finding out new things' or discovery, and a second sense of 'making' or of inaugurating things that we have not heretofore seen.

In this sense, there is no simple 'reality' of either justice or freedom to be brought out from a potential source; rather, we constantly make and remake these things. There is a *poiesis* going on here: that ancient term not only gives us our own 'poetry', but it also means something like the kinds of 'making' that we associate with all forms of crafts, makings that are material and historically substantive – just as poetry is, when poetry is properly understood as a custodianship of a shared language and its possibilities for making meanings. This most certainly does *not* require the kind of leadership so admired by Miss Brodie, a leadership that simply brings *authoritarianism* instead of authority. One key and fundamental difference between authoritarianism and authority might neatly be summed up in the words of Hannah Arendt, when she writes, against authoritarianism, that while authority certainly implies forms of obedience, it 'implies an obedience in which men retain their freedom'.[7] Such authority is, essentially, an authority that acknowledges that it requires legitimation, especially from those who will choose to obey; and, further, authority such as this obeys the demand or desire for the production of freedom and its extension. By contrast, authoritarianism implies the end of any freedom by imposing the end of any discussion or debate or dialogue or change.

The counterpart of leadership is now called, especially in the management jargon, 'followership'. Once more, we have an excellent literary example that might guide us: a poem by Seamus Heaney. In a very early poem, 'Follower', he writes of his relation with a great personal precursor figure, his father. He describes how straight a line his father was able to plough on the farmlands, and how skilled he was in leading his horse and his plough across the field and its furrows. The young Heaney writes that 'I stumbled in his hob-nailed wake', and describes himself as always stumbling along uncertainly behind, being always 'a nuisance, tripping, falling / Yapping always', even though his father sometimes 'rode me on his back / Dipping and rising to his plod'.

In these lines, we see the young boy getting in the way, slowing the father down; but we also see the father helping, untroubled by the boy – indeed, bringing the boy into the same rhythms of his own body, quite literally 'involving' him and enfolding him in the work. The final lines of the poem show what happens in this situation, when generation speaks to generation, when they maintain a tradition and transfer a knowledge or an expertise:

> I was a nuisance, tripping, falling,
> Yapping always. But today
> It is my father who keeps stumbling
> Behind me, and will not go away.
> Heaney, 'Follower'

In this moment, the poem transforms itself and its reader. It becomes a poem about memory, about bearing the weight of the past; but also about how a follower, heaving learned something, becomes a leader and, in so doing, also cares for the past and recognizes his debts. In leading, this new leader bears the weight of the past on his back; aware that he is a leader *because* of the past, and able to look forward and make his own straight lines – in Heaney's case, the lines of verse, turning back and forth like the furrows of a ploughed field. He carries on the tradition of working the lines; but, as we also know from Heaney's most famous early poem, 'Digging', he exchanges the lines of the furrowed field for the lines of verse, of writing itself, his 'squat pen' in that poem taking the place of his father's spade in his hands. It is thus – in this fundamental act of *transformation* – that this follower gains his authority, becomes an author.

This is a little reminiscent of a political writing as well. I am thinking of Marx's great opening to the *Eighteenth Brumaire of Louis Bonaparte*, in which he argues that the great events of history happen twice, as it were: the first time as tragedy, the second as farce. More importantly, right at the start of that pamphlet, Marx points out what we might now take as an almost entirely uncontroversial observation. He writes that people make their own history, 'but they do not make it just as they please; they do not make it under circumstances chosen by themselves, but under given conditions directly encountered and inherited from the past'. In this, he is pointing out that, in the search for autonomy, for the authority through which people can make and subscribe to their own laws, there are necessary limitations and pre-conditions given to us by our place in history, our location in time and space. As he glosses this, in a tone that is actually rather like a foreshadowing of Heaney (and of many others), 'The tradition of all the generations of the dead weighs like a nightmare on the brain of the living'.[8] This might also be, quite simply, a description of the process of education itself: bearing the weight of the past, but for the purposes of making and imagining a new and different future. Indeed, our task, as Marx hinted in these same pages, is to learn to 'draw our poetry ... from the future'.

These examples – from both literary and political writing – help us to understand that leadership and followership are charged with meanings well beyond the simple idea of being at the head or tail of a race, or of an army, or of a group or institutional body. In becoming a leader, one faces some fundamental issues. There are questions of responsibility to be addressed, of adequate answering for one's own past or for a more general tradition, of having appropriate experience, of being able to transform that experience in various ways (from ploughing to writing, for instance) such that something new is made possible.

To lead does not mean to begin with a Year Zero and to ignore all that has come before, but rather to have a peculiarly privileged relation to all that has come before. To lead requires a profound historical sense: a sense of one's responsibility to history. To lead is to be in a privileged position that brings with it a burden, but a burden called 'answerability'; and what is being answered is, among many other things, the very history that has made us. This answerability is infinitely more than being 'accountable' for one's present decisions; and our contemporary notions of such 'accountabilities' are, sadly, a poor and entirely inadequate substitute for a real and substantive idea of what leadership entails. Perhaps above all, to lead means to assert a particular kind of break, to effect a break that will produce the *transformations* that we saw exemplified in Heaney. In this, it is clear and should now be accepted as utterly axiomatic that the leader, insofar as they lead, cannot be simply the agent of another, more powerful force – even a force to which they are to be held to account.

We can look at what this means for various qualities of leadership within the University. In some cases, the leader in question will be the vice-chancellor, provost or president; but the leader, in these days that have witnessed the rise of the managerial class, may also be one such as the registrar. If we limit ourselves to a consideration of these roles, though, we will be taking too narrow and too parochial a view of our question. As should be clear from my foregoing examples, leaders crop us in many guises and in many situations. Thus, we need to look at the micro-level and to consider the question of leadership in relation to teachers, students, colleagues; and also we should look at the macro-level and ask about the wider authorities that shape the University institution, including funding councils or education ministers and their associated political bodies. The fundamental question concerning leadership relates to the *authority of the University* as an independent and autonomous institution within the much wider ambit of a society or a civilization, and thus to the legitimization of our search for the true, the good and the beautiful. It is only in the establishment of this independence and autonomy that any gesture towards democratization and justice becomes possible.

Let us begin elsewhere, and in another time.

1

On 18 October 1704, the philosopher Giambattista Vico, author of *The New Science*, gave one of his annual orations to the incoming student body of the University of Naples, where he held the position of Rector. The annual oration was a kind of keynote address setting the academic credentials and priorities of the University; and in each of the addresses that he gave Vico was at pains to iterate the foundational principles of his institution as well as to give leadership and to establish a kind of moral compass to guide the novices as they began their great courses and programmes of studies. He told the incoming novice students in Naples that year that the greatest benefit of learning is 'to be educated for the common good of the citizenry'. Their learning, and the teaching that goes with it, was not for private profit, but for the good of community.

Before we pass this by too quickly, let us pause to note what a refreshing thought that is. It is based on the idea that, even if not everyone follows a University education, still and nonetheless everyone benefits from the fact of it. A useful analogy is with the system of road-building or railway-building within a nation: whether individuals travel on these things or not, we all benefit from them; they unify communities in material as well as potential ways; they facilitate commerce and the transport of food and goods, improving thereby the very *fact* of civil life and culture, and even civilization itself. We might also compare this to the idea of a national health service: whether we as specific individuals are ill or not, the entire nation benefits from the fact of such a thing. Such an ethic appears to be entirely missing in the rather more mercenary ideologies to which we are encouraged to subscribe in our own time, in the mistaken Hobbesian belief that there is no alternative to a life that is individualistic, 'competitive', atomized and, as a consequence, 'nasty, brutish and short'. What might Vico's lesson here mean for the profession of the teacher, indeed for the very conditions of education as a whole; and what might it imply for the question of leadership, not just in the Naples of the turn of the eighteenth century, but much more generally?

We should begin the investigation at the most substantial part of a ground-level in terms of the material daily work of the University: the level of the teacher and their authority. In earlier versions of the academy, the beginning teacher, seeking the authority to profess the discipline, was an apprentice. An apprentice learns a craft, but is also 'bound to serve, and entitled to receive instruction' from those already established in the craft. The two-way obligation here is vital: the apprentice is bound, but, once experienced enough, will be set free; the master is likewise bound, bound to give freely of their experience. In being thus bound together, like Heaney and his father, the generations together find what I will call the *intimacy of community*, and also recognize the centrality of the question of their responsibility for the community and its future. This – the necessity of establishing an intimacy of community – is already a fundamental precondition of citizenship. The apprentice is learning a craft, but also bearing it and its responsibilities, and thus becoming the guardian of its values; the master is attentive to their responsibilities towards the future in a community that extends beyond the academy, beyond the immediate environment in which they lead the apprentice, helping and shouldering where necessary.

In this old academy, then, *all* learning is apprenticeship – be it in engineering, medicine, law, literature, languages, or any other field, be it academic, technical, vocational or crafted. Further, there is no crude distinction between teachers and learners: we all both learn and teach at once. That overlap is vital to the organic energy of the whole institution, the whole arrangement of the community that is dignified or edified by the University. The community may be that of scholars in a discipline, but equally is that large and material community that we call civic culture, nation-state or even, at one limit, international dialogue. This is apprenticeship not just in English literature, say, but also and more fundamentally it is apprenticeship in the freedom of thought, and the freedom in citizenship.

T.S. Eliot thought something similar when he wrote of how literary and cultural tradition operates in an essay of 1919. In his celebrated essay, 'Tradition and the Individual Talent', he explained that 'the new' can only be brought into being or made to happen by one who embodies a tradition. An absolute novelty, such as we might now associate with a 'Year Zero' mentality, not only lacks any kind of legitimacy, but is strictly impossible. Further, it is of necessity grounded in a falsification of how things actually are. To become 'modern', and to assert an authority and autonomy required to shape a future, we need to learn – and to carry the weight of – the past, even if we are about to break with the immediate past in an act of imaginative and material creativity that we identify as a transforming of reality. In the newspeak terminology that governs us, 'modernization' can only happen if it is based on an organic continuity with the institution that is being modernized. However, those who deploy this word in its newspeak accent appear to believe that modernization requires a junking of the past: everything begins as if we were at a Year Zero. 'Modernization' is simply the cant term that we use to try to avoid the negative totalitarian connotations associated with that 'Year Zero' mentality.

Managerial 'modernization' assumes not only that the past is another country, but also that, as another country is it underdeveloped; and, consequently, there is nothing to learn from visiting it. In short, 'modernization', often like another cant term, 'reform', is designed rhetorically to assert a force of authority – the authority of a Miss Brodie and her preferences, here, now – over the possibility of learning from the past, from education or even from rational argument. In the more measured understanding of becoming modern – that is, in my sense here of the attaining of an autonomy – the apprentice teacher worked rather more like the Eliotic poet; and so they felt themselves bound to institutions, to disciplines and to the governance of the standards within those institutions: a tradition.

The idea of tradition can, of course, be both conservative and radical. In fact, it is precisely the ambivalence of the term that gives it its value: such ambivalence means that we need to discuss it, argue about it and even struggle over it in a culture of conversation or discussion. Sadly, however, this idea of tradition is now replaced with the qualities – or, more accurately, the 'languages' – of excellence, which strain belief. This is a language that brooks no discussion or debate: 'excellence', unlike 'tradition', is such a vague term that there is no possibility of any real discussion about it. All that we can do is to claim it: who would ever wish to claim that their institution was anything less?

Ever since the establishment of a culture of mistrust of the University – a culture generated under the pusillanimous mean-spiritedness of Thatcherism in the 1980s in order to justify the squeezing of public funding out of the academy and the exertion of governmental control over it – we have decided that University teachers need to be taught how to teach; and, more tellingly, we have asserted that this form of teaching-how-to-teach will most certainly *not* involve the processes of apprenticeship and the forging of the intimacy of community. Instead, in fact, the purpose will now be to ensure that there is *no* allegiance between generations and to require that the coming generation will form an allegiance with the much more abstract idea of 'modernization' itself, now raised to the level of being something like 'professional modernization'. The Year Zero has arrived, so to speak. The incoming teacher must break with their forebears and determinedly ignore any authority that their experience might offer, and must instead endlessly 'reform'; and they will do so according to the whims of those in control of the word 'modernization' – that is, the government and its agents, now acting like an authoritarian Miss Brodie, armed not with the same charms and persuasive charisma, but with money.

It is in this way that we bear witness to the rise of an entire industry – a very costly industry, publicly funded – of various forms of teaching accreditation in the University. The titles of the units that provide this activity all vary, but they usually involve words like 'teaching enhancement', 'quality', 'development' and sometimes 'PVC' or Pro-Vice-Chancellor (reflecting the pious seriousness with which this is taken by senior management). In their work, these units all proceed entirely as if University teachers had never previously thought, themselves, about teaching. They work on the assumption that, having been students ourselves, we are nonetheless entirely virgin with respect to the very idea of teaching. Only an entirely atomized mentality ('teachers' over here; 'learners' over there) could reasonably think such a thing.

The general governing assumption in these programmes is that University teachers up until now have never really reflected on how they conduct their work in the classroom and beyond. The incoming teacher is thus placed in a position where they, too, must mistrust the existing faculty; and the procedure is one that systematically and structurally quite literally 'degrades' the teacher who has gone before. It is a form of instruction that proceeds by insulting the past, rather than learning from it. The effect of such programmes for teaching teachers becomes, in these 'units of enhancement', the same structurally and universally: they damage the community of free thought that is properly called learning and teaching. At macro-level, they become 'Learning and Teaching Subject Networks' or the Higher Education Academy (HEA): self-perpetuating bureaucracies that have lost any material contact with 'traditional' realities on the teaching and learning ground, despite their pieties about the sanctity and dignity of teaching.

Crucially, these 'innovations' work on the assumption that actual and material experience – the forms and methods of teaching in the past – counts for nought. The actual work that colleagues might have already done in the classroom is routinely ignored, to be replaced by the purely formal and abstract ideas of the *soi-disant* excellent classroom performance. Instead, then, of having the intimacy of community, the incoming teacher finds herself or himself in a situation where what is expected is a kind of pledge of allegiance to the abstract qualities of an alleged 'best practice' in 'teaching-excellence'. There is, in this, a barely veiled contempt for practical experience, precisely and paradoxically at exactly the same moment as such practice is being vaunted as the most important aspect of our work as teachers. The bureaucracy of 'excellence in teaching' bases itself upon the imbibing of abstract guidelines, abstract ideas and images – that may have no basis in reality – of what goes on in an ideal lesson. Thus it was that, for a long time, every lecture – no matter its content – had to be codified as a series of bullet points on a PowerPoint presentation; that every lecture needed the same number of slides; that every lecture needed a bit of 'down-time' when students should reflect on what the lecturer just said; and so on.

These practices – often staggering in their lack of imagination – reduce the activity of teaching to a mere catalogue of mechanical operations; and the mechanic-in-chief is not the teacher, but rather an abstract and invisible agency that feels no need to argue for its essentially whimsical or technologically fashionable methods. In this, the teacher becomes a pure (by which I mean mere) 'human resource', a simple and reduced element in the machinery, and one that has itself to be mechanized, routinized and, above all, kept in check. We will find out more about how the language of human resources afflicts and damages the idea of proper leadership below. Suffice to say, for the moment, that the reduction of a colleague to the status of mere resource is not only damaging, but is also key to the operations of the quality myth that goes by the name of 'excellence in teaching'. Crucially, here, such a position calls into doubt any authority that the teacher may have, based on their experience of the subject domain and its specific disciplinary content.

These units for the alleged enhancement of teaching and learning have the effect of driving a wedge between generations, of raising a suspicious eyebrow over our apprentices, of de-legitimizing the experience of earlier generations; and, above all, of *mechanizing* what should be the *organic* community of the University and academy. In focusing on the allegedly *generic* skills that are deemed to be the cornerstones of any and all teaching activity, they actually empty the disciplines of their traditions, and de-legitimize their teachers, precisely at the moment when they are giving accreditation to those teachers. They demand allegiance to those generic skills and the accompanying quality agenda, rather than an allegiance to a community of free thinking.

As a consequence – and this is the single most important point here – the community is being denied the possibility of establishing its own new authority for shaping the future; and that is being replaced with an authoritarianism that requires compliance with its various and multiple 'guidelines' and bureaucratically imposed 'codes of practice'. Having established Year Zero by trashing the past and its experience, modernization now, paradoxically, freezes history precisely at Year Zero: there can be no future, no possible legitimate change. Yet there will be endless 'reform': that is, there will be endless modifications made to the abstractions to which we must be made to conform. To put this crudely, our 'leaders' may change their minds about what we do and should do: leadership by whimsy is the result.

2

None of this is governed by internal leadership within institutions. Rather, that leadership has caved in under the demand for forms of compliance with an imposed 'quality agenda'. The result is a loss of independence, a loss of autonomy and, consequently and above all, a loss of cultural authority and standing for the University as an institution that is an essential part of a civilized community. The community here – that civic tradition to which Vico alerted us – is under threat. Superb teaching happens in our Universities, certainly; but it happens in spite of, not because of the quality-and-excellence agenda. That agenda, policed as it is by those who have made a career out of the de-legitimization of experience and authority, replacing it with the mediocrity of allegedly 'excellent' bureaucratic process, drives quality down to the lowest acceptable common denominator, and undermines what teachers and students are doing on the ground.

There is a consequent divorce between actual teaching and its alleged fundamental methods; and such a divorce has damaging effects for the question of leadership and authority. The model, based on the language of excellence, is replicated at other and more strategically telling points in the structural organization of the University. Just as teachers must be taught to teach (though not by qualified teachers), so also our 'leaders' also have their own form of leadership-accreditation (not based on anything called experience of an engagement with their community). In the UK, there now exists a rather large armature that addresses the idea of leadership in higher education; and one very significant body involved in this is the Leadership Foundation for Higher Education (LFHE).

The Foundation offers a number of 'tailored' courses, all designed to address the very precise and specific circumstances of each individual who will follow their programmes. This tailoring, however, itself begins to look 'off-the-peg' as soon as one consults and considers the Foundation's published materials. The organization runs a number of programmes; many of them designed in propaedeutic fashion to let a practitioner or participant move incrementally from one step on the ladder of leadership to the next. Thus, we have their flagship programme, the 'Top Management Programme' (TMP), which has been followed by very significant numbers of existing vice-chancellors in the UK. However, before undertaking this course, it will really make sense if one follows the 'Senior Strategic Leadership' programme, which is partly designed for those who are already in such senior roles, with an eye to moving on to vice-chancellorship. Yet, it might make even more sense to start at 'Preparing for Senior Strategic Leadership'; and, lying 'under' this we will find, for example, the 'Head of Department' programme. Thus, there are multiple levels of leadership established, each with its corresponding programme and each with its corresponding leader figure.

Two interesting things can be noted immediately. The first is that the materials for all these appear to have been prepared according to a standardized template: standardized and recurring features appearing for all levels of programmes that will be enjoyed by participants include things like a '360-degree feedback loop'; 'practical tools, exercises and leadership techniques'; 'cross-institutional understanding'; 'a safe and supportive environment'; and 'action-learning sessions'. It may well be the case that these all apply at each and every level; but do they not also apply elsewhere, even in the classroom, say? In other words, these are *not* in fact specific to leaders at high strategic level; *nor* are they addressing the specifics of each level. The result is that these kinds of activity are seen to be generic but, perhaps more importantly for present purposes, they are seen as the preserve of higher-level leaders; and they also serve to homogenize all leadership as if it were all much the same thing. In this, those things that are generic and abstract trump all that is the historically specific and the materially particular.

Secondly, in the programmes designed by the LFHE, all the senior programmes make use of workshops. These are interesting because the workshops are all grounded in Shakespeare plays. If you are 'preparing' for senior strategic leadership, you work on *Macbeth*; if you have prepared and are now doing senior strategic leadership, you work on *As You Like It*; and, if you've reached the Top or the TMP, you work on *Henry V*. In one way, obviously, the practising academic is delighted at this: the vice-chancellor is learning from the work of the English and Drama departments. Only, however, they are not. The plays become simply the merest allegories of leadership situations; and we are to learn an extremely limited number of things from them: the virtues of inspiration, rhetorical communication or persuasion, the ability to 'sell' an idea and secure buy-in, questions of ethical leadership and so on.

The LFHE programmes all make extensive use specifically of workshops provided by Olivier Mythodrama, an organization dedicated to the use of drama – and especially Shakespeare – to help develop good leadership in business and the public sector. In one of the sample videos that are publicly available for the organization, Richard Olivier, a Director and practitioner in the company, gives a lecture on 'The Pyramid of Power' in which he analyses Shakespeare's ancient Rome as an allegory of the shape of power. He indicates that Shakespeare mythologizes history, and quotes Joseph Campbell to the effect that 'myth is something that never was, but always is'. The lecture, as also with the lecture in 'inspirational leadership' deploying *Henry V*, proposes that there is such as a thing as an 'eternal myth of leadership'. This use of mythodrama is highly charged and highly significant.

We might set the question of mythodrama alongside other modes of learning, modes that might equally well involve an aspect of play or drama. As I have indicated in an earlier chapter, play is indeed central to learning; and, as is clear throughout this book, I believe that literature and the other arts can also offer helpful structures that allow us to understand management. However, play, with its central guiding principles of *fiction-making*, need not drive us towards a subscription to myth or archetype. Here, I take a lead from the scholarship of Frank Kermode. 'We have to distinguish', he writes, in *The Sense of an Ending*, 'between myths and fictions.' It is important to hang on to the *provisional* nature of the fictions by which we will learn. 'Fictions can degenerate into myths whenever they are not consciously held to be fictive. In this sense anti-Semitism is a degenerate fiction, a myth; and *Lear* is a fiction.'[9]

Leaving aside for a moment the troubling correspondence between myth-learning and a certain anti-Semitism, we can see now the fundamental flaw in drawing up a 'myth' (especially an 'eternal myth') of leadership. Kermode again writes that 'Myth operates within the diagrams of ritual, which presupposes total and adequate explanations of things as they are and were; it is a sequence of radically unchangeable gestures. Fictions are for finding things out, and they change as the needs of sense-making change. Myths are the agents of stability, fictions the agents of change.'[10] Right through most of the management ideologies of leadership, there is an ongoing strain of 'change-management'; but the problem is that managerialist leadership such as that promoted through the LFHE erects the *myth of the leader* as opposed to the fiction of the leader; and myth presupposes keeping things as they are. There simply is no stable or 'eternal' essence of leadership that can be bottled and sold via the LFHE or any other programme.

From this, we get the third and decisive point of interest. In all of this, the leader becomes a rather isolated, if potentially heroic, figure. This is so even when teamwork is being vaunted: the team consists of those who are the followers; the leader stands apart, 'excelling' as it were – 'exceeding' the structures that they lead – standing then above and beyond the fray. It is not that 'there is no "I" in team; it is rather that "I" am not part of the team that I lead'. This leader is heroic in that isolation, always presented as having to 'deal with' things or people that 'block' or 'stand in the way of' the vision or idea. The clear guiding principle underlying this is that the followers are nothing more than 'human resources' to be manipulated, even to be fooled by rhetorical legerdemain ('motivating' them), into the appropriate behaviour in order to fulfil the 'journey' presented by the leader-figure. The journey, however, is that of the leader alone; the 'troops' are but the resources required to get to the destination, that eternal myth called 'excellence'.

Leaders decide things – in an abstracted form; and followers have to conform. This is not only a recipe for *hubris*; it is also a recipe for an unhelpful establishment of a fundamental division between the leader and their followers. Perhaps needless to say, it also offers a rather sad and desolate image of both the leader and their follower figures. It gives us a model of 'leadership' that we can recognize as all too common in our times: the leader becomes one who *confronts* their followers or community, proposes actions or beliefs that the community rejects and then proceeds in wilful ignorance of that rejection. This is the leader who demonstrates their strength of leadership precisely by doing things that are counter-intuitive, that insult the community or that fly directly in the face of what the community clearly wants. The result is precisely that form of hubris in which the leader makes themselves the centre of the story, distracting attention from the material history that the community is required to confront.

Within the University that is in any way affected – or infected – with these notions of the charismatic, decisive and 'excelling' leader, there is massive damage being done to the intimacy of community internally. This version of things actually pits the leader (in this case, the vice-chancellor) against the followers (the academic community); and an extremely unhelpful divide is established. That division generates a sense of leaders being 'out of touch' with things on the ground (and this is all the more pronounced precisely at those moments when the leader takes a keen interest and believes herself or himself to be firmly 'in touch'). More fundamentally, it damages any claim that the University might make for the ideas of democracy or widening participation in the judgements and decisions that, once made, will take the institution in particular directions.

Of course, it need not be thus. It might be interesting if the vice-chancellor and other senior strategic leaders did indeed try to learn from the English and Drama departments, for example, and the kind of *playing* with fictions that takes place in those departments and disciplines. In such a case, there would be a much more productive interchange between leader and follower, and one in which the leading might come from the follower in some way, however slight or substantial might be that way. In every case, there would be a different relation – one of a shared intimacy of community – between the leaders and the followers. Indeed, the very fact of the discussion and debate would be something that would dissolve the potentially dangerous isolation of the leader, and would allow for a process called 'learning' to take place on all sides, a learning that would also have the benefit of being addressed to historical and material specifics, rather than to the abstractions of 'the vision thing'. Such learning, based in discussion that involves the community and its traditions, is intrinsically more democratic than the hubristic isolation produced by subscription to the myth of the strong heroic and isolated leader.

The prevailing ideology of leadership, however, precludes such a positive set of possibilities. The individual who occupies the position of leader, presiding over institutions that are forced of necessity to proclaim structural excellence, must always logically be seen to excel and thus to embody the values of the institution; and in this, they are seen as one who, in a sense, stands even above their institution. That, after all, is what it means to excel – to exceed circumambient norms – in this way. In a proper University, by contrast with this vacuity of 'excelling', I have stressed that there is an element of what we might rather more prosaically term 'going beyond what we have previously thought': the point there is to seek things undreamt of as yet in our philosophies, and this entails a widening of the scope and ambit of our thought and activity.

This, however, is very different from the excellence discourse. Because it is essentially vacuous and meaningless, this latter gives us a state of affairs in which the individual leader demonstrates their leadership precisely by establishing a distance or a gap between themselves and the very institution that they lead. Excelling, in this, means placing oneself at a remove and working in a sphere of action that is fundamentally different from the sphere in which one's followers are engaged. We usually call it simply being out-of-touch with realities on the ground; and it is out-of-touch with those realities because it has abstracted itself from those realities, preferring allegiance to an abstract sphere of excellence and supposed quality.

If we are indeed to modernize in any serious sense of the word, then we might start the process by trying to catch up with 1704, when Vico asserted – indeed, rather took for granted – that the University could establish a shared intimacy of community action, that it had a public function and that such a function implied a relation to civic authority in a way that was designed to contest authoritarianism.

3

The underlying premise for my argument here is that we are facing something of a crisis of leadership in higher education in Britain, as also in the rest of the advanced economies. That crisis has been to a large extent provoked by what we might call 'the rise of the managerialist class'; and the result of that onward march and triumph of the archetypal members of that class is that instead of leaders, we have managers; instead of followers, we have resources.

A little history can contextualize matters. In the late 1970s and 1980s, Universities – and, of course, as we are always reminded, there were fewer of them then – were centrally funded by government. There was a more complicated support system, of course, in that we had research councils and industrial bodies that helped fund research; but the bulk of funding for most Universities came, as today, through the form of a 'grant-letter' that disbursed public funds. Between about 1919 and 1979, the grant-letter came from the University Grants Committee (UCG), headed, in its latter days (1973–83), by Peter Swinnerton-Dyer, a very eminent Cambridge mathematician. Then, in the midst of his leadership, came 1979 and a general election.

One of the things that developed at this time was a kind of ideological struggle, not between class interests, but rather a struggle for something that, in another context, the philosopher Jürgen Habermas would come to call 'the public sphere'. Essentially, two views of what society is about came to the fore. Interestingly, for those of us interested in language, the struggle was in many ways a struggle about semantics, especially over the word 'individual'. At the time, among the many things, I taught Chaucer. I liked pointing out to my students that, for Chaucer, the word 'individual' meant something different from what it had come to mean in 1979. In fact, its meaning for Chaucer was rather opposite to its meaning in the more recent period. To Chaucer, the word meant something like 'indivisible from': an individual was one who could not be defined separately from their social sphere, their sphere of operations. Now, as we all know, the word in more recent times means precisely the opposite: it suggests one who is totally distinguished from her or his circumambient background. Monty Python got the paradox right in *Life of Brian*, a film that is most definitely a product of its time (1979), but whose relevance remains pertinent today.

In the film, Brian is made into a reluctant leader of sorts: he is followed everywhere. In frustration, he decides to address his followers; and he tells them that they really do not need any heroes or leaders. They repeat his words, like schoolchildren reciting their lesson. 'You don't need a messiah', he shouts, 'you're all individuals'. 'Yes,' they shout back in perfect chorus, 'we're all individuals'. At which point, a little voice pipes up, '*I*'m not.' In the film, it is the very denial of individuality that produces individuality: it is the very denial of leadership that produces the singular individual capable of leading.

In the non-fictional events of that same year, the political battleground is drawn between those who see society as a kind of arithmetical aggregation of discrete persons, each making their own way and caught in what looks a little like a primitive Hobbesian struggle with the unpleasant and graceless business of a life that is based in aggressive competition. On the other side, there are those who believe in the existence – and the necessary preservation of – a public sphere, public good, a public (define it how you will: nation, class, gender, etc.) to which they might be prepared to sacrifice their private interests for the more general good. These are members of the benevolent group, grounded in ideas of cooperation; and they are set against the graceless who subscribe to an ideology of fierce competition and the priority of something vaguely called 'business'.

It is important to note that the idea of business in the ascendant at this moment is indeed vague. No actual or specific businesses are being described; but an ethic of competitiveness and aggressive ruthlessness is being ascribed to the world of business as its presiding normative value-system. It is this kind of position that is satirically critiqued in the figure of Gordon Gekko in the 1987 film *Wall Street*, when he pronounces the fundamental ground of the new business ethics in the phrase 'Greed is good'. The idea of business behind this, however, has to remain abstract; for, in 1979 and the years that follow, it is about to be applied to all aspects of public life, including the University. From this moment on, Universities start to be described by government ministers – and, eventually, by some vice-chancellors – as 'businesses'.

Greed against civics; competition against cooperation: put like this, of course, it is amazing that the first group won out in the ongoing struggle of ideas. It is more than amazing: it is testimony to the power of a certain kind of conservative force and ideology that prefers to think of the social as, at best, parochial. As Mrs Thatcher once put it, 'There is no such thing as society. There are individuals, and their families.' In that mode of thinking, from which we still suffer, there is always going to be damage done to the idea of the intimacy of any community that takes community as something that exists beyond one's front door and, with it, damage to the existence of a University.

Among the losers in this contest, then, were all those who believed in community and, yet more important politically, those who worked in the public sphere. In order to make sure that things stayed this way for as long as possible – that is, in order to drive home their victory – the graceless put in place institutions and laws that would ensure the establishment of new norms. We usually call all this Thatcherism; but that would be to dignify one individual too much, I think. The key point is that, in the image of Thatcher, a select few – identified with the ideology of acquisitive individualism buttressed by aggressive ideas of business-competition – were able to win against all the others; and these became our 'leaders'. That is to say: new forms of social legitimation, or of legitimation of individuals in the public sphere, were established. All relatedness was to be conducted like a business, with calculation of input and output, or of efficiency and gain becoming the key motivations for any and all action.

As Walter Benjamin knew ages ago, such a situation could lead only to war: and, in the 1982 war in the South Atlantic, we established the new paradigmatic model of the leader, a model that has stayed with us and plagued us ever since: the 'war-leader', be it Thatcher in the Falklands/ Malvinas or Blair/Bush in Iraq. These leaders work essentially on the principle of a counter-intuitiveness whose effect is to place them in a world apart, to put them deliberately out-of-touch with the community that they are in place to serve, represent or lead. The hubris we see here as a determining characteristic of leadership is exactly the same, however, as we saw in Miss Jean Brodie. She, we recall, asserts her own authority in the face of everyone else by the whimsical claim that Giotto is the most important Italian painter, for the simple reason that she herself likes him. Thus, she has 'proven' her case. The paradigmatic 'war-leader' typically leads by telling us that 'if only we knew what they knew', then we would agree with them. The key, for present purposes, is that they thereby place themselves in a different sphere of operation from those of us who are followers. The intimacy of community is determinedly broken and replaced with a hierarchical and atomized fracturing of the civil or public sphere.

At the more local level of the University, we begin to see the hubris of individuals who start to style themselves not as vice-chancellors but rather as chief executive officers. These individuals believed, possibly honestly, that they were running a business; and the logic then is that they establish a fundamental principle, for internal governance as for external self-presentation, of competition, aggression, ruthlessness and the bottom financial line. This has massive repercussions. While it is entirely reasonable to make a case for saying that a University should be run in a business-like fashion, that it should have an eye on performance and on its economy, it is a fundamental category mistake to proceed by wilfully forgetting that this is but a *simile*. We can be run *like* a business; but it most certainly does not follow that we *are* a business. One could equally make an entirely reasonable case to say that a University should be run *like* an orchestra; but it would be clearly silly to expect it to found its entire operations on the musical abilities of its staff and to set itself on a par with the Berlin Philharmoniker. Birmingham University is most certainly not the City of Birmingham Symphony Orchestra, even if these diverse organizations could, in principle, be organized and managed in a similar fashion.

At the same time as this is happening in the higher education sector, there is also a further structural change going on. As I indicated in my opening chapter, the UGC mutates into the HEFCE and, explicitly here, a marked change took place: where the UGC had operated as a buffer between the State and the Universities, between government and the academies, HEFCE had the opposite brief. Its task was to grant money to the Universities, but to take with the money whatever message it is that the government of the day wants to promulgate. HEFCE becomes explicitly an agency of or an arm of government. This is the first major explicit politicization of the Universities in the modern era. It calls into question any idea that the University can now exist as an independent and autonomous authority in its own right; and consequently, it calls into question also the University's power of granting and distributing authority to a community more generally.

Now, what follows from this is a domino effect: HEFCE is henceforth an agency of government, answerable directly and solely to the minister for education; vice-chancellors, as recipients of the moneys disbursed by HEFCE, now become agents of HEFCE, and answerable to its chief executive; registrars become agents of vice-chancellors – or, more precisely, they become equally agents of HEFCE, for they now make the claim on the moneys, since they are in charge or structural and administrative organization; deans become agents of the vice-chancellor; heads of departments become agents of the dean; and lecturers become agents of the institution. In short, we no longer have staff or personnel, but rather we have now all become, in one way or another, the merest 'operatives' of an overarching system of authority. We are now, in an appalling and profoundly insulting phrase, 'human resources'. Further, in a fundamental structural shift, the 'leadership' in the University now cannot represent the interests of the academy (including those of staff and students) to the wider public sphere; rather, their task is to represent the interest of government to staff, students and public sphere, and also to ensure that those interests are properly executed.

Further, and perhaps most troubling of all, at the end of this chain of agencies, the student now also becomes an agent of government policy. Their 'task' becomes one where they are expected to use their University education in order to help fulfil a role in forms of employment that are sanctioned and legitimized by the State: their task is to contribute, directly as a result of their study, to the economy in whatever happens to be the approved fashion. This becomes a tacit *requirement*, in fact: they must make 'business', vaguely conceived, more wealthy through the generation of more economic activity. In a fee-paying regime, further and with a cruel irony, they act as this kind of agent of government, *but* they are now also expected to pay, themselves, for the 'privilege' of fulfilling the role, as agent of governmental ideology, thus given to them.

The prevailing ideology in all of this is, of necessity, an ideology of consumerism. What leadership is left is given over to a vague idea of 'market forces'. However, despite the prevailing terminology, market forces are never *free*: they are controlled and regulated, not always accountably and, though perhaps always *legally*, not always *legitimately*. These forces do not exist in order to extend civic freedom or democracy; rather, they exist in order to reduce the content of freedom and justice to matters of consumerist 'choice' and 'value for money'.

Two key shifts thus take place. First, there is the explicit politicization of the academy in which it becomes the agent of government. This has the effect of driving a coach and horses through the Haldane principle, whose effect right through the twentieth century was to keep at arm's length the relation between government and the Universities. With the demise of the Haldane principle in all but name, the University thus loses academic and many other forms of autonomy. Secondly, the registrar-manager now ascends to a key position, at least alongside the vice-chancellor if not yet higher in the hierarchy of internal authority and leadership. This is so because, in the business model, the very question of what might be the academic content of our activity depends upon our 'business plans' as academic departments. If it can be shown that we are, as a specific department, 'in deficit' according to the accounting regime deployed by the University then it follows that we are not justifying our existence; and if we cannot then persuade others to help us out by cross-subsidy within the overall business, we should be closed. I will deal with this more fully in my final chapter, on finance, below; but suffice to note for the moment that the registrar now has a key leadership role *in the academy*, for, in the business model the academy is *but an adjunct* to administration and organization. The administration itself becomes the determining and, importantly, the *controlling* centre of the University's authority.

Within all this, followers have become human resources. As a mere 'human resource', I am placed on a par with the paper clips, with the sole difference that I am classified as 'human' as my distinguishing factor. However, as a resource, I am – like the paper clips – fundamentally interchangeable with others in my category. All that is now required is that I am properly managed, not offered leadership – and certainly not offered a form of leadership that might involve me democratically in government by discussion and dialogue. The kind gloss on the terminology of 'human resources' would be to say that my humanity is recognized for what it is, in a profound ethical care; the reality, however, is that my humanity has to be minimized in terms of efficient management of the system as a whole. Thus, for example, initiative is thoroughly to be encouraged – but only as long as the effect of the initiative shown is something that conforms to and improves the operation of the existing system, helping to sustain whatever vision is proposed by the internal leadership of the academy, now itself necessarily a shadow of government policy. In order to ensure this, the human resource is required to operate simply as an element in an overarching mechanized system, the better to 'deliver' the 'product' or 'offer' that constitutes 'the student experience' and so on.

What has happened to leadership within this, especially in a sector that exists for the production of critical thought? It is surely immediately apparent that we can also see the question looming that was more explicitly in the air in those dark days of the early 1980s: the question of academic freedom, which must include the ability freely to criticize leaders, including those in government or its agencies, and also freely to criticize the ways in which one's own institution – once it is effectively an arm of government – is being run.

4

As virtually anyone within the sector now knows, we operate within a highly bureaucratized system. This, while it may appear to offer some managerial benefits, actually operates in ways that militate against proper leadership. The key to an understanding of this lies in what we can call the demise of argument or debate. One way of leading any large organization, such as a University, is to find rational principles for moving towards the future development and ongoing work of the organization. Habermas would describe this in terms of our being able to have systematic argument, from widely differing points of view. The aim is to provide legitimacy for the operation of the organization, as well as to ensure that all participants share, in equally committed fashion, the work carried out.

The way this works, in a rational fashion, is for arguments to be laid out in public in an effort to secure consensual agreement regarding the laws that might govern us. That is the literal meaning of autonomy, the 'giving ourselves the law' encompassed in the language of the *autos nomos*. The argumentative positions must be articulated without prejudice or bias, and simply as what each participant sees as the better case, based on established facts and desired endpoints. Participants then try to persuade each other, and to do so without any coercion, threat or force other than the force of the argument itself. If the parties can establish a consensus on these grounds then, according to Habermas, the result is the expression of a rational will; and, in the University environment that we are presently discussing, it will offer us the benefit of commitment from all parties and a clear sense of an agreed direction for the organization. As a further corollary, the debates must be kept under review, in case of changing circumstances or the emergence of new and different argumentations.

This is not how things happen. Given the distance between leaders and followers in our institutions, and given that they effectively operate in incommensurable realms of discourse, such dialogue and debate is never among equals. A Brodie-style authority is asserted, but very indirectly. It is rather difficult in many cases to bring about consensual agreement: conversation and persuasion both take time, for they depend upon our reflecting on matters of substance. In terms of the politics of management, the decision, in the face of this difficulty and potential waste of time, is to abandon the very pursuit of rationally agreed plans. Instead, what we have is the much quicker pursuit of agreement regarding much lower-level and seemingly peripheral matters: the establishment of agreement regarding *procedures* or *processes*. As long as such procedures are themselves content-free, there is no need to detain ourselves over matters of substance.

Sometimes the agreement in question here is even agreement about procedures for reaching agreement about plans – the plans themselves hovering ghost-like in the background, but their substantive content never being openly discussed. The logic then is that the leadership can substitute an agreement about a *procedure* for an agreement regarding a *plan*. While it may look *as if* we are debating matters of academic substance, we are in fact *limited* to a mere discussion of the 'best practice' in terms of how we reach decisions in general terms. To agree to move things in accordance with a specific set of procedures becomes *the equivalent* of agreeing to substantive change or stability itself; for, if the procedures by which the plan is agreed are shown to conform to the (agreed) processes for making decisions, no one need ever discuss anything of substance anymore. There is a systematic eradication of legitimate decision-making, and its replacement with purely legal protocols for a decision-making that will now take place elsewhere. This is a useful shorthand description of bureaucracy.

Habermas worried that many societies might operate entirely legally, but without legitimacy: that is, they establish laws, but the laws have not been arrived at through a rational process of examining substantive argument involving participants. Bureaucracy moves a step further. Instead, then, of providing an argued case for something that can have the force of consensually agreed *law*, we have abandoned the principle of having law – and certainly for establishing legitimacy – in this way. Weaker than a law is a 'guideline' or a 'code of practice'; and these are essentially matters or procedural protocol. The very terminology of guidelines and codes is indicative of the fact that, in principle, they offer such latitude that it is difficult for any reasonable individual to contest them: after all, they only offer guidance, and do not constitute an agreed set of fixed and established rules. Given that these are not *laws*, further, they do not even need really to be argued for in the first place: they are 'merely' guidelines or codes. However, once we do have such guidelines or codes, they start to assume the *force* of law, and to operate precisely *as if* they were laws that have been arrived at in rational fashion. The result is that our bureaucratized and mythic leadership may have *power*, but that power now has grounding neither in *legality* nor, certainly, in anything approaching what Habermas would regard as *legitimacy*.

Leadership and its corollary, governance, are thus established essentially on the basis of something no more substantial than occasional anecdote or 'news management', as it is sometimes called. Slavoj Žižek has written about how this operates, in his book, *The Puppet and the Dwarf*. There, he discussed the more extreme political forms that this kind of leadership has taken in world history; and, alarmingly, he finds the model in the manner of governance operated by Stalin. He points out that Stalinism operated as a 'strictly centralized system of command'; but the problem for many of the cadres was that, frequently, no clear order would be given regarding what was being actually 'commanded'. Instead, Stalin provided only vague hints and general guidelines or, in Žižek's terms, nothing more substantial than a mere 'sign' indicating a general tendency or direction of travel. The enthusiastic cadres, eager to curry favour with the controlling centre, would typically over-respond or 'excel' themselves in their response, as if the sign were in fact an order. Thus, for example, there might be the placing of an anonymous derogatory comment regarding someone or some event in *Pravda*, or some ostensibly very minor matter of culture would be referred to in praiseworthy terms; and it was up to the cadres to 'interpret', to find the meaning behind the signal. Stalin, thereby, is of course absolved of specific responsibility: he did not give the order as an order at all. There is, in fact, no need now to issue orders: the cadres intuit the general trajectory, and maintain their own authority and legitimacy by fulfilling orders that have not actually been given.

This then becomes a whole and functioning system of leadership. Citing Sheila Fitzpatrick's *Everyday Stalinism*, Žižek goes on to indicate that 'important policy changes were often "signalled" rather than communicated in the form of a clear and detailed directive'.[11] In this, the leader can get things done, can remain 'above' the fray ('excelling') and can also appear even to be critical of the actions carried out by the cadres, such criticism furthering the sense of enigma and charisma – but also the unpredictability necessary to ensure enthusiastic compliance. This leader shows, in the words of Žižek, a basic 'mercy' against the power of the law itself, a mercy that I have referred to as 'whimsy' above. He then goes on: 'Is it not a fact that showing mercy is the only way for a Master to demonstrate his supralegal authority? If a Master were merely to guarantee the full application of the law, of legal regulations, he would be deprived of his authority, and turn into a mere figure of knowledge, the agent of the discourse of the university.'[12]

Now, it would clearly be a mad exaggeration to suggest that vice-chancellors are Stalinist. However, it is not at all a wild suggestion to indicate that the methods of leadership have certain structural similarities (or, in Fitzpatrick's extremely troubling terms, that a certain Stalinist practice has become 'everyday'). Specifically, they both engender and indeed are grounded in bureaucratic authoritarianism rather than legitimate authority. Firstly, there is the 'excellence' in which the leader-figure hubristically exceeds the bounds of the institution, establishing a fundamental chasm or division between the worlds inhabited by leaders and followers. Secondly, there is the assumption of a power, but without the corresponding responsibility (for responsibility belongs to the realm of the enthusiastic cadres, or 'middle managers'). Thirdly, there is the ostensible 'enabling' of the cadres, whose 'job' is to so internalize the signs that they can, in turn, replicate the system of authority at work and, indeed, even excel in it by going further than is required. With such an internalization, the cadres of middle managers can then themselves assert an authority over institutions in which they work to be 'whiter-than-white' in terms of the way that they fulfil or interpret the 'signs' given from the controlling centre. In passing, of course, it should be noted that to be whiter-than-white is to be lying: there *is* no colour whiter than white. The phrase is lifted from the discourse of consumerism and specifically from advertising related to cleansing: it was a certain washing powder that would allegedly get clothes whiter-than-white. Finally, while all of these procedures may be legal (even if they involve lying), they lack legitimacy.

More commonly, we have that system whereby leadership now implies an identification of the local leader (in our case, a vice-chancellor, say) with a more 'central' leader (a government official, for example). The resulting version of leadership looks rather peculiar. A useful example to highlight what is at stake here comes in an address to the Association of University Administrators from Steve Smith, the President of Universities UK in April 2009, when the then-Labour administration was indicating that it was inclined to require (note the 'signalling' going on here) that all academics demonstrate fully the 'impact', beyond the walls of the academy, of the research that they undertake. The President's speech (going further than is actually asked for by government) had him assuming the actual position of a government minister and asking specifically whether the arts and humanities community had done enough to demonstrate that they should be funded according to these new impact-driven criteria: 'if you were sitting in the Treasury, you would ask: do we need 159 institutions doing humanities and social science research?' he said. The question is not one that is meant to elicit dialogue and debate.

More recently, in an attempt to defend the supposed 'independence' of the 2010 Browne Review Committee that looked into funding the University system on the UK, Julia King, one of the two vice-chancellors on the Committee, explained that, while there had been no direct interference by government, nonetheless the Review would have been doomed had the Committee not taken into account and internalized in their deliberations the fact that they expected government to be making massive cuts in the teaching budget for the University sector. The cadres were doing what they were told, without the necessity of anyone telling them to do it.[13] The structure here is akin to that described by Žižek in the political sphere; and, crucially, those who should be 'leading' their organizations now 'lead' by internalizing a logic, infiltrated from elsewhere, that has been neither debated, nor discussed, nor even established.

In the end, we have what is properly called a system of the delegation of guilt and blame. This is a further characteristic of bureaucracy. It is clearly anathema to rational leadership; and, equally clearly, it deserves no followership.

5

To be a leader, we need to have at least one follower. Far from it being the case that leaders and followers are semantic opposites, they are in fact semantically tied to each other, almost bound to each other like apprentice and master. In a peculiar – and deconstructive sense – a leader paradoxically depends upon followers to follow them, else they lose their position as leader. In other words, the followers are in an odd sense logically prior to the leader; and the leader is dependent upon the followers. You might say that the leader follows the followers in this respect.

What explains this deconstructive relation? Ethics – an ethics of leadership – I believe offers us at least one viable answer. Ethics require two things: firstly, a realization that, in any human relation, there is a kind of demand that comes from the fact that the person with whom I am in relation is fundamental to my own continued existence and well-being; and, secondly, a realization that, just as I face this other directly, so we are both part of a wider network of social connectedness and relation. Leadership, in these circumstances, is that which can be agreed as a condition of our continued and sustained well-being. In short, leadership is also the search for justice and for the increase in human freedom; and it too is governed by the demands of the true, the good and the beautiful. Perhaps a yet more pressing observation deriving from this is that, if our leadership is to be in any real sense 'effective', it has to embody the view that the institution as a whole has an ethical relation to the wider society of which it is an integral part. The intimacy of community required for good leadership *within* an institution is but a micro-level of the intimacy of community that drives the good or just or free society as a whole. This raises the obvious question regarding the role of the University in terms of social, political and cultural leadership within a wider community.

There are a great number of theories of leadership now available to us in the management discourses and business worlds. Indeed, we can trace a more or less straightforward history of the evolution of thought about leadership and the varied modes of its 'effectiveness'. It will be useful here, as we explore the question of the leadership of the University in society, if we have a brief summary of the various positions. In giving this summary, I am indebted to the work of the Centre for Leadership Studies in Exeter University, and specifically to their *A Review of Leadership Theory and Competency Frameworks*, carried out by Richard Bolden *et al.* [14]

Broadly, the history of leadership theory follows a trajectory that goes from the 'great man' or iconic and charismatic leader theories through to what is now called 'transformational theories' of leadership, in which the management of change, including changing the potential of staff, has become more central. Bolden *et al.* point out that, although there are a number of differences along the way in the various theories that have been advanced, nonetheless they nearly all share the certain common characteristic that they all think of the leader in individualistic terms.

One of the most helpful summations of the practices of leadership is that advanced in the so-called 'Leadership Grid' drawn up by Robert Blake and Jane Moulton. The grid plots the coordinates, along two axes, of 'consideration for people' (the y-axis) and 'concern for production' (the x-axis); and the gradations along each axis go from 0 to 9. The resulting 'best practice' model is that which gives coordinates of (9,9), combining a score of 9 for both 'production' and 'people' (highest concern for production allied with highest concern for people). In such a case we have 'team management' where the leader has brought about a commitment to a shared general goal, based on trust and mutual respect. Interestingly, the grid also proposes a model that is called 'authority-compliance' (coordinates of (1,9)), in which the concern for production is rated at 9 (the highest) while consideration of people rates at 1 (the lowest); and the chief characteristic of this mode is that management prioritizes efficiency and tends to regard human elements as potential interferences or obstructions to that efficiency. This, I shall note simply in passing, is what appears to be increasingly prevalent as a daily experience of the norm for ideas of leadership in the University and other public-sector organizations.

We come closer to establishing a healthy dialectic between leader and follower when we reach the theories of Robert Tannenbaum and Warren H. Schmidt, who seek to consider leadership in terms of a potentially evolving and changing balance between 'boss-centred' and 'subordinate-centred' involvement in the leadership decision-making processes. Here, we see the introduction of the idea that bosses can learn from subordinates. This is carried a little further in John Adair's 'action-centred' leadership. In this, Adair proposes that there are three elements that need to be kept in mind: the task, the team and the individual. These operate in intersecting fashion, rather as in a Venn diagram, where there are varying sizes of 'sets' (the task might dominate in some situations, the individual in others, for example) and where there are also therefore varying quantities of intersection among the potentially diverse interests. The action-leader is the person who can participate in any and all of these circles of interest; but, crucially, they must also maintain a distance, flying as if in a helicopter above the entire activity, so as to be able to take consistently the global overview.

Clearly, this last comes quite close to my own depiction of the leadership dilemma, in which the leader is essentially structurally *required* to distance themselves from activity on the ground. While it is indeed necessary for a leader to take an overview of a global whole, it is also equally important, in my view, that others can fly in the helicopter, as it were.

Bolden *et al.* conclude their survey with an attention to Robert Greenleaf's work from the 1970s onwards on what he calls 'servant-leadership'. This comes closest to the kind of idea that I am advancing here. In servant-leadership, we acknowledge that there are two competing priorities in play for those who become a leader. The servant-leader is the person who starts from the desire to serve; and, in serving, they come also and in turn to desire to lead. Key to this, though, is that the servant-leader is leading in a fashion that is informed by the demand for service to others, to those with whom they exist in the relation that I have been calling the intimacy of community. Against this is the individual who is leader first ('perhaps because of the need to assuage an unusual power drive or to acquire material possessions', as Greenleaf puts it).

The two positions here are polarized extremes, of course; and most leaders sit somewhere along the spectrum and not at either end. The difference, however, is fundamental. In Greenleaf's words, it manifests itself:

> in the care taken by the servant-first to make sure that other people's highest priority needs are being served. The best test, and difficult to administer, is: do those served grow as persons; do they, while being served, become healthier, wiser, freer, more autonomous, more likely themselves to become servants? And, what is the effect on the least privileged in society; will they benefit, or, at least, will they not be further deprived?[15]

After this brief summary of the available theoretical models for leadership, it is clear that the ideas of leadership that govern Universities in our time are simply out-of-date: we have not 'modernized' at all. The question here, though, is how we might look at servant-leadership in terms of the relation of the University as leader to the wider society of which it is an integral part.

There is a long history of anti-intellectualism in the Anglo-world; and that now manifests itself most evidently in the mistrust of the University that has been established as an ideological norm in our conservative cultures. The real question for the sector is how we might rehabilitate the University as an institution worthy of respect, treated as an institution of at least equal importance alongside the vague 'business' that our governments demand that it serve and thus able to participate in a culture of conversation that enables government-through-debate. The idea that the University is there primarily to function as a menial service-provider for this vague world of business is extremely short-sighted; and, worse, it limits the possibilities that the University might have to offer to the wider social sphere. It reduces the idea of 'service' to an extraordinarily narrow range of activities and options; and that reduction not only damages the University, but also damages the whole of the social and public sphere of which it is an integral part.

While we are now witnessing a slightly more serious understanding of the idea of the leader-as-follower, it nonetheless remains the case that a proper dialectic between the two roles has not yet been established. Instead, the dominant understanding of the leader is one based upon the 'pyramid of power' or, more generally, upon the fundamental error of establishing a hierarchy of power within the public sphere or shared citizenship. Our 'intimacy of community' is not based upon mutual respect and, at this historical moment, the University finds itself endlessly trying to justify its existence, rather than assuming a role as occasional leader and constant servant-leader of a wider public sphere. The logic of the position that I am advancing here, however, is that the leader is indebted to the follower for any power that they have; in brief, the power lies neither with leader nor follower but with their *relatedness*, their shaping of an intimacy of community in the pursuit of justice and enhanced freedom. This kind of leader establishes the kind of authority validated by Arendt, an authority that gains obedience without any loss of freedom; but I go further, to argue that leadership is leadership *if and only if* it enhances freedom and extends it. It is not enough simply to protect existing freedom; the point of leading is to offer freedom more widely.

What might this mean in the University? It means, above all, finding out what the constituency wants to do. It means *encouraging dissent* rather than conformity; and this dissent becomes the language that shapes possible futures and keeps them open. It means challenging all authorities, especially those that are illegitimate or that assume the position of a Miss Jean Brodie. At the present time, we urgently need the University to assume this kind of servant-leadership if it is to establish its legitimacy – the legitimacy of the life of the mind and even of thinking itself – as an important element in the public sphere. That is, we need the authority of the institution as a bulwark against the forms of authoritarianism that threaten not just the University but the whole of our public life, the whole of our social, cultural and political communities.

5

Assessment

Controlling Conformity

Assessment is, in many ways and for many people, the single most essential thing that a University is about. This assessment, properly considered, is not simply a matter of considering how we look at or scrutinize the performance of students in specific tasks during their student careers. Indeed, it can equally well be related to the much more fundamental issues of access and of widening participation. Many of these issues are themselves determined by assessments that are made outside of and prior to any student's University life. Further still, assessment and its surrounding practices and issues apply not only to students but also to faculty, who are themselves now routinely assessed, and who have always been assessed especially when seeking their academic post in the first place. Thus, from the reading of UCAS or other application forms from prospective students, via the scrutinizing of CVs and of prospective colleagues at job interview, on to the monitoring processes that govern the progress of both student and staff, to the summations of a career in some academic obituaries (and sometimes equally in obituaries of those directly and indirectly affected by University life), assessment looks to be a basic and pretty thoroughgoing aspect of what we do. In some ways, assessment more or less permeates University life and activity in our times.

In this chapter, I want to consider the very foundation of the idea of assessment itself, and its widespread ramifications and effects on the daily life of the University. The reason that we should carry out such an investigation into the now large body of philosophies of assessment is straightforwardly given: my case will be that we have made a rather fundamental shift, especially in the last third of the twentieth century, and one that has had effects beyond those foreseen when we made the changes. The shift in question is one that makes a move away from a system that we described by the term of 'examination' towards what we now know as the science of 'assessment'. That this is a science is, at least ostensibly, entirely indubitable: we have Centres for Research into and for Assessment up and down the land, and we have graduate and other programmes of study in it. We even have pro-vice-chancellors whose brief places assessment at the core of their day-to-day governance activity. Assessment itself can now be assessed and accredited, and can find itself both governed and governing, in various ways. This chapter will in turn therefore be a kind of assessment of assessment, so to speak; or, to put it more neutrally, it will be a scrutiny of the consequences of our move towards assessment as a routine aspect of all practices within (and occasionally beyond) a University.

The shift from examination to assessment is far from being simply a neutral changing of semantic terminology; and the growth of the 'science' of assessment is likewise far from being a simple neutral encoding of activities after the fact. That is to say, once we have agreed that it is fundamentally a science of sorts, then it follows that the science of assessment does not rely on a *description* of practice, but prefers to strive to codify an ideal and agreed *prescription* for 'best practice', and to garner support for assessment methods that have a scientific and verifiable grounding or a reasoned or 'scientific' foundational basis. This becomes a whole philosophy of assessment; and it is this – as well as the political consequences of the philosophy – that I want to look at closely in the context of the University that I have been trying to describe in these pages.

It would be an oversimplification, and indeed a misrepresentation, of the case that I am about to advance here to suggest that I want to advocate a return to 'examination' systems. It is unquestionably true that the shift to assessment is, in many ways, a profoundly positive and progressive thing. However, I will argue that this change from examination to assessment, though inspired for the most part certainly by the utmost of good intentions, has turned out to be regressive in some of its fundamental aspects, and also that it has been consistent with the very authoritarian ideology that, as we have now seen, already dogs the questions around our leadership at every level, both within and beyond the University as an institution. That implicitly individualistic authoritarian ideology afflicts the society as a whole, of course. More pertinently for our present concerns, it not only impacts negatively upon the University as an institution, threatening its very credibility as a source of judgement and legitimate practices, but it also damages, perhaps beyond repair, the possibility of our students ever gaining access to a justice and freedom that is constituted through the free play of a critical knowledge that might be founded in ideas of how we 'judge' most justly. Adopted in the interests of a hoped for 'democratization' of the examination business, assessment – in its current practices and governing philosophies – nonetheless impairs our abilities to found a democratic community of shared interest.

In what follows here, I will offer an analysis of the philosophy of assessment in its current most widespread forms and in the light of its emergent ideology. In doing this, I will argue that the predominant form of thinking about assessment contrives to evacuate our Universities of the activities (most specifically, activities of the exercising of judgement) associated with *critical knowledge*, replacing that instead with a set of practices and beliefs that seek to prioritize the efficient and controlled *management of information*. This is consistent with the tendency that we have seen – and that I have already analysed to an extent in preceding chapters – towards the commodification of education and the no-longer-creeping-but-rather-galloping marketization of the University and its core work. I will then turn from the analysis of some shortcomings to a suggestion for how we might better proceed.

1

It used to be the case that the most important thing that a University teacher did was to examine. University life consisted, broadly, of three to four years in which the student engaged with her or his teachers, with work in the laboratories, with the resources of the library, and with other students, peers and colleagues in both formal and informal activities whose summative force is best caught in the term *Bildung* – a kind of formation of the self that is grounded in the possibilities of edification that are themselves guaranteed through our social and mutual interactions with each other. Along the way, the student would undertake a good deal of work, sometimes on a continuous weekly basis (such as writing essays, conducting laboratory experiments and so on). These would be graded and would thus give the student a guide to their standing and progress; but the grades themselves would not, in this first instance, be determining of final results or degrees.

Then, at the end of this period of study and intellectual growth, the teacher took it upon themselves to ask the student to show their knowledge of a discipline in some detail and at the levels of intellectual sophistication that would be required in order to gain the candidate their degree. What was being examined here is a combination of various things: competence in the field, such that the student can demonstrate a familiarity with the basic materials constitutive of the field or discipline of study; an ability in comprehending how the discipline 'works', in terms of its legitimized protocols or normative and agreed practices; cleverness, in showing how they can manipulate materials and offer inventiveness and new discovery; and a basic sense that the relevant work has been covered in some breadth and depth, perhaps further embellished with some extra-curricular aspects of an education in more general terms: *Bildung*. In this case, should the final results be unclear in any way, the work that had been done on continuous weekly assignments, and graded, across the years could be looked at; and, at this stage, the coursework (as we would now call it) would play a part in helping determine a degree result.

This all sounds rather vague. However, regardless of how vague it sounds, it 'worked' for a long period of time and was widely accepted practice. It was even accepted when the examiner realized that, in many cases, what was at work here was a mode of judgement that might have been based upon some aesthetic categories (of 'the beauty of the well-formed argument', for example). That is to say, the element of alleged 'subjectivity' in the governing principles of 'examination' was not widely regarded as especially troubling; after all, it was thought, the examiner was examining precisely because they were already rather expert in the field and knew its protocols and expectations extremely well, indeed so well that they would also be able to recognize the value of a novel thought that stepped outside of the usual protocols.

This means that, with regard to this procedural mode and under-standing, the examiner, as the personified embodiment of their discipline and institution, had an authority and was expected to exercise that authority in their judgement. There was an expectation that objectivity would also be maintained, of course. It would be unacceptable for an examiner, as a Marxist (let's say), to downgrade an English Literature essay on the grounds that it did not take a sufficiently 'revolutionary' perspective on the poetry with which it dealt. To this extent at least, the professionalism of examining would be maintained and I, as an authoritative examiner, would exercise personal judgement, based on my experience and authority in the field, while also eschewing personal bias. I would judge the work against the protocols and practices *of the discipline*, and not against my own personal ideas.

Further, a system of 'blind' and anonymous double-marking, where two examiners grade the same work independently of each other, to be complemented in turn by accreditation through a further examiner who would themselves be external to the institution (drawn from another University), would also ensure the ironing out and evisceration of bias and prejudice. The external examiner would not only help adjudicate, but would also be in a position to compare performance between this University and the institution in which they routinely examine as one of the internal examiners, thus striving to ensure a modicum of comparability in degree validations among different Universities nationwide. In short, it was a serious business, and colleagues were enjoined to work collaboratively in order to make it work.

But when one says that all of this 'worked', we also have to ask some corollary questions. Above all, what exactly is the system that is working here, with its wheels oiled by this complex examining process? What, in short, is the fundamental thing that is 'working'? What is it that this mode brings about, what is it that it sustains, and how might it advance in any serious way the purposes of the University? There have been a number of complaints about the system of examining as I describe it above, of course. Three things in particular stand out: a) that it reproduces clones of the examiners; b) that it at least potentially lacks objectivity and formal verification procedures; and c) that its processes are obscure, partly because the judgements made are essentially 'occasional', demanded by the ad hoc nature of treating every examination activity or submission on its own terms, on its own occasion and as it arises.

Let us consider these objections in turn. First, we can look at the claim that examination is concerned above all to reproduce the already existing body of knowledge such that the student essentially becomes a repetition or reflection of the teacher. Writ large, the argument suggests that the system is designed to produce the next generation of lecturers and examiners. Writ yet more large, the argument is that this system is about the essential preservation of existing privilege by a procedure that is designed to ensure its onward self-reproduction. The allegation here is that the student 'secretly' knows that the teacher wants an examination submission in which the student essentially *confirms* the teacher's own thoughts. Were this to be true, the consequences would clearly be serious. In common parlance, of course, this was referred to as 'spoon-feeding' the student, who would 'regurgitate' the food offered. Sickening, if so; and, perhaps more importantly, such a system will necessarily downgrade the work of any and every individual who is not destined to become the next generation of academics. The system thus looks self-perpetuating and self-validating, not to mention troubling in terms of its intrinsic politics, designed to sustain privilege.

More fundamentally, what is at stake is a system whereby teachers 'teach to the test' in order to get predetermined and desired results. The roots of this, in Britain at least, lie in the mid-nineteenth century. In 1862, Robert Lowe, then Vice-President of the Education Board in Lord Palmerston's administration, promoted what was called the 'Revised Code' governing the costs of education. Fundamentally, the Code – a product of the Newcastle Commission's review on the State's commitment to the principles of providing a mass education – advanced the idea that schools should be 'paid by results': if children attended well, the school would receive some funding; and if the pupils also passed some tests in reading, writing and arithmetic, then the school would see its funding very much enhanced.

We should note something about this: whenever we see this system of governance whereby State interest in and payment for education are dependent upon performance or results (or, as in more recent times, the perpetuation of league tables and their respective standings), we should recall that its foundational roots are to be found not in any modern demand for improvement in education, but rather in a cost-cutting exercise from 1862. Further, we should also always remember that neither Lowe nor Palmerston, the earliest architects of a system of 'payment by results', were great supporters of democracy or the general democratization of society that we might now think of as being related to a widespread and generally free education system. If a University education has anything to do with the freedom and justice that we associate with increased democratization, then it would follow that 'payment by results' in any form or in any sphere of University activity would not be our preferred mode of governance or finance.

More immediately pertinent for the present argument, it would be inevitable, as Matthew Arnold and others pointed out, that in such a system teachers would, quite eminently reasonably, organize the work that they do with students entirely around the predicted demands of the test itself. This is not only reasonable in the face of an ideology of 'payment by results'; it is also almost a *requirement* of teaching in such a situation. Examination here is something for which the student or pupil is to be 'drilled', as a series of repeated exercises to be gone through. The effect – though not necessarily the purpose – of such a state of affairs is indeed to produce a certain degree of educational conformity.

At one level, a certain degree of conformity in education should be regarded as non-controversial: we should probably strive to ensure that all conform to the belief that in arithmetic two plus two equals four, for instance. However, demands for conformity are not always as innocent. Consider the question of childhood handwriting. Here, an expectation of conformity is slightly more troubling in education, for in this the motor activity of the child's body becomes involved, when there is an expectation or even a demand for a certain orthography. For some individuals, the matter of neatness of handwriting is a physical matter of such motor control. As we now also know, alongside the possibility of dyspraxia, certain cognitive activities can obstruct the easy practice of reading (dyslexia) or of computation (dyscalculia). By and large, however, the conformity in question here is untroubling, at least relatively. It is indeed good if we generally conform to the view that twice two is four, if only because it will allow us to compute degrees of economic equality and inequality in the wider society of which the University and its students are potentially leading participants.

In the more advanced setting of the University in recent times, the question of a potentially unwelcome conformity was not driven in the first instance by financial consequences; rather, it was allegedly driven by matters pertaining to class interest. The danger seen was that an education at advanced level, especially in the arts and humanities, was deemed to be something that reinforced class prejudices by cloning the faculty. The student 'passed' to the extent that they had successfully internalized the values of the teacher; and that teacher, themselves the product of earlier conformist thinking, was typically middle-class. Examination was the means of legitimizing middle-class values as normative. Examination, in these terms, was clearly seen to be potentially damagingly 'political' or at least to be a practice shaped and given norms by a tacit political ideology; and so the move to call its protocols and practices into question derives from a sense of required respect for other class positions, for multiple points of view and for an awareness of diversity among the student body. The period when this begins, unsurprisingly, dates from the expansion of the University sector, the beginnings of a substantial increase in the student population, from diverse backgrounds, and the settling in of the post-Robbins era institutions.

The process of University expansion in the UK that we usually trace back to Robbins in 1963 had in fact already begun prior to the commission of the Robbins Report, and was really partly initiated by the new settlement at the end of the Second World War. Indeed, a number of the Universities usually thought of as 'post-Robbins' initiatives had already opened (Keele, for instance opened in 1949, as the University College of North Staffordshire, before becoming renamed as the University of Keele in 1962; Sussex opened in 1961; East Anglia in 1963; Essex had been planned for opening in 1961 and so on). However, a yet more significant thing brought about by Robbins was the granting of degree-awarding powers to a number of Colleges of Advanced Technology. The constituency for these new institutions, which then started to flourish and grow at a rapid pace in the later 1960s and through the 1970s, was much more diverse than had previously been the case in the more homogenized University sector. Further, we already had, at this time, relatively large numbers of sizeable 'civic' institutions as well. The class composition of the student body, then, is becoming increasingly mixed.

In an earlier age, when University education was more solidly a preserve of the upper-middle class and aristocracy, it was obviously not considered to be a matter of troubling concern that those attending would have their existing class positions and prejudices confirmed through examination. That was, in fact, largely the point. Examination was the process by which they were validated, their identity legitimized, precisely as members of a class or at least of a social elite. Now, however, a constituency drawn from a much more diverse background caught the spirit of the times, and began to question – to judge adversely – the centrality and normative standing and authority of Establishment values. In the University, these Establishment values were thought to be encoded in the system of examination. If examination was the means whereby the Establishment would sustain itself by demanding conformity to its norms and values, then 'to pass' was to internalize and therefore unquestioningly to endorse those values. In an expanded system, with greater diversity and a burgeoning sense of democratization, this quite rightly comes under extreme pressure and speculatively critical scrutiny.

The second ground for concern was that the system lacked objectivity. In some ways, this follows directly as a consequence of the first concern discussed here. If it is the case that examination produces conformity, it follows that the values inscribed within the examination system are not themselves subject to the kinds of scrutiny that might permit substantive change. The examination is a kind of absolute authority here, not subject to criticism or questioning, not open to critical assessment of its own procedures. The kind of 'new thinking' that might be available from the new diverse student body would not be allowed to disturb the secure truths already established by those in authority – the middle-class teachers, legitimized by their position not as teachers but as representatives of an Establishment, and enforcers of its values. It is then a short step to suggesting that the already established values are not only old-fashioned but also that they are specific to a particular class and thus essentially subjective, endorsed by a necessarily partial (and thus blinded or at least myopic) point of view. This is what we have already seen in the figure of the Jean Brodie of my previous chapter.

The fear here is that teaching and examining are done according to the silent rules that govern what Pierre Bourdieu once called the 'aristocracy of culture'. There is a parallel between the mercantile world and the world of culture. Both rest on kinds of capital; and, in both, those who control the capital have a certain position of authority and power. In the academy and, indeed, in all areas of the public sphere dominated by questions of intellectual capital, the members of the aristocracy of culture, Bourdieu argued, have their positions of power and authority not because of anything they actually *do*, but rather simply by dint of who they *are*. They are *essentially* always right: the essence of who they are is identified with what are proposed as eternal values, and these values in turn are what constitute the very identity – the *being*, not the *doing* or actions – of the aristocracy.

Thus, it would follow, in this account, that the hypothetical 'aristocrat-teacher' of the set-up has no need to justify their judgements in examining: the judgements are intrinsically correct because of who is making them. The judgement is a manifestation of the intrinsic rightness of the teacher themselves as an individual. It simply endorses again their identity, takes no significant account of anything else, and certainly takes no account at all of the possibility of historical change. It is only the vulgar – the examinee, from this newly diverse range of backgrounds – who have to define themselves by their actions. The fact of having to 'prove' themselves not by what they are but by what they do in and by examination is *ipso facto* proof of their intrinsic vulgarity, and thus a manifestation of the fact that they are excluded from the aristocracy, and rightly 'judged' by that self-sustaining aristocracy.

That is, the vulgar are thus excluded unless and until they 'prove' themselves by passing the exam, which means confirming the subjective identity of the teacher. The structure necessarily endorses a hierarchical view, but one based upon subjective being and not upon performance or activity or the action of the examinee. 'Vulgar' here, deriving from the Latin *vulgus*, meaning 'of the common people', is a term that, for political reasons, is to be rehabilitated in a move against the acceptance of the class structures that tacitly shape examination ideology.

Thirdly, all of this is, unsurprisingly, obscured from immediate view by the 'vagueness', as I already described it, of the system as a whole. The examinee does not know what is required of them, for there can be no published criteria for the examination process. What is examined is not what one does, but rather how 'what one does' reveals 'who one is'. Thus, the examinee has to second guess what is going on; and there can be no published criteria, for the simple fact that the criterion for passing does not depend upon action but upon being, upon identification and consolidation of a pre-existing identity, the identity of members of the Establishment or 'aristocracy of culture'. In some ways, the change that was required here is the most far-reaching. In an ideology of 'openness' that emerges essentially from the ideas of self-revelation (either deriving from the 'letting it all hang out' themes in the hippie parlance of the period, or – more sinister – from a post–Cold War anxiety about espionage and subterfuge), there grows a demand for something called 'transparency'. Transparency will ensure that nothing untoward is going on, that there is no class bias or prejudice of any personal kind, that every judgement will be validated and justifiable; and, above all, that judgements can be measured and legitimized by reference to criteria for examination that are fully out in the open, known by and available to all participants in the process.

The inevitable demand for change from all of this negative examination ideology goes hand in hand with the growth and distribution of University education, with a watering-down of class prejudices and Establishment certainties, and with an ostensibly democratic demand for an opening of the doors of opportunity to all. In many ways, this last aspect of the change is the most telling: it relates to issues of access. The 'examination', as opposed to a system of 'assessment', essentially was considered as a kind of bar to further progress: intrinsic to its system, it requires failure in order to allow a number to proceed further, 'qualified' now to various 'degrees' by their examination. The exclusivity of the process was seen to be consistent with the closing of doors, the closing of opportunity; and the very movement – a politically inspired movement – of opening the doors and opening new Universities required a different and even opposite system. Instead of measuring qualification by failure, the idea now was to assess and to measure the extent of what participants could do, rather than to discover their limitations and what they could not do, or to judge who they are. Assessment is the first ideological step towards what is now termed 'competency criteria', which is the latest manifestation of what has become, essentially, a disregard for 'qualification' and the authorities that are invested in such qualifications.

2

In the contemporary world, we do still live under the very same 1862 ideology of Palmerston's administration where we organize education in terms of 'payment by results'; but we refer to it now as 'competitiveness', and signal its force through the existence and encouragement of 'league tables' at regional, national and global levels, and through competitive bidding for limited funding for all of our educational activities. Bids for such funding, of course, have themselves to be assessed; and we also now have a large armature of 'Peer Review Colleges' and the like, designed to regulate the competition. It might be noted, in passing, that peer-review, in these situations, is a system that requires the academic community to enforce cuts upon themselves: it is now our peers who judge us as lacking either in our research bids or in our research assessments. This is a further example of what I have called a delegating of the blame for what is going on: if we now fail to find adequate funding, it is because of our peers and their judgements about us; and governments that actually impose the cuts that require this remove themselves from responsibility. The single most important thing to note here is that, in order to secure funding – sometimes for even basic work – we are required to participate in the competition; but the rules governing that participation require that it is we ourselves who inflict the financial cuts. That is to say, we are required to internalize the ideology, like the good cadres that we saw at work in my chapter on leadership.

This generalized competitiveness is now so intense, and so finely granulated, as to require that not only do we have league tables, but we even have league tables *of* league tables. (Is the Shanghai Jiao Tong index 'better' than the *Times Higher Education* world-rankings? Or vice versa?) In this, it is important that we ensure a certain 'profile' from our institutional 'results': the more high-quality degrees we award in our individual institutions, the greater the prestige of the institution – and the obvious financial consequences follow on from this. As in 1862, it becomes almost incumbent on us to have an eye on the future safety of our institutions; and that will now require a careful attention to matters of degree results, and to ensuring that we have sufficient numbers at a high degree of excellence, at the end of our programmes.

We are moving towards the establishment of a normative acceptance of 'assessment' as a replacement for examination. Assessment is also how we are enjoined to judge institutions as well; and thus, as a practice, it permeates our system as a whole. This will necessarily give a positive view of the institution, since what it measures is the positive aspect of achievement, rather than the more negatively inflected measure of failure to qualify. The change involved is more than a simple change of nomenclature: it is also a change of ideology.

An examination, technically defined, is the 'testing of the proficiency or knowledge of students or other candidates for a qualification'. In other words, it operates primarily as a kind of gate or bar, barring some people from being 'qualified' to do something, while allowing others to practise. It is concerned with *qualification* and thus with *quality*. To assess is (again, technically) rather vaguer: it is 'to estimate the size or quality of something or someone'; and estimation, its central defining term, requires *quantification* (or measurement). The intended consequence of the change from examination to assessment is one that is determined by the desire to let more people 'cross the bar', as it were; and it will do so by prioritizing questions of measurement.

The idea – entirely admirable in principle at least – is to widen opportunity for progression such that more people can go further with their education without being excluded through a failure to qualify. In passing, however, we should note that we lose the determinations of quality and of the attendant legitimizations provided by 'qualification'; and we now replace the solidity and assurance that this gives with the rather more vague idea of 'progression'. In principle, progression implies an ever-onward and positive movement; but it also indicates that the qualification (or endpoint, point of 'arrival') is less important than the 'journey' that the student now makes. Further, the University career becomes but a stage in another, longer 'journey', the ideology of which we have already seen in the chapter on experience.

I have already indicated that the shift comes about because of the quite proper demands for the massification of the higher education sector; but, despite the primacy of that demand, the change here has little to do with increased democratization. There are a number of reasons for the growth of higher education worldwide at the end of the twentieth century; and all such reasons for this growth are intrinsically political, but with a rather small 'p'. That is, the growth is not governed by any serious (and probably consensually agreeable) demand for a better educated citizenry, but rather for more local reasons pertaining to political preferment in elections and the like. It may be the case that, as in the 1980s and early 1990s, especially in the UK but also in other advanced economies, there was a strong political need to reduce the numbers figuring on public registers of youth unemployed; it may be the case that 'modernization' of a general economy is tied, for political reasons and especially in those cultures whose industrial base is eroded or non-existent, to a supposed 'knowledge-economy'; or it may simply be that the University is now seen as itself an 'industry' of sorts, requiring 'growth' to justify itself in political cultures that believe economic growth to be more important than the sustainability of an ecology. In all these and similar cases, the driver for change, therefore, is not primarily pedagogical, but rather political; and there is thus a primarily political consequence for this change. It will follow, however, that the political change attracts further pedagogical turbulence in its wake, as I shall show.

It would indeed be a fine thing to have more people more highly educated, for, as Aristotle believed, knowing is *eudaemonic*: it makes you feel good and improves the *quality* of a life. We might even go so far as to argue that, indeed, knowing such as this improves the quality of *lives* or of our *living together*. However, such well-being, grounded in the idea of qualification and quality, is not our priority in the present climate. Rather, in the conservative ideologies that drive the now corporatized model of the University, it is taken for granted (or rather, it is rather rashly imagined) that there is some direct link between a University degree in a specific subject and highly paid employment in a field related to that same subject. The journey here takes us straight from University study in a discipline to paid employment in that same discipline; and the only real difference is that, in the earlier stage, the student pays their fees while, in the later stage, they are paid for the application of the same work that was done in study-form. Thus, the argument goes that education is indeed *eudaemonic*, but *only* in the sense that people feel good when they are more highly paid than others. Such a view presupposes a highly atomized society, in which lives interrelate only through market mechanisms: the individualized 'atoms' collide only when they compete for the greater individual benefit or profit.

The case that drives the argument of this present book, however, contrasts profoundly with this. Not only does it accept that there is indeed *no* such direct link (not everyone following an engineering degree becomes an engineer; not everyone doing English becomes a poet or an English teacher; and so on), it also accepts that the quality of life in question is determined not simply by a kind of neo-Hobbesian greed or demand for individual advancement over others. However, the case I put forward here is that, even if a graduate (or anyone else, for that matter) is unemployed, it is better for the life of the public sphere that, as a citizen in that public sphere, they are well-educated and thus well-*qualified* for taking as full a part as possible in that democratic civic community. In this way, a more general *eudaemonia* becomes possible.

The sad fact today, however, is that although more and more people attend institutions that are designated as a University (or have the fabled 'student experience'), it does not follow that we are thereby substantively educating more people: rather, we are engaged in a primarily *political* process whose determinations are not primarily ethical, nor, actually, to do with the quality of life. As many will acknowledge, in an age of mass education, when there has been a systematic and repeated reduction in the unit of resource, it becomes increasingly difficult, if not impossible, to attend to particulars – including individual students carrying out specific and particular exercises or work – in ways that were the norm before. Of course, it is also difficult to acknowledge this, for in doing so, the lecturer opens themselves to the charge that they are admitting to not doing their job properly. And, crucially, as we also know, in the culture of 'payment by results', lecturers as much as students are ripe for assessment, with their performance to be monitored and measured.

The industrialization of the University, however, driven by codes of 'efficiency' and 'performativity' – as if we were a widget-business – tends to make the expected codes of conduct and behaviour within the institutions approximate precisely to the conditions that govern such industrial businesses: the task becomes one where, tacitly or not, we are expected to shift units in a highly productive fashion (lots of undergraduates and graduates) with maximum quality of output (highly classified degrees) and consequent sustaining of the brand (your own University name goes here, usually with a strapline indicating excellence in some generic way).

This – the brand and our sustaining of it – is what will be 'examined' now in the marketplace in which the University is to find and make itself. One consequence is a growing expectation that teachers will be prepared to observe a primary allegiance to the institution and its institutional brand rather than to the scholarly discipline and its protocols, of which they should properly be guardians. At the level of assessment, the task now is not only to give more people access to our mythic 'student experience', but also to measure or assess the quality of that experience and, crucially, to ensure that it is as homogeneous as possible and as highly evaluated as possible. If there is heterogeneity, there will be potential ground for complaint in that some people are being given 'better' (biased) treatment than others; and, of course, it is precisely this that was wrong with 'examinations'. In scrutinizing this student experience, we need to assure the same excellent quality for all. How, then, do we discriminate among participants?

For many, the answer to this question is straightforward: we do not and should not discriminate in any serious fashion at all. We should not award classified degrees; but we should rather limit ourselves to a transcript that describes work done and, at most, a local rather general grading that is not very finely granulated. In this, there is a transparency of sorts, and there is no validation of an aristocracy of culture. We simply indicate that the student in the case has more or less satisfactorily completed certain requirements. However, this does not yet answer the problem regarding the 'cloning' of students, in which the student essentially rehearses what the teacher has said. To address this, we do indeed need some level of discrimination and distinction.

To maintain transparency and the supposed democratization of this system, while also addressing the issue of cloning, we need to publish the criteria that need to be fulfilled for the ascription or awarding of each grade: 'grade-description' is the technical term for this. *Information* in the form of such description becomes the driving force for this aspect of our move towards assessment. We inform the student of the criteria for each grade by providing a clear or transparent description of what is required to secure the grade; and the student, in principle at least, could thereby effectively grade themselves, for all they need do is compare the submitted work with the published criteria, match it up and pronounce the grade. We thus eliminate also the possibility of any human interference (such as the activity of external judgement) from the process: the straightforward means of elimination of potential human error turns out not to be the elimination of error, but elimination of human intervention. In sum, it is in principle possible for the student to secure their own 'payment by results': the result in question has its clearly designated 'price', as set out on the label marked 'grade-descriptor'. Yet this itself, apart from an obvious queasiness about the validities of such self-assessment, raises a crucial issue: the issue of supposedly transparent information and its political import.

The demand for transparency – ostensibly an ethical good, ensuring that nothing untoward or covert is going on – becomes a key driver for the prioritization of information (which can be transparently given) over knowledge (which is, of necessity, less secure and murkier, a matter of dialogue and debate). There are large implications for this.

Information has become our poor substitute for knowledge, in exactly the same way that *transparency* has become our poor substitute for truth. The two, combined, form a deadly conjunction through which any demand for justice – which depends upon human intervention and *judgement* – can be safely circumvented. Instead of the difficult work of judging that would be required for any proper 'examination' of whether a specific outcome is just or not, we have a self-perpetuating and self-validating *system* against which there can be no real appeal, for the system's legitimacy is given and guaranteed because it is (allegedly) transparent and replete with information. The relation of knowledge to information, as the relation of truth to transparency, is related to our central question in this chapter: how and why and what do we judge?

3

The so-called 'knowledge-economy' that is allegedly the main economic determinant for these changes in our practices is, as it happens, no such thing, for what we have in our time is not an increase in knowledge but an increase in *information*, aided and abetted by technology. The political economy, in general, has little time for knowledge (which tends to be provisional, relatively unclear, open to argument and debate); but it is by contrast obsessed with information (which at least has the appearance of stable certainty and resembles the solidity of the Gradgrindian 'fact'). Further, it is the very structure of assessment (as opposed to examination) that encourages the *confusion* or *confounding* of knowledge with information, such that the key to success becomes one of having access to information, sometimes processing it, always 'managing' it, but rarely ever thinking about it or knowing anything as a result of finding it. Many cannot distinguish between knowledge and information – one reason why plagiarism is rife, of course. There is also an ideological dimension to this as well, related to technology.

Andrew Abbott, in a speech called 'The Future of Knowing' to the University of Chicago Alumni on 6 June 2009, makes a distinction between what I have called information and knowledge, but he recasts it in his own terminology as a distinction between knowledge and knowing. The latter – knowing – is what a University should be about; However, the former – knowledge (or what I call information) and our supposed measuring of it by assessment – is what structures all our teaching, especially via the prioritization of assessment over examination. Abbott points out that the present generation of students is the first to have gone through almost all their education in an electronic and computer-driven world. He argues that, in this world, knowledge has become something that students think of as being 'contained' in the data on the Web and that, essentially, students do not know how to manipulate that knowledge to make it into knowing.

We can easily recognize this as an ostensibly conservative neo-Platonic argument about technologies of memory: Plato, in *Phaedrus*, questions the technology of writing, saying that it damages human memory. Writing, it is alleged, provides a kind of repository of knowledge that can be located outside of the self, a self whose identity, in an oral culture, is given precisely by the interiorization of knowledge and the necessary memorialization of it. While an oral culture identifies the self with her or his body of remembered knowledge, a literate culture divorces the self from knowledge; and the feared result is a loss of the faculty of memory itself, memory which is vital to self-knowledge as much as it is to the everyday business of practical living. Walter Ong once argued something similar, suggesting that 'modern' thinking (he means post-Renaissance thought) is shaped by what he calls 'place-logic'. As he puts it, in an argument concerning the technology of print and our earlier shift from oral cultures to literacy: 'We ourselves think of books as "containing" chapters and paragraphs, paragraphs as "containing" sentences, sentences as "containing" words, words as "containing" ideas, and finally ideas as "containing" truth. Here,' he concludes, 'the whole mental world has gone hollow.'[1]

Abbott, however, takes the logic of this further. He conducts a series of classroom experiments, through which he discovers some interesting things about how his students tend to read. First, many read electronically: that is, they do not have the physical book, but read e-copies of the work on screen. Further, when reading for study, they often 'read' by cutting and pasting. In the texts that they study they come across passages that they think contain keywords; they then highlight these passages online and paste them into a Word document. They then construct occasional sentences to see if they can link the pasted collage of passages.

Asking his students how they read, and whether they prefer print to screen, he finds some interesting results. He gives the example of a reader who describes the process of reading online very well, explaining how he has gone through chapter one of *The Great Gatsby*. Then, the student writes:

> I finish a page and there is a link at the end of the page to connect me to the next chapter. I double click it but before I can go on to the next webpage I am shown a Google ad with an opportunity to win a getaway cruise ship online. Reading a hardcopy of the novel would have saved me from this absurdity.

Yet the absurdity, of course, is the point, as Abbott argues: webpage design is structured to reduce the space for genuine independent thinking: instead, we 'surf'; and we surf in order to be persuaded to buy things. Abbott says:

> My point is that our students have been brought up spending much of their time – the time that we spent reading magazines, second-rate novels, and the occasional piece of fine literature – surfing an internet that has been optimized in terms of these retail-oriented principles of web-design. That's where their model of cognition is formed. Ours was based on rubbish texts, to be sure. But at least they were texts. The current generation of students has been raised on a cognitive form that is deliberately designed to be as indulgent, as 'user friendly,' as preorganized as is humanly possible, all in order to hold the reader's attention long enough to sell him something.[2]

These, of course, are the students that we are now enjoined to bring into the University: consumers, rather than students. The commodification of knowledge here is validated by procedures of assessment that do not require the student to demonstrate 'knowing', as Abbott terms it, but rather to demonstrate solely that they have gained access to the database of 'knowledge' (or, in my own terms, 'information'), and that they have then manipulated or 'managed' that knowledge in its organization of cut-and-pasted parts into a new whole.

The economy in question here is not in any serious way a 'knowledge-economy'; and it is not governed by the exercise of critical judgement that is of the essence of any form of assessment (or, indeed, examination). Rather, what is at stake here is the 'cloning' of shoppers, so to speak. The task, in fact, is to prioritize rapid consumption of unexamined information and, correspondingly, to de-legitimize the slow and inefficient use of time that is required for us to 'assess' a text or any other kind of information. Consumerism such as this justifies itself simply by looking at growth in sales: it needs no further philosophical validation. As the self-proclaimed 'realists' would have us believe, this is just how it goes in our contemporary sphere, and we should learn to live with it or to adapt to it. For us, however, in this present argument, it is vital to note that the reduction of knowledge to information is consistent with the demise of any form of assessment at all.

It may be that we have inadvertently found, here, the reason for another aspect of the 'economy' of the knowledge-economies: inflation. Specifically, it begins to look as if our mechanisms almost essentially *require* that we show such inflation in terms of grades awarded for work. If we make a move away from 'qualification' and its root in something called 'quality', to arrive at something called 'quantification' (or 'estimation') and the question of measurement; and if, further, it is increasingly incumbent upon us to attend to 'the brand'; then, *ipso facto*, it makes sense to give the results of the measuring in rather inflated terms. Thus, it is not so much the 'knowledge' that grows, but the 'economy' itself; and the word for that is, simply, inflation.

Behind the turn to assessment, then, driven as it is by a system of 'payment-by-results', it is entirely rational that grades should be inflated in various ways – many, if not all of them, entirely legitimate. The legitimacy lies in the fact that what we are now enjoined to do is not to examine knowledge, but rather to record the management of information. If there *is*, in an assessed piece, a body of information of a measurable quantity or size, and if there is also a *managing* of that information that is consistent with the procedures described in the grade-descriptors, then the likely consequence is, indeed, this kind of inflation. The number of 'first-class' degrees rises; the 'brand' prestige rises; payment – in terms of intellectual, academic, and financial capital – is secured. The inflationary cycle is then repeated, in more and more bloated form. In all of this, however, the amount of education in question may not have risen at all: that is, now, an entirely separate matter from the recording of processes in which the managing of bits of information, and the transparency with which such managing and recording is done, has become paramount.

4

One of the main issues affecting the question of examination and assessment is legitimation: how do we ensure that people are being graded properly, and therefore being given the opportunities that assessment was designed to offer them? As I indicated above, in the times of 'examination', this was straightforward (if also, as we now know, troubling and concerned with exclusivity). Judgement was key; and the judgements in question were grounded in prior experience and the authority that such experience gives. The judgement, in short, is legitimized by two things: the qualification of the examiner, and their accumulating and accumulated experience. This, however, turns out to be precisely the problem: the judgement, determined by human input in this way, is not guaranteed to be 'objective' and neutral. Humans rarely are 'neutral', especially when judging matters in fields where they have expertise and experience, given that it is precisely such experience that constitutes their authority *and* their identity. Their 'identity' is thus confounded with their 'experience' or authority.

In the first instance, then, examination is potentially contaminated by bias and prejudice. There is a necessary determination to try to preclude such poor judgements. The consequence, in the first instance, might respectably turn out to be argument and debate, even a *thematization* within the discipline precisely of the terms and nature of the debate. Indeed, at one time, this is exactly what happened, when the specific ideological bias of particular critical positions, especially in the arts and humanities disciplines, was exposed. We once called this 'the theory wars', in which there were not only 'competitions', as it were, between various theoretical positions but also a much more fundamental battle between those, on one hand, who denied that there ever even was a theory governing their position and those, on the other, who saw all positions as being 'situated' within presiding ideological stances. These 'wars' never really resolved anything, largely because the opposing camps essentially ignored each others' work.

Moreover, at the institutional level, no argument was ever really enjoined at all; rather, the consequence was an argument that suggested that, rather than adjudicate between the two camps, we should adopt the more 'nuclear' option and remove the possibility of human bias entirely. Thus, the so-called 'theory wars' became just another paper or module within the degree or disciplines, ripe for assessment. How do we remove human bias, systematically? We do that – we did that – by delegitimizing the prior knowledge, experience and, indeed, qualifications of the examiners. This is why I refer to it as a nuclear option, a razing of the ground itself. That qualification and that experience – indeed, behind this the very institutional authority of the University as a whole – now become the problem that assessment will counter and overcome; and so, instead of benefiting from it, we establish an allegedly 'neutral' system, based upon the supposed self-evident ethical goodness of *immediacy* and, above all, of *transparency*.

We now live in a culture that has no time for professional experience or knowledge. Perhaps the main issue here is again that of time: we live in a kind of foreshortening of time itself, and, as I have indicated before in this book, the result is that we give no time for learning or teaching or thinking. In line with the immediacy of electronic forms of communication, we also want our assessments to be immediate, which in some ways means also 'unmediated'. The most common form this now takes is the entirely reasonable demand for a fast turnaround of assessed work submitted by students: it is indeed right that this work should be assessed with a high priority and returned promptly to the student. However, immediacy also means much more than this. At its extreme limit, it means that we should not be assessing now work that was done a year or two years ago: that is to say, the moment for assessing definitively is when the module itself finishes. No time is to be given for any further meditation, or work, or reflection on that work. For the Quality Assurance Agency for Higher Education (QAA), this immediacy of assessing was once deemed to be best practice; but it meant that the student was effectively precluded from making cross-references among or between separated modules of study. Denied that possibility, the student is also denied the chance to make their own judgements about priorities in the wider scheme of their degree. The thought to be assessed, then, is also thought that cannot be 'mediated' by the student who takes the time to think more deeply about the work being done, the discoveries being made.

Against any sense of a judgement that can be made in a proper and mediated fashion – that is, a fashion that takes time – we have been told to prefer a judgement that can be as quick and as efficient as the delivery of a webpage at the touch of a button. The result is all; the mediation – or study – required to get there is eliminated in the demand for immediacy and transparency. For judgement, we no longer call on human intervention; rather, we make appeals instead to an abstract system, devoid of the possibilities of contamination by human thinking. In this, we are no longer professors, but rather (and rather insultingly) 'human resources', operating within a prescribed system; and, as human resources in relation to assessment, we become not examiners but 'operatives of the assessment function'.

This, of course, now goes well beyond the confines of the academy; and it may well be the case that this discourse originates elsewhere and has been inappropriately imported into the academy. In the language and norms of 'human resources', it is important that, instead of attending to a candidate's curriculum vitae, say, that would reveal prior experience, we turn instead to 'competency criteria'. That is to say: the CV might possibly prejudice an employer to favour one candidate over another, precisely because they have demonstrated the requisite experience for the job in hand, while other candidates may not. Such a move, it is argued, potentially prejudices me as employer against the less well-qualified candidate – that is, it does so *unless* I ignore that experience and authority, establish a 'ground zero' basis for comparison and turn to assess competence instead of prior qualification. I then, of course, need to set competency criteria; but the primary assumption is that these criteria will somehow themselves be 'neutral', and that, of course, is impossible. The criteria, set by me as employer, are inherently biased by *my* subjectivity. The only way around this would be to eliminate also my own subjectivity as well and to become 'the employer function'. This way, we effectively strive to eliminate humanity entirely from the process and from our relations with each other. Thus, also, assessment and judgement can now only be assessments of *processes* and not of *content*. The ideology contained in the very terminology of the 'HR' language tends to ignore such a difficulty; yet it is the basic difficulty in question more generally, for it is the difficulty regarding *legitimation*.

In passing, let us note the further development of the trajectory that I have traced here. I have already argued that we have moved from an interest in knowledge to an interest in the management of information. This shift, however, to 'competence criteria', reflects a further shift. No longer are we interested in information itself (the CV, for example); rather, we will develop a bare questionnaire that allegedly allows candidates – regardless of their knowledge or experience or authority in a field – to show a supposed competence. We might pass over the fact that all that this shows is competence in filling out a form; or, perhaps, we should not so glibly pass that fact over. This – the ability to operate within an abstract system by manipulating forms – is exactly what our emergent bureaucratic cultures now prize. As with employment assessment, so also with assessments in the University that has been infected with this pernicious language and modes of thought.

Within the University, however, there are yet more pressing immediate concerns. The question for the student, once they receive the grade, is not any longer 'What can I now do? What am I qualified to practise?' or 'Where did I go wrong?', but rather, 'Did the examiner get it right?' In other words, now that any principle of legitimation by 'qualification' is removed from the scenario, we can now also examine the examiner. The examiner's knowing, experience and authority – their qualifications – are now, literally, out of the question; but the examiner themselves is very much *in question*. So, we have a system where the examiner, in principle, can be examined – by a second-order examiner (who may be the student, but may equally be a further institutional 'authority', such as a 'quality assurance agency'). However, it follows logically at this point that the same logic would apply, surely, to this second-order examiner; for this second-order examiner is also or should be, at least in logical principle, subject to precisely the same kind of scrutiny in turn. In the end, we face the ancient Ciceronian question of who judges, *Quis custodiet*; and we should add the other prime question asked by the great orator, the question of who stands to benefit from the judgement made, *Cui bono*? To avoid the obvious infinite regress, we simply and at a stroke get rid of the 'who' here. The answer is: the system and processes of examining themselves. We are no longer as interested in the *content* of assessment as in its *processes*, its carcinogenically proliferating and bureaucratically self-justifying modes.

In relation to this, consider here the arguments advanced by Sally Brown, for example, an eminent pro-vice-chancellor in a large institution in the UK (one that prides itself on widening participation in University, and in teaching, learning and assessment). In September 2008, in a piece in *Times Higher Education*, she argued that, for today's student, 'the value of work is tied to the weight of assessment', with the unsurprising – if rather shocking – consequence that 'students regard marks as money'. Her response to this is not that we should aim to correct or even to question for a moment such a narrow view of assessment and its signifying 'currency' in marks or grades; instead, rather, Sally Brown appears simply to accept it. So, she argues, 'if we want to influence student behaviour we need to indicate the value we place on certain types of activity by weighting marks towards what we regard as important'. At one level, of course, such a statement is entirely non-controversial. In assessing someone's familiarity with nuclear physics, say, we may well place more emphasis and give more marks to their description of the Hadron Collider than we will to the accuracy with which they have numbered the pages of their scripts.

Yet, in this context, remember, marks are *currency*, and this affects how we can understand the question of *value*. Essentially, we will see here that we have an attempt to legitimize the translation of *quality* into *quantity*; and, crudely, the question now for the student is not a question about 'knowing' at all. Instead, the focus is on an entirely different question about the 'value-for-money' that they are getting for their investment in the University degree programme. Do the 'marks' given by the institution represent the proper value in the eyes of the consumer? Behind this, we can easily see the threatening shape of 'inflation' once again; but the inflation, while affecting price (or marks) has now no relation at all to value; and this is so, paradoxically, precisely in the middle of a discourse regarding the value of assessment itself as a practice.

Sally Brown is absolutely right in stressing the importance of assessment; but the logic of the position, at least as advanced in her argument, is one that does not value assessment for what it can do, but rather values the processes and procedures of assessment for the granting of wishes to candidates. It is a 'purchaser-provider' model of assessment; and the resulting danger is that students can be told – or even that they *should* be told – exactly and only what they want to hear, or what they have 'paid' for.

The argument advanced by colleagues such as Brown depends on an idea of the University as a repository of data, which we call knowledge, and which the student buys or, better, invests in: the University as 'bank', so to speak. She subscribes to the prioritization of what Abbott called 'knowledge' (my *information*), and her prioritization of assessment over all else precludes the very possibility of 'knowing'. The key thing here now is the quality of the University brand: its value in the marketplace. Of course, in the UK, we have a means of legitimizing this quality: the Quality Assurance Agency.

This logic is one where knowledge is measurable and quantifiable; and we have simple ways of legitimizing our evaluations and measurements. We argue that the transaction that goes on here is transparent: that it becomes supposedly self-evidencing. The way we do this is through the proliferation of those QAA-required grade descriptors, whose function is now clear. They are there to indicate to a student the 'price' of each grade that they will achieve. Thus, while an 'A' grade shows or 'contains' qualities x, y, z, p, q and r, a 'B' might only contain x, y and p. In this, what is happening is that assessment is reduced to a legal and mechanical process: it is no longer a matter of judgement or legitimation at all, in fact, much less 'qualification' to practise something (as in an exam).

The examiner is now the pure functionary of a system, and they are also to be held to account for the way in which they operate the system. This last aspect is what we usually recognize as an intrinsic 'appeals' procedure, itself now backed up in the UK by the large and expensive armature of an Office of the Independent Adjudicator. This Office can explore processes and procedures of assessment, ensuring that institutions do what their schedules and assessment protocols say they do; but it cannot reassess. There is logic here: they cannot reassess because the question of the human judgement that awarded the grade has been entirely eliminated from what is seen to be the substantive business of assessment itself. There is nothing to reassess other than the mode in which the system of assessment has been operated. Given that the Office of the Independent Adjudicator, as a court of last appeal (before legal processes themselves actually begin), now stands *over* the system, those 'operating' the system – teachers and assessors – lose their own authority and standing. Once more, authority is to be vested in the management of processes and a transparent system for ensuring their transparency.

In assessment, we are in a position where nobody judges, in fact; and this is a perfect description of a bureaucracy. We have established instead a system, based purely and simply on a crude logic of mercenary exchange – marks are money, remember – and the task of the examiner, and the student likewise, is to preserve the sanctity of the system itself. 'Save the banks', even if that means damning the community that the banks are there to serve. It's a bit like any mercantile system: no single individual is in charge; but nonetheless, there are classes of people that rise to the top. In this case, the class in question is the managerial class, the bureaucrats who devise the systems, but never claiming any conscious agency. They see themselves – with good reason – as being slaves to, or at least honest servants of, the systems as well.

We have lost the very possibility of critical knowing here; we have lost the possibility of genuine exploratory dialogue and debate about value. Thus, in this state of affairs, we do not have assessment at all – remember, assessment means estimating quality – for we have no one actually estimating anything. We have replaced examining with something closer to bureaucratic monitoring. This, the other side of transparency, is surveillance. It is to this that I now turn.

5

Delegitimized, de-authorized: this is the version of human being that I am about to pass on to my assessed students. But let us look, in these final remarks, at what is at stake in this new orthodoxy. We can begin from the work of Phil Race, an eminent figure in the new managed assessment structures that cripple British and other institutions. He argues that there are three types of learner: deep learners (the kind that get actually to know things, but with a tendency to specialize and get a bit lost in thought); surface learners (those who skim the edges of lots of things, without ever really getting to grips with first principles on anything); and strategic learners (those who know what they need to do, pragmatically, to pass exams and get good grades, and who behave accordingly). Although he actually seems to favour this third, his case is that, in the move to the plethora of new ways of assessing everyone, we must strive to be just, to avoid systematically favouring one type of learner (for example, she who is 'good at exams') over another.

So, logically, given that there are multiple types of learner, it follows that we should multiply our modes and manners of assessment according to this. In such a multiplication, everyone, regardless of their standing or character-type, can 'come to market', as it were. Instead of having 'finals', that one big blow-out of formal exams after years of time spent in study, thinking and (all being well) learning, we now have continuous assessment as well. This was the first diversification of how we measured performance (and that phrase is itself now telling: it is a machine that is performing, and we are but cogs within it). Race lists at least fourteen kinds of assessment that he urges us to use. Here they are: exams; open-book exams; structured exams; essays; reviews or annotated bibliographies; reports; practical work; portfolios; presentations; viva voce exams or orals; student projects; posters or exhibitions; dissertations or theses; and work-based learning.

Now, with this proliferation of assessments, happening continuously and virtually constantly, every single move a student may make is monitored and assessed: *everything* becomes measurable and thus needs its 'code of practice', its mode of operation. The student cannot move for assessment – and importantly, she has no time to learn, to study. She is, in fact, radically disabled from learning, for she must always instead show how she is behaving in terms of the logic of whatever assessment her work or present activity is geared towards. That trusty old foot-soldier, Private Study, is dead; General Knowledge will soon follow to the grave, for such knowledge is not specific to the matter being monitored through these diverse assessment practices.

As if this were not enough, Race argues that the student must also now *replicate* all this, this time in the form of self-assessment. That is to say, she must internalize the ideology, or put herself under these same forms of scrutiny. It is important to remember, though, that what is at stake in all this is not the human person making judgements; but rather the preservation of the sanctity of the system. So, rather than ask, 'Have I got the content of this test right?', the question becomes, 'Am I doing this kind of assessment properly? What are its protocols?' We sometimes make the mistake of calling this 'enabling'. Actually, of course, it is a structure that we have seen in fiction: Winston Smith, tortured by surveillance in George Orwell's *1984*, is told by O'Brien that he must learn to love Big Brother – not to pretend to love Big Brother, but actually to do so. What is enabled by it, what is made operational by it, is the system of overall surveillance, now made more efficient because individual students can internalize it.

My joke is that 'private study' is dead; but this signals something more important than a poor joke. What I am getting at here is that the realm of the *private* is now also under threat. The systems that I have explored elsewhere in this study have revealed that prevailing ideas of the University have served the purpose of doing an extensive damage to the idea of the public sphere, with the atomization of society into individual acts of purchasing things. However, when the public sphere is so roundly attacked, directly or indirectly, and when that attack is carried on in tandem with an ideology of 'transparency', the result is also an attack on the realm of the private. The question is whether we can maintain the idea that education, or something that we might call the life of the mind, can ever be allowed the private space and time within which to flourish or to be enhanced or to find edification. Are we allowed now to have our own thought? When everything we do is to be assessed, and when we need to keep ourselves under surveillance to ensure that we can guarantee that we are doing things according to the presiding published and transparent criteria (or 'grade-descriptors'), then we have lost the sense of ourselves as private individuals entirely. We are now (at best) representatives of something else, something more abstract: we become 'agents' of the existing social order. This is yet more totalitarian than the very system of examination that we tried to escape so long ago.

As if to prove this, finally, suggests Phil Race, after all that external assessment has been redoubled at the level of self-assessment, we need to add the final twist of peer-assessment. In the situation in which we find ourselves, this maps very easily right on to those feared characters in *1984*, the Household Spies. As in that novel, the end result is the same: a demand for complete conformity and totalitarian homogeneity, where the possibility of independent thought is as crushed as possible, usually under the Newspeak that we would now recognize in its forms of 'Managese'. Thus, something that begins with the entirely admirable drive to find ways of rewarding diversity ends up by instilling a normative power of conformity. We are now reduced, all of us involved in assessment, to being agents of a presiding bureaucracy and system. This, of course, is not to say that good forms of assessment – those that can enable people to learn and to find authority for their autonomous activity – do not happen; but it is to claim that such good assessment happens despite the prevailing ideology of assessment whose effect, if not purpose, is to preclude the possibility of genuine social and cultural justices and freedoms. These things require the intervention of human judgement, with all its attendant risks; but we should recall that one of the first principles governing the University, at least as I am arguing for it here, is precisely the *search* for justice, and that search, like any quest, involves risks of getting things wrong. This, however, is also one of the conditions of our being or becoming human at all within a civic culture; and that culture shows its civilizing force in its benevolence and grace in the face of possible error. We usually just call this something like discussion or debate; and, in the University, we call it research, learning, teaching – and the search for good judgement.

In the end, the whole ideology of assessment goes hand in hand with a surveillance society. It is as if we cannot trust our students to become independent citizens, with thoughts of their own: rather, we have to make sure that all thought is managed, all criticism is reduced, and all people are constantly keeping themselves under surveillance. Needless to say, this is anathema to the very idea of academic freedom.

At the core of the whole issue is the lack of trust. It is not just that the prevailing ideologies do not trust our students to become independent citizens. More than this, it is also the case that we do not trust teachers. Yet more, it is also the case that we trust *neither* students *nor* teachers to become *the kind of independent citizens* that 'we' want. Of course, the 'we' in question here needs to be identified; and it usually can be identified in terms of whatever is the presiding centre of power and authority in a society. In many cases, that will be government; but in too many cases, the government itself is not as independent as it might be of others who determine the 'mood' of the nation, including, for instance, various media outlets that are closely identified with specific business interests. In the UK, for example, it is difficult for any party to gain political power unless it has the backing of News International media; and that is a business interest that does not have, as its primary aims, the advancing of the kinds of autonomous independent search for freedom and its extension that I have characterized as a primary goal of the University.

In the face of the lack of trust, a lack that was enthusiastically encouraged in the UK in the 1980s, when the Thatcher government was determined to ensure that there would be no alternative sources of authority in the society to rival the government's own claims and grasp on social control, it was decided that we really needed a mechanism to restore trust, or to 'assure' the population of the 'quality' of what was going on in Universities. Thus the QAA was born, first of all as a sub-agency of HEFCE and becoming, inevitably, an independent body after the Labour administration came to power in 1997. The QAA does what its title suggests: it acts as an agency (but an agency answerable to whom?), is concerned with 'assuring' (not with 'ensuring') and is organized around a general idea of 'quality' (but a quality that is to be measured and thus rendered into quantity).

QAA is certainly concerned with standards. However, the one abiding slippage that seems to found all its activity is the slippage that confounds 'standards' with 'standardization'. Thus it is that, in collaboration with the Higher Education Academy, through which it encourages the internalization of its norms by new lecturers, it endorses the activity of setting things like 'benchmarks' that will help us to assess performance, not just in the graded performance of student activities but also in just about everything else. The benchmark then becomes a standard; and the standard then becomes something that needs itself to be 'standardized' across and between institutions. The inevitable drive here is towards homogenization. Once this becomes normative, we have the enormous armature of practices that require us to be standardizing everything.

This helps explain why it is the case that modules have to be computable and exchangeable: their 'content' needs to be standardized in terms, say, of the time it will take a student to engage with the work each week. The demands of exchangeable currency – those CATs that I discussed earlier in this book – require that we know the size *and currency value* of the tokens (modules) that we now insert into the economy of the degree. Yet more fundamentally than this, we have to be 'assured' that if a module in final-year bioscience takes ten hours of a student's time, then it is somehow *equal* to a second-year module in economics that also takes ten hours. The actual content of what is being done for those ten hour periods is erased in all of this; and, again, we are left with an abstract equality that bears no relation to actual experience or actual activity. This affects, and infects, assessment, whose quality is now focused around these standardized practices and measures. In the end, the idea is that we should ideally be assured that 'a First is a First is a First': no matter if it is a First in Medicine from University X or a First in Comparative Literature from University Y. If a First is a First is a First, then the business community of employers (and the taxpayer) knows what it is getting when it employs the First-class graduate.

Gertrude Stein, the somewhat abstract author of modernist texts such as *Tender Buttons*, wrote that 'a rose is a rose is a rose'. Hearing this, Ernest Hemingway replied that 'a rose is a rose is an onion'. Here, we have two different attitudes to the ways in which language might relate to reality. Stein's language is hypnotic and lulls us into a rhythm whereby the semiotic aspect supplants the semantic: the way that something is chanted becomes the message itself. Hemingway (paradoxically, given his usually rather bare style) stresses the inevitable metaphorical nature of the semantic itself, and draws attention to the necessity to establish difference as the very foundation of our making semantic sense at all. The key question for us, however, is as basic as this: why do we want to believe that all Firsts are the same, as if there existed somewhere an absolute essence of 'the First'? Importantly, even if there were such an essence, it would now be an essence given to us by the processes of crudely abstract mathematical standardization, and not by any more material authority, such as that of an experience grounded in and displayed by acts of judgement.

Is there a way beyond this? In concluding here, let me state a fundamental principle that I suggest as a governing purpose of assessment. Assessment is about legitimate authorization. Many will agree with something as basic as this; but many will also misunderstand it in terms of thinking that I am arguing for an assessment that is concerned to 'enable' in a very general sense. I need to offer slightly more precision, and will do so by looking at a determinedly 'enabling' model of assessment that has already gained significant traction in the United States and that threatens to surface in the UK and elsewhere: the assessment that is based in the idea of the 'Ability-Based Learning Environment' (ABLE).

ABLE has been pioneered especially in Alverno College, a liberal arts college in Milwaukee. Alverno has an emphasis on what it describes as learning those abilities that students need in order to be able to put their knowledge to use. In principle, this sounds fine, of course. In practice, we need to examine what it entails. ABLE is codified, for there are precisely eight specific *abilities* that are highlighted and made central to the entirety of the College's practices. The eight abilities are: communication; analysis; problem-solving; valuing in decision-making; developing a global perspective; effective citizenship; and aesthetic responsiveness.

There is obviously nothing objectionable, at least in principle, to our students in general having certain kinds of 'ability' in all these things. However, the question I raise is a simple one: what happens to the *specifics* and particularity of our different kinds of knowledge when they are subsumed under these more generic and generalizable abilities? Is it the *same thing* when I consider 'effective citizenship' in a class on maxilla-facial surgery and when I consider it in my teaching of Joyce's *Ulysses*, say? My point is simple: as with the demands of the QAA in the UK, we have here a drive towards a homogenization of the student body in terms of an eventual assessment practice that will no longer measure proficiency in a field, but rather will attend to the kind of person that we now are. Education becomes a means to produce a specific kind of human being or human behaviour, and one that is homogenized as far as is possible according to the determining whim of an overarching ideology.

There has been a drive in the UK in recent times that actively parallels Alverno's ABLE education. In the UK, we have been asked to prioritize something called 'transferable skills' or, more pointedly, just 'skills' in all of the modules that we propose for validation. In other words, we cannot teach the particulars of our field now without ensuring that those particulars themselves are in some ways subservient to this skills agenda. These skills tend to be rather vague and generic: it is not the case that the government has suggested that an English department, say, should help its students to develop a skill in Althusserian Marxism, or Derridean deconstruction, or in the analysis of *Ancrene Wisse* or *Paradise Lost* – or, indeed, in *anything* that might be thought of as specific to English. Rather, English modules, 'licensed' by QAA demands, cannot be taught unless they demonstrate, for random examples, skills in 'teamwork' or 'problem-solving' or 'effective communication' or 'leadership' and so on. These randomly selected skills, however, start to look less random once laid out: they are broadly recognizable as the skills supposed to be central to effective business management. That is to say: English is here reduced to or translated into 'Managese', and the potential 'critic' becomes, instead, a skilled 'manager'.

I have suggested that the ABLE agenda and the skills agenda are effectively as one, but with different explicit formulations. ABLE wants to produce a particular kind of graduate. Explicitly, ABLE does not use anything like a traditional examination. Its curriculum, it says, does focus on measurement or quantification, but it stresses that this is always 'measurement that's about you, and only you'. In its explanation of the ABLE curriculum, it states that 'The lessons you learn are applicable in real life, they become part of who you are'; and this 'real life' is one that is 'competitive' but focused specifically on three key areas: 'the worlds of work, family, and civic community'. In passing, let us note that Alverno itself presents itself therefore not a part of 'real life'; real life happens outside of the College and it is a space of *competition* involving work, the family, and civic community. ABLE assessment is thus guided by whatever ideology it is that shapes a real-life world that is apart from this learning; and this is why the College has to stress that the learning that is done within its walls is 'relevant' to a reality elsewhere.

The learning becomes practical, but only in the sense that it 'prepares' the student for the competitions that it claims to be constitutive of reality; and the assessment is practical, too, but only in the sense that what is assessed – by the student who keeps herself under scrutiny – is the measure to which she fits in with the ethos of competitive work, competitive family, competitive civics.

Our own UK skills agenda performs the same function. The skills agenda helps divert attention away from the specifics of academic or intellectual content; it places a responsibility for self-monitoring upon the learner; and it requires a mode of assessment that drives us towards the priced evaluation or the quantified evaluation not of academic work but of personhood *in a marketplace*. This, I hope needless to say, raises questions of ethics and morality. The question is whether it is the responsibility of the University to produce the good consumer, as this ideology seems to propose; or whether we might think of education at this level as more edifying than this, or at least as endowed with a greater scope and ambit.

Alverno might find a justification for what it does in its religious foundation: it is a College founded by and grounded in the beliefs of the Franciscan Order, with its explicitly Catholic ethos determined by the School Sisters of St Francis, who chartered it in 1887. Outside of this religious kind of foundation, however, and in the more general tendency towards assessment as self-monitoring, we have a parallel of Catholic self-examination going on; and the project is one where we are driven to conform to an alleged external standard, really a standardization. The incipient totalitarianism of assessing persons – as our potential labour force especially – rather than performance is, at least, potentially pernicious. Yet this is what lies behind our transferable skills/transferable knowledge agendas.

Let us rehabilitate assessment; but let us rehabilitate it as something that enables a student to engage more deeply in the first instance with their field of study. There will no doubt be adjacent skills that the student learns; but these will vary, of necessity, with the individual student and with what they may bring to their programmes of study. More importantly, it is an error of political importance to confound the assessment of an academic performance with the assessment of an individual person in terms of the kind of person that we 'produce' from our institutions. In the end, we do not 'produce' at all in this way; but we can teach, and we can assess – and even examine – what we teach. That is to say, we can legitimize certain kinds of thinking; and we can, through that legitimization, bring our students to the point where they can exert their own authority. In this way, they do not become 'agents' of a government agenda, but rather they become authorities in their own right. Further, in this way, instead of government assessing its population, the people can properly assess its government. Assessment, if it works at all, can measure its own success by considering how well the graduate can learn to judge critically the world that they inhabit and can help to invent; assessment works, that is, if it searches for and tries always to extend justice.

This is at the root of an assessment grounded in justice and in democratic extensions of freedom; it is this that we should encourage. Within the classroom, we can do this by attending more directly to modes of assessment that are specific to, and that address the particularities of, our separate disciplines and academic practices.

Sally Brown writes that 'your intended learning outcomes should serve as a map of your teaching programme'. This mechanical procedure reduces us to human resource, refuses the organic life of the mind or of learning. Only a bureaucratic mentality could come up with such crude and unhelpful ideas. It is intended to ensure that there are no loose ends, no 'play' within the engine-like mechanisms that 'drive' us and our 'motivations', and that everything can be accounted for. Yet more importantly, it commits the fundamental error – a kind of category mistake – that sees the University as an agent of governing ideologies; and sees the role of assessment as one that polices the kind of social agents that we produce, ensuring that we produce only people capable of conforming to whatever government, business or other external forces demand. An assessment that is grounded in the legitimization of our students' authorities will help us to a different kind of outcome: one where democracy and freedom can be extended, and where assessment becomes, genuinely, a matter of radical empowerment.

6

Finance

Money for Value

It is possible that you, who are reading this book, might be a vice-chancellor or a broadly equivalent senior University officer somewhere. It is also equally possible that – whether you are or are not such a senior manager – you may always prefer to describe yourself as a 'realist' or a 'pragmatist'. In these cases, I would be willing to bet that, having glanced at the contents page of this book, you have turned to this chapter first. That, I am afraid, is probably your fundamental problem: and it is your 'pragmatist-realist' attitude that makes your problem into ours. I respectfully suggest that you return to page one, and that you prepare to address the question of finance by engaging with some matters of principle. The idea is that, by considering such principles, we can start to think about finance in terms not of a crude and programmatic 'value for money', but in terms of *money for values*.

Despite your self-description, it is, of course, neither 'realistic' nor 'pragmatic' in any fundamental sense to start from an assumption that finance – increasingly described by the advanced economies simply in terms of 'scarcity' – must axiomatically be a problem against which any resistance is futile. The financial starving of the University sector worldwide is not in any sense a natural state of affairs but is a matter of ideological preference. That preference is the expression of a conservative political will that fears the extension of freedom and the demand for justice; moreover, it is a will that knows that such principles have their roots in the University properly understood. Starve the roots and you can starve the growth; but, while a bonsai might be a nice aesthetic ornament, a University cannot be legitimately reduced to the status of ornamental adornment to a government. We are not a laurel to be draped upon an imperial head. Finance, as any economist knows, has at least a potential relation to growth; and in this area, the oak might be preferable to, and might also be more sustainable than, the more delicate and easily harmed bonsai.

So: off you go back to chapter 1.

1

Now, welcome back to our vice-chancellors and other realistic senior managers (now perhaps slightly more realistic than before); and here we can proceed with the argument.

When we consider how we should finance a University system, we should ask what it is exactly that we wish to fund, and for what purposes. That is to say, we might properly begin from a question of what it is that we *value* in this activity. As we do so, we might also start to see that we can entertain the possibility of a different organization of higher education as a whole, in which the University plays a significant part but is not the whole story. At least two kinds of economics – or, perhaps better, two different attitudes to the economy – can shape the argument or outline its parameters. Let us consider them in turn.

We can adopt the view that the University is a key driver of the more general political economy of a State. To a large extent, this is certainly true. The worlds of business and commerce, not to mention the general public sector, all benefit very substantially from activities that originate in the University. The actual figures change from year to year, but the fact always remains the same: the University yields a very substantial net profit to the State and, in addition, provides resource to industry and the commercial private sectors, often at rates that are much cheaper and more efficient than those offered by private-sector concerns. Many FTSE 100 CEOs are in their positions at least partly thanks to things that they learned in a University education; and many use that education well to make decisions that are of general benefit to the nation's economy. It is very important that, at all times, we remember this simple fact: the State invests public money in the University, and the University returns it, *with massive interest* and in ways that support *both* public- and private-sphere activities.

As a part of this case, in which the University is seen as a major player in terms of national economic growth, we should understand that one of the single most important aspects of the University's identity and profile is its performative efficiency. Governments, aware of the fact that they are investing public funds, want to ensure that the institution that receives the investment maximizes return to that public; and, accordingly, it will ask stringent questions regarding performance and will demand certain outcomes in terms of efficiency. This much is straightforward and ostensibly relatively non-controversial.

Yet the prioritization of performative efficiency has a rather old-fashioned feel to it. It is, of course, a relic of an earlier model of industry, one that has its roots (like so much of our general educational system and apparatus) in the burgeoning industries of the Victorian period in England.

In this model, the key measure of efficiency is not just the quality of output, but also its quantity and – yet more importantly – its standardized consistency. As customers in Victorian and post-Victorian England, learning to become modern consumers, we want to be 'assured' of the 'quality' of the 'product'; and, as business-leaders with an eye to profits, we want to maximize the numbers purchasing the product. The key to delivering both these outcomes is to ensure conformity to an ideal model. The end-user ('customer' or commercial sector) needs to know exactly what it is getting for its money when it buys or invests in the product.

However, at this point, we should be asking some obvious questions. First, in what way do graduates resemble 'products'? After all, we do not 'sell' graduates. Then, in what ways can knowledge, with its always shifting parameters, be quantified and priced? Moreover, the more fundamental question presses itself upon us: the question of whether this is indeed what we want from our University. Put simply, do we want to encourage consistent conformity among our graduates? There are some circumstances in which it can be argued that it might be appropriate to encourage conformity. These might include certain aspects of military procedure, for instance; but even here, conformity is unadvisable at the level of strategic or higher-level thinking and planning. There are also some circumstances in which it can be argued that our task is to prepare people for a more general conformity with social life, as in the example of trying to rehabilitate a prisoner, for example; but even in these cases, it would be inappropriate to reduce the prisoner's potential by narrowing the scope of their activities. There are, of course, some within the educational political establishment who welcome the militarization of school life; and these would also welcome the opportunity to reduce human potential to a status whereby the school-leaver simply 'fits in', a modern euphemism for the Victorian political quietism involved in 'knowing one's place'. However, none of this is in any way consistent with a so-called 'knowledge-economy', an economy that is allegedly to be driven by inventiveness, innovation and fresh critical thinking. Its place in the University is therefore questionable, to say the least.

Against such a model of prioritized performative efficiency, then, we might propose a different way of thinking about the economics of higher education. We can take our source for this from a great literary example, that of Shakespeare's *King Lear*. Lear is well aware of questions of power, economy and leadership. The play opens with him setting up a new model of governance, central to which is a fundamental act of economic measurement. 'How much do you love me?' he will ask each of his daughters in turn; and he makes it clear that the size or quantity of their dowry – and their power – depends on the answer. There is to be a more or less directly proportional relation between land controlled and amount of love shown by his daughters. He expresses this in terms of an emergent idea of meritocracy that will contrast with what has been thought of as a kind of naturally given privilege. As he puts it: 'Which of you shall we say doth love us most, / That we our largest bounty may extend / Where nature doth with merit challenge?' In other words: whose performance now will we reward or merit, regardless of your position in the natural family, regardless of ideas of inherited rights and privileges?

Lear, however, is starting off at this point – a point that is not so very far removed from the first 'performance-measurement' economic position outlined above – only to undergo a significant lesson through the play. Having split the country into smaller managed units, denounced Cordelia, and left all power to the charge of Goneril and Regan, he quite rapidly turns to these two elder daughters, looking to them for some care in his old age. He will go, each month, from one daughter to the other, attended by a retinue of 100 of his knights. Or so he thinks and says. The daughters, as we know, have other ideas; and these ideas are based entirely upon ideas of performative efficiency. In one of the most harrowing scenes in English drama (2, iv), we see King Lear quite suddenly and barbarically facing what we would now call an ideology of economic cutbacks, stripped of his attendants and reduced to nothing: he begins the scene with a grand retinue of 100 knights and ends it alone, with none.

Goneril has refused to accommodate Lear's retinue, saying she will accept only fifty knights in her house. Outraged, Lear turns to Regan; but she endorses Goneril's economies of scale, and then goes further, reducing Goneril's fifty to five-and-twenty, on the grounds that anything more than this might be potentially disruptive to the efficient running of the household (literally, of course, the 'economy', from the Greek *oikos*, meaning household or where we stay, and *nomos* meaning law). The gradual reduction and stripping of Lear then continues apace, with Lear at this stage still endorsing the crude economics of an input-output efficiency model. He turns to Goneril and says, 'I'll go with thee. / Thy fifty yet doth double five-and-twenty, / And thou art twice her love.'

Goneril's reply, though, drives home to us exactly what happens in any kind of 'efficiency drive' taken to its logical conclusions: 'Hear me, my lord. / What need you five-and-twenty? ten? or five? / To follow in a house where twice so many / Have a command to tend you?' And, before he has a moment to reply, Regan completes the manoeuvre, with 'What need one?' Lear sees his resources (his retinue) reduced in this way, ostensibly entirely reasonably; but it is only reasonable in terms of a kind of crude performative efficiency that tries to quantify quality, that turns 'love', say, to a certain measure of land or that quantifies affection in terms of numbers of knights. It is at this point that Lear not only learns something crucial but also offers, suddenly and with great power, an entirely different version of economics.

He explodes with a powerful argument about what we need to be human at all. When Regan asks 'What need one?' he turns on her, saying, 'Oh, reason not the need! Our basest beggars / Are in the poorest thing superfluous.' The argument is simple, but devastating: it pits efficiency against humanity; and it pits the crude meanness of 'need' against something we might call 'generosity of spirit' or 'grace', seeing these as being constitutive of the essence of human being itself. For Lear, the grace in question is a recognition of our human nature: 'Allow not nature more than nature needs, / Man's life is cheap as beast's.' It is against this crude reduction of the human being to the status of an abstract beastly 'factor' in a calculation that Lear now rants. He is right to do so.

The example reveals, in a simple way, the two kinds of economics that should be in place when we consider what it is that we are funding when we think of how we will pay for the University. We can argue for a model of higher education funding that is driven by the conformities necessary to the efficiencies that maximize industrial growth in a nineteenth-century culture; or we can argue for a model driven by the demands of an essential humanity – grace – which might simply mean something like a generous opening to future possibility. As it is the case that the University already 'gives' to the State in terms of the financial investment, it is right and proper that we look to the University – and its funding models – themselves to be founded in grace, graciousness and giving. What is it that the University can give, not to private individuals or to a nineteenth-century economy that is long gone; rather, what can it give or offer to futurity and posterity? What is the dowry, as it were, that it offers to those committed to the extending of human freedoms? This is the question that shapes how we might productively and profitably (I use the words determinedly) set about financing the sector.

The realist/pragmatist probably rails already at what they will call the 'unreality' of this kind of approach ('what does a packet of grace cost?'); and the argument will be put against me that I am asking for an unlimited giving of public funds to an already privileged academy. However, that is very definitely not what I am arguing. I accept fully that there are also some more basic economic questions that still need to be addressed. However, I am suggesting a way of addressing them, a mode or *mood* of address; and the mood and attitude that I advance here is one of a certain promise, the kind of promise that we find written on our currency, the promise of *value* as opposed to the abstract question of unadorned *sums*.

In sum, then, we find ourselves in a position where our preferred funding systems at the present time are those that were deemed appropriate for an early industrialized society. They are anything but modernized, preferring instead a nostalgia for an earlier social vision, founded in and for the production and further extension of social inequalities. The University, in this way of thinking, becomes akin to, or at least modelled upon, a factory for the efficient production of consistent conformity. The preceding sections of this present book have also revealed this production of conformity as a guiding principle – if an entirely silent one – that shapes most present governing ideologies of the University. My analyses and scrutiny of things as diverse as learning and teaching, research and leadership all reveal the same underlying drive towards a production-model of efficient 'quality assurance' regarding consistency in 'outcomes' or output.

Perhaps the moment is right, in the present near-global fiscal crisis, to start to expose such a model as profoundly unhelpful, not just because it is outdated but also because it fails to address the present historical condition of our societies. Yet more importantly for my own present argument, we might start to consider a funding model based on the concept of grace, understood as an idea of giving an opening to the future, to potential and to possibility; and giving such an opening in a fashion that is unconstrained, liable to produce diversity instead of uniformity, liable to release invention and innovation. In short: it is time to replace a funding model that produces nineteenth-century conformity, and conformity to models of the production line with, instead, a funding idea that will release people into their diversities in an unconstrained fashion. To do this is to begin to address the necessity of our production not of widget-conformism (where everyone will take their assigned proper place in an overarching social system designed for inequalities), but instead our production or imaginative making of freedom, justice and something that we might properly call democracy and democratically widened participation in our society.

In recent times in the UK, we have seen some attempts at rethinking the question of finance. With the production of the Browne Review, a report into the sustainability of the University sector, launched in October 2010, we also have a model that appears to be in tune with the presiding ideologies of present-day assumptions. The Browne Review is, in some ways, a perfect example of all that is wrong with our thought about funding; and I shall take it here as paradigmatically exemplary of a massive failure of imagination. I might also describe it is a failure of political will, except for the fact that it actually represents a *determined exertion* of a political will, and one that is profoundly undemocratic, deeply reactionary and driven by an ideological dogma that sustains inequalities in our society. I shall show how this is so in what follows here. What we will see is that, in higher education as a whole, we have the establishment of a simple but true aphorism: if you want to produce harmless conformity and to maintain the existing social order of inequality and damaged democracy, you prioritize efficiency and 'value for money' in your financial strategies.

Lord Browne considers the University almost entirely in terms of the nineteenth-century model of production, whereby it is an eternal handmaiden to something that is seen to be more substantial, more 'real' in some historical and material sense: commercial activities, economic stimulations and a vaguely generalized realm of 'business', usually simply meaning private-sector commercial activity. For the student, the University becomes nothing more than a gateway to personal wealth, and thus a means of consolidating and, indeed, of extending economic inequalities in the society. The substantive identity of the University is anorexically reduced in this, and its status is correspondingly impoverished. Throughout the Review, there is a number of references made to the social and public good brought about by a University education. However, in all cases, these are either swiftly brushed aside or briskly translated into what the Review takes as the more meaningful idea of private financial gain.

The attitude is best summed up in a phrase dropped, almost in passing, in the chapter where Browne evaluates the present system of funding the sector in the UK. There, we find first of all the casual breezy assertion that 'everyone agrees' that graduates should make a contribution to costs (although unstated, the assertion clearly implies that it is also agreed that this should be through a system of fee-incurred debt); and this is then followed by the further assertion that 'The primary reason for this is that graduates benefit directly from higher education. The public also receives a benefit but this is less than the private benefit.'[1] This is an assertion repeatedly made, but never actually examined in anything like the requisite detail, and never backed up with the required substantive evidence; and it is a highly contentious assertion that is open to much debate.

Consider, for example, the University education of a GP or other medical professional. She will almost certainly find employment, and may gain a high salary as she progresses through a career. Now, consider seriously the claim that it is the graduate herself or even graduates in general who benefit from her higher-level degree-status education. We are at a car crash, and our HE-trained doctor arrives on the scene. Before treating the victims, the doctor does not ask whether the victims are graduates, to ensure that only graduates gain from the education that she has received. This is a very simple case, obviously; but it is offered as an example to show that everyone benefits from a higher education system.

At this same car crash, there is a firefighter who has no higher education training at all. The firefighter is able to cut the victim out of the car, having first of all made the scene safe – for everyone, including our doctor. We can all also equally well benefit from the training and education that those who have *not* attended a University bring to our society as a whole. The activities carried out in a University are but one part of a more general state of affairs in which a society can demonstrate its commitment to social being, to our sharing in the life of a community.

Remember, Browne asserts that the 'private benefit' of the individual doctor *outweighs* the public good. Clearly, in this example, nothing could be further removed from the truth. Moreover, as my example also shows, the value that we accord to a higher academic education should not in and of itself axiomatically be 'higher' than the value that we accord to other types of education. Education, training, work itself are primarily valuable because of the public good that they yield, or because of the ways that they enhance the public sphere and our lives within it. Education, in this respect, is not a business, certainly not a commercial activity, nor is it even remotely 'like' one, nor should it be reduced to being the condition of a transactional medium responding to private avarice. Remember this doctor and this firefighter: they will return later in my argument.

Browne, however, prefers a more atomized view, in which we all operate as entirely discrete individuals, 'paying' for an education if and only if we are 'assured' of its 'quality', and measuring that quality in terms of a financial return that is mine, all mine. In short, Browne fails entirely to address the very idea of our being a community at all or of education happening in any kind of social sphere. Whenever the community is mentioned, it is thought of simply as a kind of arithmetical adding-up or agglomeration of discrete individuals, never amounting to anything like a geometrical shape where one part of the whole might affect or be held in tension with any other.

This is for the simple reason that Browne lays bare the idea of a market principle that governs his idea of the University, a market idea that is indebted to the most banal version of what he himself called a 'morality'. In defending his Review against the charge that it appeared rather crude with respect to any ethical considerations about education, Browne asserted that 'morality lies in giving people choice'.[2] This is the market version of 'freedom', applied, with vigour, throughout Browne to the University and its constitution. Freedom, for the panel of this Review, as for those who have adopted the instrumentalist 'performative efficiency' model of economics, is simply the freedom to continue shopping, in which we are all reduced to the fondness (literally, madness) of a King Lear measuring how much land in return for how large a statement of love. The suggestion is that, by putting consumerist choice in the hands of individual students-to-be, the quality of higher education will be improved; and, somehow, this is construed as an ethic. That argument is simply negated: do we go to the supermarket for our morals? Are we more 'free' if there are three different brands of tomato soup on the shelf? Does the fact that we choose between two different supermarkets make the world a more 'just' place?

This issue of 'student choice' as the key determinant of the system proposed by Browne is extended further by David Eastwood, Vice-Chancellor of Birmingham University and a member of the Review panel. First, there is a yet more radical act of 'atomization' than we have seen before: the argument is that 'students don't pay; graduates do'. This neat legerdemain does not just break society up into discrete individuals; it adds further to this by breaking those individuals themselves up into fractions of a life. Eastwood goes on from this to welcome a state of affairs in which he claims that 'students now decide' things; but if we follow his own logic of atomization, students do not make choices at all. It is not the case that the student comes to a University and then starts, by a process of consumerist choice, to drive the University agenda and curriculum; rather, those choices are made when the student is typically still at school, aged seventeen or so; and, indeed, entry-level qualifications are decided by the 'choices' of fourteen-year-olds preparing for public exams. We thus have a position where the vice-chancellor is driven by the choices of school pupils. Eastwood has used a simple metaphor here, suggesting that this ideology puts the student 'in the driving seat'. What he fails to add is that the reason Browne needs to propose a massive increase in fees is because government has withdrawn all State funding for arts, humanities and social sciences, and has reduced funding for everything else. If the student is in the driving seat, it is in a car that has just been emptied of petrol.

The ideologically driven model of 'student-choice consumerism' might be fine, if we could assume that the school pupil, like any other consumer, is able to make entirely disinterested rational choices, untrammelled by any other influences or persuasive forces that assault the consumer as a matter of course. However, this simply does not happen: there is no such thing as a pure or ideal consumer, a consumer whose choice is driven entirely by reasoned argument. Things like ideology, advertising, television, controlled media and so on all affect and even shape the 'choices' one makes. As Martha C. Nussbaum pointed out already for us, often when we speak we do not speak entirely in our own voices, because peer pressures, parental influence, social pressures and so on all help determine what we 'freely' choose to say.

Finally, however: one might have assumed that one of the reasons why an individual attends a University at all is precisely so that they can learn *how* to argue and debate reasonably, in the pursuit of things that we call true, good or beautiful. Eastwood's 'logic' proceeds as if these things are already known definitively, and that school pupils can now reasonably determine the future of the University and of our society by choosing to 'buy' them in various different specialist shops, called Universities. What happens when these consumers all choose to study English literature, for instance? How will we get the engineers we need to build our roads and bridges, the architects for our buildings, the scientists to help us understand our environment and so on? The answer given by Browne and Eastwood is that the market will be set up in ways to ensure that we do, as a society, get enough well-educated engineers and scientists: that is to say, like any so-called 'free' market, it has to be rigged to produce certain outcomes; and, rigged like this, it simply insults its consumers while pretending to place them at the centre of all choice and political will.

The 'argument', in its wilful deceptions, is barely worthy of any intellectual attention; and it is a sad measure of how far this ideology has become ingrained within our institutions that it can be proposed at all as a serious 'philosophy' of the University and its sustainability. If anything, it is a further indication of how far our 'leaders' have removed themselves from material actualities on the ground, both institutionally and socially.

The questions I pose here are obviously all rhetorical questions. If there is any increase in freedom in this consumerist model, it is remarkably low-level and indicative of a quite extraordinarily impoverished sense of what freedom or justice might mean. Issues of sustainability, world hunger, privilege among developed nations over less developed economies; all of these are held in suspense as we ponder which brand of jeans or beans to buy. It is for this reason that the Browne Review – and, much more importantly its underlying ideology, shared with all those who believe that the economics of University funding should be driven by performative efficiency – is parochial and pusillanimous. The assumptions governing the Review, further, are a million miles removed from realism or pragmatism: the Review, in seeing individuals in an atomized fashion, unrelated to each other except by monetary transactions, gives a purely 'idealized' version of human being. Browne fails to consider or to realize that this idea of the single human is a pure abstraction, and has nothing to do with material and historical realities. It is also equally unrealistic to assume a clear correspondence, especially construed as a causal correspondence, between a University education and the acquisition of private wealth. Such a stance is entirely inconsistent with a University that is interested in widened democratic participation in the pursuit of freedom and justice.

The nineteenth-century performative model is, then, simply inadequate to the present day. Its inadequacy, however, does not derive simply from its old-fashioned nature. Rather, it derives from the fact that it fails to acknowledge the complexity of the social and public sphere in which the University exists. This is one key reason why a modern University system should, in principle at least, be financed through public funds. However, it is also equally true that not all taxpayers can make the same levels of contribution to that funding. If – and this is the big if – if we do indeed decide to have a large University system, then it follows that we also need some political will to bring it into being and to sustain it financially. That political will should be shaped partly by an explanation that the University exists primarily for the public good, and not for personal financial gain or greed. It is not a simple service-industry, beholden to business; and nor should it be an agent of government. However, since it yields such benefits to society as a whole (producing, for random examples, teachers, doctors, lawyers, architects, linguists, engineers, physicists, pharmacists, dentists, vets and all sorts of other actors who offer promise and future possibility), it is right that it should be funded by society as a whole; and, in this instance, that means the State.

Behind this lies a further political ideology, of course; and that is the ideology governing the viability of a system of progressive taxation. It is entirely fair and progressive to ask our doctor, in my car-crash example above, to pay a greater percentage of her salary in taxation than our firefighter, on the simple grounds that she earns significantly more. Were the reverse to be the case, it would be equally appropriate to ask the firefighter to make up the positive differential. There are many factors alongside a University education that lead to massive differentials in earning power among individuals. Those discrepancies often also lead to significant differences in the commitments that individuals might have to the common polity; and it is *that* differential that a progressive taxation system tries to address.

It is important to stress that such a proposal – for a funding model based on progressive taxation – is *not* a deviation from a more 'natural' state of affairs in which we supposedly live now. The present condition is one where we have a system of taxation that is designed and structured in such a way as systematically to transfer wealth into the hands of a small number of people. It is a system made by political choices and wills. It need not be the norm. It is not at all self-evident that the super-rich, many though not all of whom have benefited from education, should pay proportionately less of their wealth as a tax-based contribution to the public good of the community that will continue to allow them to enjoy that wealth.

It is a measure of how far along the regressive road that we have travelled in recent times that this idea is probably regarded as shocking to some. However, the principle of a fees-structured financing is entirely negative, entirely historically regressive. The argument, at one level, is simple; and it has to do with widening participation, to which I will now turn.

2

Let us begin an alternative to all this from the realization that education is expensive; and a mass education even more so. We can also add the well-known aphorism, though: if you think education is expensive, then you should try ignorance, which is infinitely more costly. A society has to decide, as an expression of its political will, whether or not it is willing to do whatever is required to have such a mass educational system. As this book has made clear, I believe that the education of our population is a good thing. What makes it a good thing, however, is that it is much more than a driver of GDP and the associated growth in economic activity of a nation. Accordingly, as with Gandhi on 'western civilization', it might well be a good idea if we could get it started. Further, as far as higher education is concerned, it might also be a good idea to extend that education as widely as possible. The proper place to begin the exploration of finance, therefore, is at the question of access and widening participation.

However, it does not follow axiomatically from my foregoing argument or position that all our population should take the same kind of education, even at advanced levels. Widened participation is better understood itself more widely, more expansively; and it is better understood in terms of a graceful happiness or a sense of belonging to – participating in – something greater than the atomized individual self. Ken Robinson, well known for his views on the place and importance of creativity in education, gives a poignant example of what I mean. At a book-signing, a man asks him to sign one of his books, and Robinson does so, asking the man, in passing, what he does for a living. 'I'm a fireman.' Robinson asks how long he has done that job. 'Forever,' the man replies. 'I *always* wanted to be a fireman. Every child's like that; but I *really* always wanted to be a fireman.' The man here goes on to explain that his desire to be a fireman was sometimes a cause for embarrassment;

and the example he gives relates to his schooling. His teacher at school, driven by an ideology of improved 'aspiration', told him that he was setting his sights far too low, that he should be doing something more academic and going to College. He was mocked for his ostensible lack of ambition; and he felt exposed and slightly ashamed; but his desire to be a fireman persisted and he followed it. Robinson was visibly moved by this. The man then went on to tell him how he had recently met his teacher again, some decades after being mocked for his lack of aspiration. 'Really?' asked Robinson. 'Yes,' the man replied, 'I did indeed come across him again recently. In fact, I saved his life. I also saved his wife. They were in a car-wreck, and I was the fireman called to the scene. I cut them free, and gave them resuscitation.'

The point here, made by Robinson, is that people are different, that they have different ways of participating creatively in a more general community, that they have different ways of attaining fulfilment and happiness. I would add to this, perhaps most importantly, that they have different ways of contributing – graciously giving – to our societies. These different ways do not all require that everyone attend University; and it should not be a mark of shame that one prefers some other way of participating in the society. The clichéd thought surrounding 'widening participation' suggests that not only is there a social hierarchy that places mind above body, but also that those who serve the social sphere and the public good in ways that are not, in the first instance, 'academic' are somehow less worthy participants in our democracy. That is clearly an abomination; and it is to be exposed and then resisted.

'Widening participation' is a phrase and an idea that deserves thought. It usually has been taken to mean something like extending privilege, the privilege that a University education is supposed to represent, to those whose class position or economic standing usually makes such participation in privilege difficult if not impossible. That is to say: widening participation, as a term in our contemporary political jargon, means bringing other, less financially well-off people into a University that is inhabited by the middle classes. Thus, it is argued, we encourage social mobility and offer the possibility of life-transforming experiences to the many and not the few. In principle, no one could reasonably argue, I think, against this admirable position. It rather fits my own biography, in fact; but it is important to say that, without a system of grants, including discretionary maintenance grants, there is no way that someone from my own background could ever have contemplated attending a University.

However, as we have seen, given the focus on the student experience and associated ideological mythologies, we really do need to ask a further question now. What is it, exactly, that the new entrants will be participating in? How wide do we want to be? Maybe the better question is given by a phrase such as 'participation in widening' or more specifically and helpfully, 'participation in widening the franchise'. If we do this, we see immediately what is at stake, I think. It is a question of enfranchisement; and one that has been an abiding concern ever since we widened the political franchise beyond the class of the landowning gentry and the gendered class of men. In short: 'widening participation' is, as my inversion of the term makes clear, fundamentally the dominant question of democracy itself.

That is to say, there is now a two-stage argument. We cannot properly attend to issues of finance of a mass education system without also asking about access and widening participation; but we cannot properly address the issue of access or of widening participation without also attending to the idea of democratic suffrage. The ability to pay fees, or, in its attenuated form, the ability to consider bearing large burdens of debt, is our new version of what used to be the 'property-owning' criterion for taking part in the vote. Before 1832, in Britain at least, very few people had the entitlement to take part in our democracy; and the criterion, essentially, was an endowment of wealth, usually in the form of the ownership of land. Thankfully, we moved well beyond this and, by 1928, we managed to extend the franchise to all adults, regardless in principle at least of gender or of their property-owning status. The imposition of fees for attendance at University is now threatening to set this back; and, interestingly, the imposition of a fees-basis for financing the University takes us back again to that early industrial model.

It is not enough, against this, to try to advance the kind of sophistry that we see in Browne and his supporters, in the suave assertion that 'students do not pay; graduates do'. This is rather like saying that, with a mortgage, houseowners pay nothing, and that it is instead the banks and lenders who pay. It is a wilfully dishonest deception. There is a burden of debt that hangs as a shadow; and that burden weighs more heavily on some than on others, depending on personal and historical circumstances; and it hangs on some to the point where, as with houseownership, it simply cannot be entertained. In short, we should not be advocating such a historically regressive move: the University of the future is a twenty-first-century institution and should not be modelled on the socio-political foundations of a mid-nineteenth-century industry. If we embrace modernization, we reject fees.

A similar argument is sometimes advanced in relation to the transition between school and University. In the UK, for example, out of the 80,000 children who are entitled to free school meals, because of the precarious financial circumstances of their family life, the number of these who proceed to study in Oxbridge is typically rather small (around 40 in 2009–10). This, it is argued, is a disgrace; and the Universities should do something – or continue to do something – about it. While it may be a disgrace, there is a yet more pressing fundamental question to be answered by those who chastise the University in this way: what kind of society – what kind of politics – is it that tolerates a state of affairs in which so many thousands of its children are in such poverty that they need to be given free meals, while many others instead dine routinely at vast expense? The scandal here is more fundamental than any question regarding University admission; and yet, it has a profound relation to the function of the University as an institution concerned with enfranchisement and widening the participation in a democracy.

At its most basic, then, this question of finance, and of paying for our education system, is best approached through a question concerning the values of democracy. This, however, is not really the way that our present arrangements and thinking seems to work. I have long pondered what Napoleon meant when he apocryphally described England as a 'nation of shopkeepers'; but it is only in more recent times, and especially given recent debates about the financing of education at tertiary level, that I have indeed started to understand the implications of the phrase. We are driven by the practices of a famous English shopkeeper, Alfred Roberts, grocer, small businessman, alderman and father of a British Prime Minister who once vaunted a return to Victorian values in our society and our education. It is his ideology that shapes a Thatcherism whereby all social and civil activity can be seen as a rather parochial financial transaction of sorts. Now, after Browne, we no longer have vice-chancellors; rather, we have people who think of themselves primarily as some kind of specialist retailers. In this, the idea of the 'student-led' University gains traction. The University becomes subject to the whimsy of market choices, themselves at the mercy of prevailing and passing fashion. However, this mentality reduces the University to the status of shop or outlet, the vice-chancellor to a retailer, the lecturers to shop assistants and – the single most important aspect of all of this – it reduces the vast significance of the concept and actuality of freedom to small matters of consumerist choice.

The pretence that there is a morality to this has already been trounced by Dickens in his 1839 novel, *Oliver Twist*. There, Dickens might well have been describing our present predicament when he shows the sophistries involved in the reduction of freedom to a question of choice in this way. His narrator in *Oliver Twist* talks of the civic governors who, as board members, organize the Victorian workhouse in London, and points out that. 'The members of this board were very sage, deep, philosophical men; and when they came to turn their attention to the workhouse … they established the rule, that all poor people should have the alternative (for they would compel nobody, not they), of being starved by a gradual process in the house, or by a quick one out of it.'[3]

Enfranchisement used to be determined by wealth, inheritance and privilege. We should surely have moved beyond such a pernicious condition. Democracy is not subject to price; justice cannot be reduced to spurious choice; and freedom means significantly more than the freedom to buy through having more wealth than my neighbour. That is to say, freedom is not measurable in terms of amounts of money that I have. The assertion that 'money means freedom' is wrong-headed, especially when we consider the issue of 'widening participation'. Such formulations once again try to render qualities in terms of quantities; and they do so in ways that are guaranteed to embed inequalities within our society.

3

If we are to take the issue of widening participation seriously, then we must see that it does not in and of itself constitute an argument for a mass higher education system. Rather, and more importantly, it raises the issue of how we can widen the participation in society itself, and the issue of the place of a higher education within that desire. As I have repeatedly stressed, I take the view in this book that education at the highest levels is an intrinsic good thing: as Aristotle observed, it is indeed more conducive to happiness that we know things rather than that we are in ignorance. However, we do not all need to know the same things; and we do not all need to live in ways that make an advanced knowledge central to our happiness and participation in a social or public sphere that exceeds our own atomized space. Some individuals are at their most fulfilled when they are working with their hands, say – sorting out a faulty plumbing system, maybe, rather than designing a new water pump. We should respect this simple fact; and the corollary of that respect will be that we acknowledge that our participation in the public life of a society is fundamental to a communal well-being. Higher education is a part of this, but not the whole; and the University, within higher education, is likewise a part of a part. As the philosophers might say, it is a necessary but not yet or in itself a sufficient condition for the establishment of a common good.

The other aspect of this is 'access'; and the corresponding question again is 'access to what?' It is here that we can begin to open the issue of the types of institution that we might have. Thus far, I have written of the University as if it were the sole location of a higher or advanced education. However, it need not be. As my preceding paragraphs here – and Ken Robinson's fireman – make clear, there are many kinds of education, and many levels, that are also necessary parts of the desired whole. An abiding problem, however, has been the issue of status: it is a simple fact that our societies in the advanced economies have valued what is called an 'academic' educational institution differently from what are termed 'vocational' kinds of institution. We need to look at this.

First of all, we need to recall that, historically, the University was a vocational type of place. This remains the case with some of our most highly rated or highly esteemed disciplines. Medicine, for example, is a vocational degree, as is law, or veterinary medicine, or architecture. Technical design is, likewise, vocational; but it has tended in our times to have a lower status socio-culturally. Why might this be the case? The difference in how we have valued these things relates to the values that we ascribe to certain forms of intellectual capital, certainly; but it is also related to certain social factors that have nothing to do with intellectual capital and everything to do with established powers or forces. Some of my examples above – medicine, law, for obvious examples – have 'professional' accreditations as well as academic qualifications; and they also have their own professional bodies, such as the British Medical Association (BMA), or the Bar, that have managed to establish themselves as key figures or sources of authority, at least for the central echelons of the Establishment within our societies. While it may equally be the case that the construction industry also has its accreditation bodies, the BMA is held in higher regard than the Master Builders Association; and this for the simple reason that colleagues within the BMA sit closer to those who manipulate the levers of political power. Thus, while those in the so-called 'higher' professions (higher here simply now meaning in potential intimacy with government ministers) are taken as being *constitutively* important, by contrast, in this mentality, the designer (for example) is only as valuable as their last design. The mentality, quite obviously, is flawed.

Design, to remain with this example, is, like medicine or law, extremely important for the quality of our living. Good design is never purely functional; and it has repercussions well beyond its local occasion. As is well known, a good deal of our kitchenware is indebted to the designs and materials that were developed for the moon landings in the late 1960s. Likewise, our inhabiting of our very domestic spaces themselves – including those kitchens where we use our space-age machinery – is at least partly determined by design and technology. One recent example of a technological design and invention that has a purchase beyond its immediate use might be the Dyson bagless vacuum cleaner. In this instance, the immediate occasion for use is the cleaning by vacuum of a carpet or floor; but the design is such that it is able to remove not just regular household dust, but also mites and allergens. As a result of a design innovation, we save money in terms of medical care: a cleaner household environment promotes better health. Its effect goes well beyond its immediate application. I am content to pay for this for in doing so I do not 'just' get value for money; instead, I contribute money for values.

One can say similar things about many aspects of higher or advanced education in all fields, of course. One simple way of giving higher prestige to areas that are not regarded, at first blush, as high in intellectual capital, is simply to give them that prestige. In our regular social hierarchies as a whole, the University itself is regarded, at least in principle, as high prestige; and some individual Universities are regarded as higher prestige institutions than others. One reason for that alleged difference in standing is the perception that some institutions carry out more significant research in their fields than others. Let us suppose, then, that we had specialist advanced institutions where, for example, design and technology were among the central concerns and practices; and let us further suppose that these institutions had a relation to a national system of higher research institutes in design and technology. In other words, we can transform the standing of some disciplines by simply giving them high prestige through the establishment of, in this instance, a series of (let us say) four Advanced Institutes for Research in Design. Such institutions would need to be distributed across the country; but their brief would not be regional. Rather, the brief would be international, placing design on an international research stage, attracting scholars and students, and gathering together, in this now national system, the most advanced work in design. As well as having a centripetal force, bringing advanced work together in each of these centres, there would also be a centrifugal force, as the centres distribute their developments internationally, either as pure research or as invention capable of yielding a commercial return.

As in the case of design, exemplified here, so also we might be able to find or make prestige for activities such as architecture, or various crafts, or music. As soon as I suggest this, of course, it will be argued that we already have such bodies for we have, for example, music conservatoires and architecture institutes of outstanding reputation. My point, however, is that we might think of generalizing this, and making out of it a system that gives intellectual and other forms of cultural capital to the institutions and their activities. It is one thing to say we have excellent conservatoires; it is another thing entirely to say that the society highly values these things or values the life of classical music, seeing its importance as part of a 'widened participation' society. If the

Bar can sit close to the centre of governmental power, then why not also the conservatoires, the design institutes, and so on?

If we do indeed have different types of institutions in this way, dignified by their dedicated 'Advanced Research Institutes', we might also reasonably expect there to be different streams of funding and resource for them. It would not be axiomatically the case that these all should be funded from general taxation in the way that I argue a funding mechanism for the University. Some things follow from this.

First, let us briefly revisit the argument for the funding of the University from general taxation. Our 'realist pragmatist' readers, if they are still with us, will now trundle out the big figure designed to arrest any further argument, debate or even thinking at this point: the Taxpayer. 'The Taxpayer' operates, as a phrase, rather like the refrain of 'We're waiting for Godot' in Samuel Beckett's play, a refrain that recurs whenever one of the tramps explains to the other why they can't move. The phrase explains nothing, but always produces the same reply of 'Ah,' indicating that nothing else need be said or even can be said. The invocation of 'the Taxpayer' arrests the possibility of any further dialogue.

There is a certain mythology that grows up around this Taxpayer figure. It is presented in many cases as if it were one paradigmatic or typical individual, first of all: a rather miserly individual, who feels that his hard-won resources or money is being constantly threatened by ill-willed and unfair robbers. Further, even when the Taxpayer becomes a generic figure, and thus representative of many actual people – 'the Taxpayers' in the plural – no distinctions or discriminations are made. Thus, the argument goes that the Taxpayer, especially the less well-paid Taxpayer, should not be handing out money to the well-off middle-class student in order that that they can enjoy a University education that will make them yet wealthier while the Taxpayer remains impoverished.[4]

This might be fine, if it had any truth in reality. However, a progressive taxation system is one where the poorly paid axiomatically do *not* pay as much tax (and in some cases pay none at all), while the better-off pay more. In a progressive system of general taxation, the wealthy, who can easily afford to pay more, do so; and they do so because their greater wealth means that they are able to make a proportionate and correspondingly greater contribution to the general public good. It is simply not the case that the poor subsidize the rich in such a system; or, better, it is not the case provided that we genuinely do have a proper progressive system of taxation. The problem is that we do not: tax policy, at least since our emergence in the UK from rationing after the Second World War, has been guided by a political will that leads to ingrained inequality, by systematically protecting the wealthy from taxation. My argument depends on a fundamental correction of that. More importantly, the very future of the University, as an institution that can contribute to a widened participation in democracy and in society, also depends upon it.

However, it might be the case that we could offer tax incentives to the wealthy, either considered as individuals or as organizations, exempting them from some duties provided they invest in our Advanced Institutes or other centres of activity in a mass higher education system. It might be seen as reasonable that some element of a raised corporation tax, for instance, could go towards the funding of 'vocational' institutes such as those organized around technological design. Alternatively, what about, for large corporate organizations, a *reduction* in corporation tax proportionate to whatever contribution such organizations might make to higher education in whatever way, such as the sponsoring of teaching or other posts? Given that the reward for businesses and commerce is potentially massive, such investments would seem to be a good use of money, profits and resources. Once more, all would benefit from this.

Likewise, and especially in the present climate, it might be equally reasonable to expect that some large banking institutions could afford to fund some aspects of our system: perhaps helping sustain a conservatoire, or providing funding for an 'Advanced Institute of Government', or some such. This would be a much better use of the moneys currently distributed as a 'bonus', amounting to many millions of pounds, given to already very handsomely paid individuals on the grounds that they are, well, just doing their job, actually. It is possible to give an indicative figure here. As I write (December 2010), in the middle of a near-global fiscal crisis caused primarily by banking and the private sector, Barclays Bank in the UK has announced that its bonus pot for the festive season 2010–11 is to be £1.6 billion.[5] That sum is just under 33 per cent of the *total* funding for the entire University sector nationwide provided by government for teaching prior to the Browne Review's recommendations (£4.9 billion; which Browne proposes reducing to £700 million by cutting the entirety of funding for teaching in arts, humanities and social sciences). This is just one bank: there are many others. The question to be asked is not just about the scandal of the bonus culture; it is a question about political and civic priorities. The law of 'competition', we are told, requires that bankers receive such bonuses, else they will flee abroad. The responsible thing to do here is not to accede to the threat, but to bid farewell to individuals who, having brought the economy crashing, nonetheless continue to prioritize private greed over everything else and thereby already divorce themselves from our society and public sphere. They cannot *all* go to New York, for the law of competition that they say requires such massive remuneration determines that there is already only a very limited number of jobs there.

Given my own limitations as an economist, it is not appropriate that I try to put too much flesh on all of this. All I am trying to do here is to establish some founding principles for the financing of higher education. Specifically, I claim that the University – which might now start to resemble a liberal arts kind of institution – should be funded from general taxation. And, in further self-justification in relation to my limited expertise in economics, I will also add that Browne, for example, also gives no actual funding detail either: that report too also sets out some general principles that are not subject to precise accounting. The main thing is that what I advance here is diametrically opposed, as a point of principle, to Browne. Remember, also, that when I target Browne here, I take the Browne Review and its authors as a paradigmatic example of an entire ideological frame of mind. It is up to the accountants and economists to imagine, in more detail, what is possible here. Above all, however, it is up to the political class to respond, with a political will, to the reasonable demand for a widened participation in our democratic society, and to follow the logic of that will through to its entirely reasonable conclusions.

4

Access, then, might mean access to different kinds of activity; but above all, it means or should mean access to democracy itself. Education, and higher education within this, is but one part of how a society achieves this. It is not in and of itself the simple and single key to achieving a just democracy and the widened participation in such a democracy that is surely the goal of any activity that seeks to extend freedom and to work towards justice through an engagement with the true, the good and the beautiful; but it is nonetheless a valuable part of it.

However, after all this, I will need to accept that there is no political will that expresses itself in the desire to pay for the University sector from public taxation funding. Or, at least, there is not the will to fund the number of Universities that have been opened in the UK since the abolition in 1992 of the 'binary divide'. That abolition doubled, at a stroke, the number of institutions that were called Universities; but it did not double the funding, preferring instead to continue the same policies as before. The result is that we now institutionalize 'competitive funding' for every aspect of our existence. This applies not only to the competition that we once called the Research Assessment Exercise (later Research Excellence Framework), but also the competition for teaching funds, the competition among ourselves for students, the competition with other Universities worldwide for airtime and space; and the competition between alleged separate interest groups ('Russell Group' versus '1994 Group' versus 'Million+'; or, in the United States, 'Ivy league' against 'Liberal Arts' against 'State'; or, in France, *grande école* against 'University'; and so on across the developed and developing nations).

What, then, should we do? I have a radical but simple preliminary solution. We should accept the fact that the political will for a mass higher education as a public good does not exist at the moment. How do we continue, therefore? One solution is to reduce the number of students and Universities; but this would run counter to the value of having an educated population, and so should not be followed. Nor, of course, would any government be prepared to face the political fall-out that would follow a slashing of student places in this way. Instead, let us accept the policy of our having diverse activities, including those that currently go on in Universities, but also those that are designated by other names, such as vocational, technical or craft activities, for examples. I propose that we welcome different types of institution, not all of which will be entirely (or even in some cases, mainly) funded by the State.

Let me remain with the idea of the University as such, leaving aside for the moment my hypothesis regarding Advanced Research Institutes and the like. By this point, we might be renaming this, in an inversion of thinkers like Newman or Jaspers, and proposing a 'University of the Idea'. My claim throughout is that the University should be projected towards an imagining of future possibility; and, in this respect, the University is there in order to create an idea. We should therefore aim to have, to sustain and to cherish our Universities. If these institutions follow my first principles above, they should have at least the three faculties I described; and provide both a general education and also a high degree of specialization within that generalist approach. The corollary of this would be that a degree would take probably around four years of study (as opposed to the more standard three-year programme that dominates the English system).

The four-year duration is called for not just because our disciplines have all grown exponentially in modern times (there is simply more stuff to cover), but also for more fundamental pedagogical reasons. Perhaps the most detailed description of what is at stake here is that advanced by George Davie's depiction of what he called 'the democratic intellect'. Davie's argument relates to the difference in higher educational systems as between England and Scotland. The English tradition, he says, is founded upon early specialization. In this, a student finds their academic niche at a fairly early stage, and their education then focuses more and more intensely upon it. The result is an extremely high level of specialized and technical grasp of a field. Against this, the Scottish tradition (with degrees taking more typically four years) is much more generalist, and it rather delays specialization for as long as possible. The English student might typically study one subject or discipline at University (or, at most, two relatively cognate disciplines); and they will reach a high level of expertise. By contrast, the Scot will usually undertake study in significantly more fields, usually therefore not at such an advanced or specialized level, and usually from a much broader range of disciplines and faculties. While the English student gains an outstanding proficiency in Greek, say, being able to translate effortlessly between modern English and the ancient Greek texts of the classical tradition, the Scot is reading some English literature, some French, some higher level maths and maybe astronomy or philosophy or history. The Scot may not be so good at doing a word-for-word translation; but they will understand much more about the translatability between cultures, the philosophy of language and of communication, and so on.

Davie's argument is that the difference here is fundamental and that it has a political charge. The 'generalist' tradition, operating at a lower level of expertise, opens itself to wider participation within the community precisely because it is not over-burdened with the technical demands of specialist expertise that is grounded in an atomizing of knowledge. In this way, and by allowing for an engagement among a number of disciplines, its student has to be able to develop not a specialized intellect but rather an intellect founded in the establishment of a foundational type of philosophy. By contrast, the English produces a narrower and essentially more bureaucratized 'elite' whose interests are not necessarily shared widely among the more general community. The real key to the democratic credentials here, though, lies in the fact that the student has to see the relations among disciplines and fields, thus adventuring in imaginative and speculative fashion, to generate the possibility of debate among disciplines and between individuals. To facilitate this, it is necessary to have a structure where the first few years are devoted to this generalist approach, before eventually specializing in a way that allows the individual to emerge as an intellect distinguished from the general but yet grounded in it. Typically, in a Scottish institution, the first two years would be thus generalist; and they would then be followed by a two-year programme (rather like an Oxbridge 'Part Two' or a regular English University degree) whose results would yield the degree title.

The result of this is not just a better educated population; but instead a population whose very intellectual foundations and modes of thought are intrinsically democratic, opening to dialogue and debate, not overly swayed by alleged specialist expertise.

Obviously, this is expensive; but the real question is whether it is valuable. I'll conclude with a brief consideration of the idea of our getting 'value for money'.

5

Attaining value for money (VfM in the jargon) means obtaining the maximum benefit from goods and services acquired and provided, within available resources. The VfM agenda has gained a good deal of ground over the last decades, and many organizations routinely have a VfM committee either at the heart of, or at least as an adjunct to, their auditing processes. As the phrase, first of all casually intruded into political discourse, gets repeated, it also starts to fix itself into a specific set of meanings. In time, VfM comes to be understood in terms of three Es: 'economy', 'efficiency' and 'effectiveness'. It usually assumes a certain scope, aiming to deal with matters such as costs and prices, a generalized idea of quality, the jargon of 'fitness for purpose', timeliness of procedures and activities, and convenience of activities when viewed from the point of view of customers. It thus develops a large armature of practices and these give it a certain mythic status or mystique.

An attention to 'economy', in these terms, means, in essence, the application of procedures that systematically and repeatedly reduce funding for activities. 'Economy', in the VfM language, means that those who hold the purse strings will always be looking at cutting resources and thus making cost-savings simply by reducing expenditure, as a matter of guiding principle and not related to any financial necessity governing the activity. In short, if the activity cost £100 last year, this year it must be done with £50. This is King Lear speaking again.

An attention to 'efficiency' means that those who carry out the activity now have to do the same work but with this reduced resource. The input is reduced, but something has to happen within the mechanisms to ensure that the output is not itself reduced as a result. Perhaps needless to say, at this stage, creative accounting of activity has to take place, for it is simply impossible to achieve efficiency in a *systematically repeated* manner. The idea of eternal and systematic improvement in this is, of necessity, a myth; and one can see that this is so if one simply takes the logic to the extreme, in which the input is reduced to zero while the output remains as it was when the input was infinite. As Lear himself said, 'Speak again, Nothing will come of nothing.'

The attention, finally, to 'effectiveness' suggests that, miraculously, despite the economizing of resource, the careful attention to efficiency will mean that the activity is *even more effective*, that it has greater impact, than it had when the resource was richer. Once again, a creativity is required here to make it appear that the outcomes have improved whether they have or (more likely) have not.

The efficiency of the VfM activity itself, of course, is now to be verified and validated by the way in which the application of these three Es does indeed secure greater effectiveness from reduced resource. The logic then is that, if it has worked already with this first tranche of cutbacks, then we should apply yet more rigorous cutbacks again and again. The final logic of VfM is one where we get something for nothing, therefore. The word that we usually apply to that, however, is 'theft'; or, in terms of the operation of a workforce in a factory, something like slavery – or, in its contemporary terminology, the 'unpaid internship' that so many graduates now have to take as their only route in to eventual employment.

Given the dubious propriety of this kind of agenda, therefore, we might want either to get rid of it entirely or at least to modify it. What better, then, than to suggest that we simply rethink the whole process by keeping the terms but reversing them: why not attend to matters of distributing money or resource for values that we want to advance? That is, instead of establishing organizational principles on the base of our getting 'value for money' – a system that neutralizes the immoralities of theft, the transfer of public wealth into private hands and a work-based version of slavery – let us instead ask ourselves more fundamentally reasonable and honourable questions about what values we have and how much we will contribute in order to advance them. In short, let us abandon VfM and replace it with an organizational principle of 'money for values'.

If we value the extension of freedom, the search for justice and a democracy that is concerned to widen the franchise with a view to involving more people more fully in these moral goals, then let us also have a system of governance that matches this. The University, in this way, becomes the place where we deliberate, not for the sake of doing things more 'efficiently', but for changing things for the good much more generally.

What price freedom? What price justice? What price an increase in and extension of these things? It is the task of the University to seek answers. It is the task of all members of the community to decide whether we wish to pay for this promise of an enhancement and edification of our lives in the public sphere, a sphere in which we must live in cooperation, not competition.

Afterword

Post-Browne

At 5.41 p.m. on Thursday 9 December 2010, the University, as a major public UK institution, found itself assailed to its very core. It was at that moment that a teller in the British House of Commons read out the result of a vote, which the governing coalition (of Conservatives and Liberal Democrats) won, by a majority of 21 votes: 323 to 302. The vote – carried by some 28 Liberal Democrat MPs who had been mandated by their constituencies explicitly to vote against such an increase, and who had pledged to vote against any proposed rise – tripled University tuition fees at a stroke. It did this in the wake of the Browne Review, focusing on the sustainability of the University sector. However, this was but the first strike in a more sustained attack on the very principles governing our idea of a University and of the principles of a University education. Fees have to be trebled for the simple reason that Universities are to have their funding cut by the coalition government: the budget allocated for teaching will be reduced by 80 per cent and the funding for teaching in arts, humanities and social sciences will be cut by 100 per cent. Fees are being imposed at this inflationary level in order to fill that funding gap.

The political backdrop to this is the financial crisis that hit the advanced economies in 2008 and that produced recession among those economies. The problem was caused primarily by the private sector in our economies and most specifically by the banking sector. The problem was so huge, however, that the only reasonable way of beginning to solve it was by helping out the banks, through the use of public funding: that is, money that had been raised from general taxation. Once this was done, then a fundamental slippage occurred that has had massive repercussions for the entire public sector and for the arena within which the University operates. Tax revenue diverted to solve the crisis produced from bad (and sometimes wicked) activity in the private sector leaves us with a shortage of public funds. Thus it is that a crisis made in the private sector becomes a problem for the public sector. Thus it is that the public sector has to carry the cost of the losses made by a private sector that continues to enjoy governmental backing and support. Thus it is, finally, that a Conservative-led administration can find cover for the advancing of an ideological programme that it now claims is a necessity rather than what it actually is: a choice.

However, fees themselves are not new in this post-Browne system. The idea of students paying more or less directly for a University education begins in the UK at an earlier date. It was a Labour administration that brought in the fees system in 1998. That was also brought about by a vote in the House of Commons, but that earlier vote was won by a margin of only 5 votes. In other words, had 3 people out of around 650 voted differently, we would not have introduced the fees system at that time. The narrowness of these majorities (3 votes then; 11 in 2010) indicates how contentious this whole ideologically driven procedure for funding the University has been, historically as well as in the present time.

At that earlier stage, the fees regime was slightly different; but its principles were grounded in the same logic. The argument advanced in favour of a fees regime is that a University graduate will benefit financially from their education. Accordingly, they should be required to pay for that education, which is now construed less as an education and more as a business investment. The logic presupposes that there is a direct link between the specifics of a University education and higher-paid employment; and it also presupposes that the system of general taxation will not be intrinsically progressive enough to ensure proportionate payment through that route. That is: it accepts that general taxation will favour the retaining of excess wealth in the hands of a relatively small number of individuals and that such wealth will excuse those individuals from playing a full contributory financial part in the social formation or public sphere within which they gain their wealth.

In the work that helped the then Labour administration to secure political agreement for the imposition of fees, its key architect, Nick Barr, points out that the inspiration for the system is to be found in the work of the economist Milton Friedman. Friedman began his career as a Keynesian, but, by 1965, had started a process whereby he more or less completely reversed his economic and political views. By this time, he was well on his way to the position with which more recent governments became familiar, in which he argued for the primacy of a kind of competitive acquisitiveness as the driver of all social activity. In his more extreme moments, Friedman provocatively suggested that a kind of neo-Hobbesian *greed* was the driving force of human activity as such, almost to the point where greed became the foundation of a kind of ethics. To be human fully was to accede to the foundational force of individual acquisitiveness that would set us at an advantage over others: greed became the first principle of ethical relation.

Now, this is a political position, and one that has been argued for in many arenas. However, what I argue here and what I have argued throughout the pages of this book is that it is a drastic over-simplification and one that, in its crude simplicity, essentially *falsifies* the description of our human or social being in the public sphere. The fundamental problem with it – quite apart from any moral revulsion that we may feel – is that it ignores entirely the *complexities* of human motivation. I am certainly not going to take a simple opposition to the 'ethics of greed': it is not the case that the motivations for all human activity are founded in a spirit of *benevolence*, any more than that they are all founded in or explained by greed. Rather, I will assume that it is more or less self-evident that human motivation is much more complex than either of these crudely simplified positions would have us believe.

Throughout the 1980s, this Chicago School economics, advanced by Friedman and others, was in the ascendancy. It combined with a preference, among governments in the advanced economies, for 'market' solutions to social and other problems that those governments were facing. The combination of greed and an allegedly 'free' market yielded a heady mixture that was supposed to give freedom itself to participants in the markets that now appeared in all walks of life. One key question that we would have to pose, however, is the question of how 'free' the free-market itself actually is. Markets can be 'free' if and only if their activity is undertaken in some kind of ideal fashion. They presuppose an ideal consumer, one who is not shaped by anything other than their own rational processes regarding the choices that they might make within the market (including the choice of whether to participate or not). This has to ignore any and all forces and influences that might shape our ideal consumer. Those forces, of course, include things such as a general ideology, fashion, peer pressures, family histories, somatic pressures such as thirst or hunger. In short, they presuppose that the consumer is an entirely discrete individual, separated off from any such force. However, there *is*, according to the synthesis of free-market and Friedmanesque individual, a force at work: the quasi-instinctive force of greed itself. There is, thus, a logical self-contradiction at the very heart of this ideology; and the ideology thus makes not only for a falsification of the actual state of affairs, but it also produces a rather toxic version of the individual, as one disfigured by a greed that separates them from the public domain, the very sphere in which markets actually – as opposed to ideally or abstractly – exist.

However, for the sake of argument, let us here assume that Friedman is right and that greed is a founding condition of our being. Now, let us add politics. Politics, if it has any function at all in this state of affairs, is there axiomatically and by definition in order to combat the kinds of negativity that will alienate us from the polis, from the public sphere. Politics, as the very word suggests, is that activity that binds us in a polis and that combats atomized isolation from the community as a whole. Now, throughout the 1980s and leading up to our present crisis, we have had a choice in the advanced economies. Either, we can have a government that celebrates – and in some case venerates – individual acquisitiveness and greed (and in the UK, we might identify that with Thatcherism); or we can have governments that see their task as one whereby they accept that greed drives everything, but that they should limit themselves to moderating and regulating its effects (and again, in the UK, we might identify that with Blairism).

That is to say: political discourse around this question has effectively been lost. Politics, as a matter of preserving the polity, has now disappeared. Both positions outlined above have ceded the argument and the ground entirely to those who wish to evacuate politics of any real meaning or actual purchase on material realities. Politics has become something divorced from the historical realities of everyday life – or, at least, that is what the prevailing 'non-political' ideology would have us believe. That is to say, we are encouraged to believe in a kind of *natural* condition, one that is non-political, in which isolated atomism is a norm. The argument of this book is that it is time to revive politics in relation to the question of the University. It is time to exercise a political will *for the University*.

Notes

Chapter 1 First Principles: The University of the Idea

1 For a discussion of this movement, written in the heat of the moment, see J. Sauvageot, A. Geismar, D. Cohn-Bendit, J.-P. Duteuil (1968), *La Révolte étudiante: les animateurs parlent*, Paris: Éditions du Seuil.

2 See Daniel Bell (1970), 'Quo Warranto? – Notes on the Governance of Universities in the 1970s', in Stephen R. Grabaud and Geno A. Ballotti (eds), *The Embattled University*, New York, NY: George Braziller, p. 233. This is also the source for the Bell quotes that follow.

3 For some of the historical background to this, see R.D. Anderson (1995), *Universities and Elites in Britain since 1800*, Cambridge: Cambridge University Press.

4 See Bill Readings (1996), *The University in Ruins*, Cambridge MA: Harvard University Press, p. 65.

5 It is perhaps worth noting, in passing, that the play addresses the relation of education to debt. Specifically, it sees that debt in a wide context that involves not just money, but also a debt between generations. Strepsides laments the fact that his son, Pheidippides, is a wastrel whose activities increase the family's debts. In our time, we are bearing increasing witness to a situation whereby established adults are visiting debts on to their offspring by *requiring* them, as individuals, to be in financial debt to the State for their University education, through the structuring of fee-paying arrangements. There is more on this later in this book.

6 See Martha C. Nussbaum (1997), *Cultivating Humanity*, Cambridge, MA: Harvard University Press, p. 2.

7 Nussbaum, *Cultivating Humanity*, pp 28–9.

8 Perhaps the most significant advocate of this position, where criticism is aligned with sceptical oppositionalism, is to be found in the work of Edward Said. For his most succinct expression of this position, see especially Edward Said (1984), *The Work, The Text, The Critic*, London: Faber and Faber, p. 28.

9 Nussbaum, *Cultivating Humanity*, p. 19.

10 John Dewey (1916, reprinted 1985), *Democracy and Education*, Carbondale and Edwardsville, IL: Southern Illinois University Press, p. 103.

11 Dewey, *Democracy and Education*, p. 93.

12 Hannah Arendt (1972), *Crises of the Republic*, New York, NY: Harcourt Brace & Co., p. 5.

13 Aristophanes (1973), *Lysistrata, The Acharnians, The Clouds*, trans Alan H. Sommerstein, Harmondsworth: Penguin, p. 136.

14 F.R. Leavis (1948), *Education and the University*, London: Chatto and Windus, p. 24.

15 Leavis, *Education and the University*, p. 25.
16 Leavis, *Education and the University*, p. 28.
17 Alain Badiou (1997), *Saint Paul: La fondation de l'universalisme*, Paris: Presses universitaires de France, p. 11 (author's translation).
18 Jacques Rancière (2009), *Moments politiques*, Paris : La Fabrique, p. 92 (author's translation).
19 Rancière (2009), *Moments politiques*, p. 92
20 See Alain Touraine (1994), *Qu'est-ce que la démocratie?*, Paris: Fayard, p. 24 (author's translation).

Chapter 2 The Student Experience: Living Learning, Living Teaching

1 See Jonathan Swift (1976), *Gulliver's Travels and Other Writings*, ed. Louis A. Landa (Oxford: Oxford University Press, p. 301. For the philosophical position behind this, see Michel Serres (1994), *Eclaircissements*, Paris: Garnier-Flammarion, p. 76.
2 Who would vaunt themselves as a Gradgrind today? Well, in the time since I originally wrote this sentence, it occurs to me that we do have an answer: Michael Gove, currently Secretary of State for Education. In addition to this Gradgrindery, he has also recently proposed a new solution for improvement of childhood schooling: bring in the retired military as teachers to help instil a bit of discipline. As with Gradgrind, there is no grasp of material reality in such fantasies.
3 Charles Dickens (1977), *Hard Times*, reprint, Harmondsworth: Penguin, p. 48. There is a larger question here: facts, or data, are important, certainly. However, data becomes 'information' only once inserted into a sentence that makes a claim about them; and 'information' becomes 'knowledge' only when those sentences are debated and discussed. Too often, in our present predicament, 'data' has become a proxy not just for 'information', but also for 'knowledge'; and we usually call the resulting situation 'league tables'. It is worse, of course, when the data are false: judgements are questionable because they are based not upon knowledge, nor even information, but mere data – or false data.
4 See Walter Benjamin (1999), *Selected Writings, Vol. 2: 1927–1934*, Cambridge, MA: Harvard University Press, p. 731.
5 See Dewey, *Democracy and Education*, pp. 146–7.
6 Dewey, *Democracy and Education*, pp. 147–8.
7 Dewey, *Democracy and Education*, p. 148.
8 Dickens, *Hard Times*, p. 50.
9 Dewey, *Democracy and Education*, p. 148.
10 Dewey, *Democracy and Education*, p. 153.
11 Said, *The Work, The Text, The Critic*, pp. 28–9; italics added.
12 Dewey, *Democracy and Education*, pp. 154–5.

13   See Theodor Adorno and Max Horkheimer (1979), *Dialectic of Enlightenment*, trans. John Cumming, London; Verso, p. 148.
14   G.W.F. Hegel (1975), *Aesthetics*, Vol. 1, trans. T.M. Knox , Oxford: Oxford University Press, p. 2.
15   Hannah Arendt (1968), *Between Past and Future*, Harmondsworth: Penguin, p. 106.

Chapter 3   A Terrifying Silence: Spaces of Research from Discovery to Surveillance

1   All quotations here come from Dwight D. Eisenhower (2005), *Public Papers of the Presidents: Dwight D. Eisenhower, 1960–61*, Ann Arbor, MI: University of Michigan Library, pp. 1035–40.
2   Jean-François Lyotard argued this, in a different context, in his essay on 'Time Today'. See Jean-François Lyotard (1984), *Selected Writings*, Oxford: Blackwell.
3   See Karl Jaspers (1959), *The Idea of the University*, ed. Karl Deutsch, trans. H.A.T. Reiche and H.F. Vanderschmidt, Boston: Beacon Press, p. 21.

Chapter 4   Leadership: Legitimation and Authority

1   See Muriel Spark (1965), *The Prime of Miss Jean Brodie*, Harmondsworth: Penguin, p. 10.
2   Spark, *The Prime of Miss Jean Brodie*, p. 44.
3   Spark, *The Prime of Miss Jean Brodie*, p. 29.
4   Spark, *The Prime of Miss Jean Brodie*, p. 32.
5   Spark, *The Prime of Miss Jean Brodie*, p. 36.
6   Spark, *The Prime of Miss Jean Brodie*, p. 11.
7   Arendt, *Between Past and Future*, p. 106.
8   Karl Marx (1978), *The Eighteenth Brumaire of Louis Bonaparte*, Peking: Foreign Languages Press, p. 9.
9   Frank Kermode (1977), *The Sense of an Ending*, Oxford: Oxford University Press, p. 39.
10   Kermode (1977), *The Sense of an Ending*, p. 39.
11   Slavoj Žižek (2003), *The Puppet and the Dwarf*, Cambridge, MA: MIT Press, pp. 105–6.
12   Žižek, *The Puppet and the Dwarf*, pp. 110–11.
13   The Smith example, and the King example here, are both as reported in *Times Higher Education*, April 2009 and October 2010.
14   R. Bolden, J. Gosling, A. Marturano and P. Dennison (2003), *A Review of Leadership Theory and Competency Frameworks*, Exeter: Centre for Leadership Studies.The text is available at: http://centres.exeter.ac.uk/cls/research/abstract.php?id=29 [accessed 24 March 2011].
15   See Robert Greenleaf (2002), *Servant Leadership*, Mahwah, NJ: Paulist Press.

Chapter 5   Assessment: Controlling Conformity

1 Walter J. Ong (1958), *Ramus: Method and the Decay of Dialogue*, Cambridge, MA: Harvard University Press, p. 121.
2 This paper is available from Andrew Abbott's University of Chicago webpages. I am grateful to Nigel Thrift for drawing the paper to my attention.

Chapter 6   Finance: Money for Value

1 Browne Review (2010), *Securing a Sustainable Future for Higher Education*, http://www.independent.gov.uk/browne-report, 12 October, p. 21.
2 As reported in *Times Higher Education*, October 2010.
3 Charles Dickens (1838), *Oliver Twist*, London: Richard Bentley, chapter 2.
4 Stefan Collini made some very similar points regarding the Taxpayer – often ideologically presented as a kind of sullen ogre figure, protecting his hoard, as Collini put it – when he addressed the conference on 'Why Humanities?' at Birkbeck University, London, October 2010.
5 As reported in the *Guardian*, October 2010.

Name Index

Subject Index